MW01259078

Extrajudicial Execution

The Dying Testimony of
Michael James Lutterschmidt

Wisdom Editions

Minneapolis

Wisdom
Editions
Minneapolis

FIRST EDITION MARCH 2020
EXTRAJUDICIAL EXECUTUION
Copyright © 2020 by Michael James Lutterschmidt
All rights reserved.

Printed in the United States of America.
10 9 8 7 6 5 4 3 2 1

Cover and interior design: Gary Lindberg

ISBN: 978-1-950743-20-9

Extrajudicial Execution

The Dying Testimony of
Michael James Lutterschmidt

Authors Note

To the best of my knowledge, I, Michael James Lutterschmidt, solemnly swear that the following story speaks the truth, the whole truth, and nothing but the truth, so help me God.

I have chosen to change the names of the people and the organizations involved in this true story, not to protect them but to provide a measure of legal protection for me. The forces that are set against me will nevertheless try to sabotage and destroy my life in every way possible and prevent this book from reaching you, the reader. They do not want you to know the savage and sadistic information I am about to share.

Introduction

Most stories contain messages or ideas that shed a light on hidden truths, although many people refuse or are unable to see or accept those truths. The movie *Fire in the Sky*, for example, was based on a true story about an alien abduction. Although the pretext stated that it was based on true events, how many people today believe the story to be true?

The movie *Jaws* was based on documented shark attacks in the early 1900s in which victims were mangled and killed by a large bull shark. The movie twisted and altered the real-life events for entertainment purposes, but the truth remains—many people were killed by the same rogue shark.

The Exorcism of Emily Rose was also a movie based on true events. When we see or hear ghost stories, we all interpret these stories differently. Some people absorb a story as fictional entertainment. I take it in as communication.

In the Bible, stories we call parables are told to communicate a message or a lesson. These stories, like Aesop's fables, are fictional but are based on a truth of some kind. No matter how much a story has been altered to entertain or attract attention, the idea behind it developed from some original fact or real occurrence.

Now, think about movies like *The Belko Experiment*. I believe the story is a message hidden in plain sight. This is a story that sheds light on covert human implants. If you do the research, you will discover real companies are requiring employees to accept the injection of hand implants. If you read the latest medical journals, you will discover that more and more newborn babies are being implanted with an electronic chip. When I tell you my story, if you pay attention with an open mind, you will learn how hundreds of targeted individuals are being tortured by nanotechnology, body area networking, and RFID chips.

Consider the movie *The Matrix*. Dumb down this science fiction movie a bit and consider how it portrays our society today, a society in which everything you do is observed and scrutinized—what you watch, whom you call or text, what you shop for, where you spend, how much you spend, and where you go are being recorded.

Television maker VIZIO was recently sued for tracking networks and channels that were viewed by customers who purchased a VIZIO television. How exactly do you think the viewing choices of these customers were being observed? If you haven't heard about this massive conspiracy and others like it, I believe it's because someone out there has the power to keep stories of this magnitude out of the news, and thus out of your mind.

If you run a stoplight in some cities, you'll not only get a traffic ticket in the mail but also a photograph of the offense with your picture and license plate to match. We live in the Matrix. Technology imprisons us without us realizing the fact of the imprisonment. We are being brainwashed and experimented on without our consent.

I challenge you to watch the documentary *Unacknowledged*. The truth is right in front of you. The decision to seek reality is your choice. Will you break away from a Matrix created to silently contain and control your own being? Or will you seek to discover what is real and being hidden from you?

The cable series *Better Call Saul* was a spin-off of the original series *Breaking Bad*. In this show, Saul had a brother who was a highly respected attorney. Saul's brother complained of becoming violently ill from electricity. He wouldn't leave the house and wouldn't allow any electronic devices to enter his home. He wore foil-lined clothing and covered the walls of his entire home in foil sheathing to prevent electronic microwaves from entering his home. Normal people watching his behavior would consider his character to be paranoid or psychotic. As a targeted individual like Saul's brother, I immediately knew that a message was being revealed. His character is a truth hidden in plain sight.

Many targets I speak with are being tortured by directed-energy weapons, microwave guns, and Wi-Fi from 5G weapons. These individuals and I frequently chat online and provide each other with help and support. Some of us go as far as building Faraday cages, wearing lead helmets, foil blankets, and on and on. In *Better Call Saul*, a scriptwriter knew some truth and chose to expose that reality in plain sight.

Ask former FBI Chief Ted Gunderson why he chose to expose these crimes and the use of these inhumane weapons. Oh, but you can't, because Ted Gunderson passed away. Ted died of cancer on July 31, 2011.

Chapter 1

A Day in the Life

"The CIA and FBI are behind most, if not all, terrorism."
—Ted Gunderson, former FBI Chief

I have never written a book before, and I can probably count on both hands just how many books I've read from start to finish. But now I have written a book in the hope of saving the lives of myself and countless others. I need to tell my true story before time runs out.

Will you help prevent me from being murdered in plain sight? By the time you read this, I truly hope it is not too late

My name is Michael James Lutterschmidt, a forty-year-old man living in Pennsylvania. I am what Dr. John Hall describes as a targeted individual (TI) in his book, *A New Breed: Satellite Terrorism in America*. A targeted individual is a person who has been singled out by a criminal syndicate for covert surveillance, gangstalking, financial ruin, physical injury and mental impairment until the human prey is discredited, incapacitated or dead. Biological, electronic and no-consent medical techniques may be used to produce "no touch" torture, while illegal psychological methods create trauma, confusion and disability. Many of these monstrous techniques were detailed by a TI named Richard L. Cain in his lawsuit against the government (*Richard Cain v. Department of Defense.*) Cain eventually won a multi-million-dollar award for the charged abuses.

Because TIs so often end up dead, either physically or mentally, I call this criminal targeting "extrajudicial execution" because the assassination is not mandated or approved by any legal judicial process, but rather by an individual or organization with cruel and illegal intentions. Whether the motive is retaliation, punishment, the discrediting of an accuser, or simply a sick desire to inflict pain and suffering, the result is always devastating for the prey.

To help you understand the depth of despair suffered by a TI, here is an account of a day in my own life. But be warned—what I am about to describe will sound insane at first. Understand, however, that both apparent and real insanity of the TI is a major goal of the program, which has three desired outcomes: incarceration, commitment for mental illness, and finally suicide. The controllers of the program will not stop until there is a successful outcome, or they are forced to abandon their mission. For nearly four years I have been suffering inhumane torture. I hope this book will force them to abandon their plan for me.

Here is an account of my Tuesday, which unfolded like most other days.

After one-hour intervals of fitful sleep, painful pressure in my head finally forces me to get out of bed at four o'clock in the morning and go outside. Sitting on my building's front stoop, I try to blow out a glue-like silicone substance from the back of my sinuses. When a clump of it emerges, I tug at it with disgust and it bounces back into shape when I release it. This weird, alien-like goo has plagued me since the beginning of my painful adventure.

As I sit silently in the darkness, only a nearby streetlight and a dry cleaner's neon sign illuminates my short road, which connects two main streets. Before I moved in, the short road and the alley behind my building was used almost exclusively by apartment dwellers. This morning it is peaceful for only a few minutes.

And then the harassment starts. Vehicles begin to light up the short road—at 4:10 a.m.! This strange form of organized stalking has become immensely intimidating. Over the years, though, I've come to anticipate and understand the pattern. The first vehicles to show up are everyday cars driven by local "pawns," I call them, most likely the lowest paid of the stalkers.

Behind several of these cars, two more vehicles race down the short road crisscrossing in opposite directions. As one of them turns off the road, another turns onto the road in front of me from the opposite direction. Before long, a vehicle stops and parks in front of me. Fully exposed to me now, the driver holds up a cell phone and begins tapping the keypad. About thirty seconds later, the car speeds off and almost immediately I feel a tingle on the left side of my head produced, I know, by electronic impulses initiated by the cell phone. A few pawn vehicles pull into the building's parking lot, sit there for a minute, then pull out and drive past me, only to go around the block and do it all over again. It reminds me of that scene in ET: The Extraterrestrial in which numerous glowing orbs begin to dance above nighttime observers until finally they all evacuate the sky.

After about ten minutes of this nonsense, the big guns arrive. These are more experienced and presumably more highly paid stalkers driving special "priming" vehicles. Priming is a form of brainwashing and is often used to train targets to associate vehicles of specific types and colors with the mysterious organized stalking effort, which produces great fear, dread and anxiety.

This morning, I am again haunted by a few types of vehicles. Today they are white pickup trucks. Seeing them sends chills through my body. For four years, when starting my car, a white pickup truck would often drive down the short road. When I would turn onto one of the main streets, a white pickup truck would approach me more often than chance would allow. When I would exit a highway, white pickup trucks would turn exit alongside me. If I stopped at a semaphore, a white pickup truck would frequently pull up next to me, or behind me. It's literally driving me crazy.

Remember the goals of this intensive intimidation program: incarceration, commitment for mental illness, and finally suicide.

Early on, I'd often speed up to the white trucks, flip off the driver or curse at him. What "they" wanted most of all, I believe, was to provoke me into an act of road rage so they could videotape me and call the police. Incarceration, right? Creating a police record? But I've learned from experience and from studying their playbook not to fall for these tactics.

Another purpose of the "controllers" or "handlers" who organize the intimidation events is to incite me into telling many people that "white pickups are following me"—a paranoid-sounding complaint sure to suggest I've probably lost my grasp on reality. Mental illness, right? Creating a mental health record of instability?

As I sit on the stoop, priming vehicles start to merge with the pawns. My priming vehicles consist not only of white pickup trucks, but also black and red ones. And, white vans—the creepy child-molester kind with no windows. There are others too, including Jeep, Mercedes, Discovery and Range Rover vehicles. I'll explain their priming symbolism later.

Unfortunately, this 24/7 vehicular stalking is not simply psychological warfare. The vehicles are equipped with all kinds of new and fear-evoking technologies including directed-energy devices, microwave guns and 5G wireless devices for precision attacks. The most indiscriminate and disabling weapons, however, are sprayers connected to tailpipes that blow out bio-agent mists. The various species of fungi and mushrooms growing all over the yard are highly suspect.

During the few minutes since the first pawns appeared, twenty-one vehicles have crossed my path—and the sun won't rise for another hour.

By now, you may be wondering who would care so much about me that they'd spend such a staggering amount of time, energy and money to harass me like this. How could Michael Lutterschmidt be so important? Well, I will fully explain how and why all of this started, but a little later—I promise. You may also be wondering why I don't just hide from these enthusiastic stalkers inside, right? Well, their electronic devices and bioweapons can attack and poison me wherever I am, even in my apartment. I've tried hiding in hotels, tents, even different states. Stay with me and you will learn the surprising reasons.

It's four-thirty now. I take a last sip of coffee and head back to the apartment. I stumble into the living room, lie on the floor and pour a vial of albuterol down my left nostril. I snort and jerk my head in different ways, trying to loosen up the glue-like crap that is causing so much discomfort. I squirt a half-bottle of saline spray into my left nostril and violently sniff it down, trying to work the goo out of my head. Suddenly I can feel the rubbery sludge slide into my throat, and I cough it up. In the bathroom, I spit into the toilet and the muck floats there like a poached egg in boiling water.

Then, as I do too often, I overdose on Flonase to get some relief. Then I grab a second cup of coffee and put a leash on Abbie, my girlfriend's dog. We go outside and Abbie does her business, but before she's done headlights appear from both directions.

It's nearly a quarter past five now and the sky is beginning to illuminate. I can see the usual morning traffic as neighbors and people start to blend in with the army of stalkers driving in my proximity. It becomes hard to differentiate the stalkers from people just driving to work.

I watch a garbage truck pull into the adjacent parking lot and pretend to pick up trash by putting down the lift and making a terrible screeching noise. But there are no garbage containers here. What should I make of this? Then I see a FedEx truck pull down the alley. Yes, two FedEx trucks driving down the very small alley that adjoins to the street. I know FedEx doesn't even start delivering until six o'clock, but what do I know? The stalkers clearly don't have to do all the work. By priming me psychologically, they have stimulated my doubts so now I may be falsely suspecting a garbage man of stalking me. Or maybe not. Almost all the normal traffic now makes me fearful.

I give my nose a final, violent blow and watch a slimy ball fly out and smack the sidewalk. Angry at my plight, I gently tug the leash and direct Abbie toward the apartment building. As we are walking up the private sidewalk, a prolonged, obnoxious bleat from a car horn causes me to shake my head. This clearly is part of the noise intimidation, which I'll explain later.

It's now close to six o'clock. Inside, I stuff my left nostril with tissues, take a few aspirin and recline on a sofa to binge on a Netflix series. I hope to doze off, but I begin to itch all over. My head begins to feel congested and the room starts spinning. My body temperature rises so suddenly my body is clammy even though the air-conditioner is running. Suddenly, my fish in the aquarium becomes agitated and starts to splash around, almost leaping out of the tank. Mr. Plecko is a sixteen-inch Plecostomus, so when he splashes, it's quite an event. Though my brain feels clogged, I try to figure out why he's trying to jump out of the water?

I try to relax—there is no point in overreacting because that only leads to more problems, as I've learned the hard way. I know better than to tell someone that my fish let me know he was being attacked by directed-energy weapons and microwaves. Mental illness is what everyone seizes upon, even the authorities, when behavior or comments becomes even slightly odd. I have tried contacting local police that cars and trucks were following me around. This desperate attempt to get help only contributed to false perceptions.

After I've watched a few episodes of my new series, *Daredevil*, it's time to accomplish something. It's now nine o'clock, so I return my attorney's phone call from the previous day. He tells me we have a lot to go over. He's representing me as I battle through several fraudulent PFAs (a Protection from Abuse order,) an ongoing six-year divorce, and visitation rights for my nine-year-old daughter, Lala, who I haven't seen for over three years. I make an appointment with the attorney for the following week, thinking, I need this short-term goal. If I can just make it to that appointment, maybe things will get better.

I start thinking about documenting my story, but I need the right tools. I need a notebook, a computer bag, and a new computer mouse. I triple-check that I've locked the doors (maybe I am a bit paranoid) that Abbie is safe in the house. I find my car in the parking lot, put the laptop into the trunk, and as I slam it shut, I hear the roar of an engine. A white truck is racing down my street. I theatrically smile and wave at the woman driver. Yes, a woman was driving an obnoxiously oversized white pickup. Kindness always seems to piss off these guys.

I put the key in the ignition and the car starts. I'm astonished. I've had three alternator belts cut, many slashed tires, a fuel pump rigged to leak gas, and fluids drained out. A woman friend who turned out to be unreliable once told me that poison was being put into my car. My symptoms confirmed this to be true.

As I pull out of the parking lot, I'm forced to wait for traffic—a white van, a black Chevy truck and a bicycle all pass the lot together. Remember, my street isn't exactly Grand Central Station. Finally, I leave the lot and attempt a right turn onto the main road when another line of traffic blocks me—two white trucks, one creepy white van and three motorcycles, each flapping a large American flag on the back, another priming message I've become familiar with.

I turn onto the street and head for a Dollar Store a few miles away. Several drivers coming toward me are blatantly pointing their cell phones at me and smirk as they drive by. I'll explain more about this later, but for now it's enough to know that cell phones with 5G Wi-Fi are being used as weapons against TIs. About every fourth vehicle seems to be targeting me. I tell myself it's just my paparazzi—I'm that special—but in truth it's disturbing to be surrounded by this many people who obviously want me dead. This kind of gangstalking has been occurring around the world, but what did I do to deserve this attention?

The Jeep in front of me has a state university sticker on the bumper, a famous cartoon mouse head over the antenna, and a license plate that starts with KLL. I get license plate messages everywhere I go. This message tells me I'm being killed. I shake my head and say to myself, "Yeah, I know."

The Jeep signals for a right turn onto a road from which another white pickup quickly races out in front of me. The truck's license plate starts with KLC, reminding me that I'm being killed with cancer. These priming and subliminal messages are meant for me alone to understand, and I've become alert to them through a process of selective perception. I can't get around the white truck, so I tailgate and notice a sticker for the state university—a major source of research resulting in many of the hateful targeting techniques— well as a "VC" sticker on the tailgate. The female driver looks at me in the mirror as she strokes back her hair with her right hand. Another woman driving an oversized truck—what a coincidence!

As I continue to follow her, three white trucks pass in the opposite direction, this time with no other vehicles between them. The white truck ahead of me turns left and I race up to the car ahead. This one is a two-door Volkswagen—not a priming vehicle—but the back bumper has a "VC" sticker on it. I looked that one up because I get primed with it all the time. It means "Vacation Club."

At the Dollar Store, I park in a spot toward the back of the lot and immediately two dark SUVs pull up with illegally tinted front windows. One parks beside me and the other picks a space two rows away. Simultaneously, the two drivers—both women—get out and walk toward the store.

I enter the store and head for the stationery aisle, passing one of the stalkers, a woman in her forties dressed as a business professional. She is walking aimlessly around the store with an empty basket. I find the other woman standing dead center in the shampoo aisle tapping on her cell phone. She doesn't look up. I walk to the stationery aisle, grab a green notebook and some pens.

Another customer has reached the register ahead of me. As the clerk checks him out, I see the woman who had carried the empty basket around the store now leaving empty-handed.

Most people wouldn't ever notice these ordinary but telltale events, but after four years of being targeted I've learned to observe everything. Maybe my life now is like the movie *The Bourne*

Identity, but instead of being brainwashed and acquiring fighting skills, I got *A Beautiful Mind* downloaded instead.

While the customer ahead of me pays for his merchandise, the second stalker walks up and stands right behind me with a box of crackers. She is still tapping on her phone. Suddenly, I get a tingling pain in my left sinus and an instant headache. Experience suggests that a 5G app on her phone has triggered a painful response from an implant in my head—more details to follow, I promise.

I remind myself that no reaction is the right action. If I said something, who would believe me? If I angrily knocked the phone out of her hand, I could be confined to a box. So, I compose myself and carry on.

I leave the store and notice that the woman who had left the store empty-handed is now sitting in her car staring at her phone. As I step into the lot, I'm forced to wait for a black pickup that is slowly driving past. It is driven by a man with a huge beard. My next breath is abruptly shortened, as if I've suddenly gone underwater. I choke and cough, bend down and put my hands on my knees to take a normal breath. Then I stand up and take a deep breath, which feels like I've just inhaled itching powder into my lungs. I get dizzy and my vision blurs. Finally, I look to my right and watch the black truck accelerate into the street and disappear in traffic.

My lungs are still itching, but I can still think. I quickly conclude the truck had driven into the parking lot to spray me with a poisonous concoction. The stalker in the car was probably communicating with him via cell phone to coordinate the timing of the attack. As I approach my car, which is parked next to the stalker, she looks up from her phone, gives me a glance—never making eye contact—then quickly exits the lot.

I still need a computer bag and mouse, so I drive toward a thrift store down the street. As I approach a red light, a creepy, "priming" white van coming toward me is signaling a left turn. I decide to be a nice guy, so when the light turns green, I give a hand signal for the woman driver to turn in front of me. She sits there for about five seconds as I continue to wave her on. Finally, I give up and step on the gas. As I approach the middle of the intersection, the van starts to turn, heading right for me. I stop, trying to stay calm, and wave her on once more. Again, the white van just sits there. And again, as soon as I move forward, the van comes right at me. I swerve to avoid her and then go straight ahead toward a shopping center parking lot.

I conclude that the whole episode was intentional. So, I repeat to myself, "No reaction is the right action." This is useful self-talk because two Bethlehem Police cars are parked at the entrance to the parking lot as if waiting for something to happen. If I had stopped and screamed at the van driver, or had an accident, paid witnesses would have emerged to tell her fabricated story.

As I drive into the parking lot, I give one of the cops a salute and head toward the thrift shop. I park next to a shiny new black Jeep. Yes, the Jeep and its color indicate it is a priming vehicle. The space next to my car is empty. As I get out and walk toward the thrift shop, I notice the Jeep has a Florida plate, which is extremely prevalent in these stalking vehicles. A tan sedan with an oversize American flag attached to the passenger-side window drives past. The driver is a woman with a masculine haircut.

I buy a bag, but the thrift store has no mouse for sale, so I pay and leave. During this brief retail encounter, a large, black truck, which has been jacked up about eight inches, has pulled into the space beside my car. It's so close I can't get into my own car. It has a big Semper Fi front bumper plate. The driver is reclined back in the driver's seat as if he's sleeping. He also has an ugly, long beard. (What is it with these beards?) I was only in that store for a few minutes, and this big truck wasn't there when I pulled up.

The two cop cars that were previously by the lot entrance are now parked on either side of the Walmart, where I am now headed. I shake my head, squeeze into my car, and refuse to allow this stalking campaign to dampen my plans. I park next to a Walmart shopping cart return.

As I enter the Walmart, three moms with their little girls walk into the store at the same time. The girls are about nine, the same age as my daughter, Lala. The mom ahead of me, a Hispanic woman, stops just inside the door and looks at her phone. The other moms and daughters filter into the store. When I'm a few feet past the Hispanic woman, she calls out to her daughter, "Lala! Lala! Look at this picture of your daddy, Lala."

I stop dead in my tracks, then turn and look at the woman. She makes eye contact with me and makes an odd smirk. Her daughter reaches for the phone and says, "Let me see," but the mom never shows her any picture. Suddenly, she grabs her daughter's hand and leaves the store.

As I stand there, paralyzed and in tears, one of the police cars drives by and I whisper to myself, "The only reaction you will get out of me is a tear." I wipe my eyes with my shirt and proceed to the electronics department.

I miss my daughter so much it hurts, and "they" know how to inflict emotional trauma. At this point, I choose to be blind. I refuse to see any other stalkers or priming symbols.

I quickly pick out the least-expensive mouse, pay for it at the checkout and obnoxiously hold the receipt in my hand as I exit. Naturally, the alarm goes off. I shrug and go back inside and patiently wait for a clerk to check my receipt. Walking toward my car, a police vehicle slowly rolls in front of me. The officer refuses to make eye contact.

I MapQuest the closest Panera Bread, figuring that would be a good place to start working on this story, but the drive there is depressing. I'm now emotionally spent. The reminder of how much I miss my daughter drains me further. I just can't believe I've been placed into such a cruel program, and I can't grasp that I'm being murdered in plain sight. What did I do to make so many people despise me?

I pull into Panera Bread and notice priming vehicles already parked there—a Range Rover and two black pickups. Since I used MapQuest, it was simple for "them" to know my destination and stage the next event. I buy a cup of Panera coffee and claim a lonely table in a back corner to set up camp. The first hour of writing is amazing. I notice the stalkers, of course, and the peacocking of priming symbols makes it obvious "they" are always with me. But I don't care. I am in a zone.

As I enter the second hour, I begin to feel odd symptoms. Someone in Panera, I think, must be triggering them—but who? There is a guy sitting at a table next to me with his back turned. He has three devices on the table—a laptop, a touch-screen computer and an iPhone—all connected to each other. I try hard to ignore it, but it's distracting. He has a goddam NSA computer lab set up on a table right next to me. He is well-groomed and dressed in business attire. He slowly sips a small cup of coffee, which he places to his right, and periodically wipes his left palm down his left leg. His right leg nervously bounces up and down. One could perceive this situation in numerous ways, but my intuition tells me he's not drinking enough coffee to be jittery, the dominant right side is showing signs of an unconscious impulse, and the wiping of his left hand down his left leg may demonstrate a sweaty palm. I perceive him as nervously uncertain.

I try to ignore him, but I start getting a tingling and itching on my legs and arms. I swat myself, as if a fly were landing on me, but there is no fly. The tingling transforms into the sensation of bugs crawling up my legs. I work through it, but when the left side of my sinus starts to burn and my left ear starts to ring, I know my new writing spot has been infiltrated and it's time to pack it up. As I stand up, I glance over the guy's shoulder. He acts like a little kid in school as he leans over his computer and blacks out the monitor. I have a fleeting impulse to beat the shit out of this guy, but the real me says to him in a stern yet playful tone, "You have yourself an awesome day."

Outside, I notice that the Range Rover and black pickup truck are still in the lot after two-and-a-half hours, but who knows? Maybe the minimum-wage workers can afford a fifty-thousand-dollar vehicle.

Now I hope you have a sense of a typical day in my life. But I need to address a few more things so you can understand of how totally screwed I am.

Priming doesn't just involve vehicles. The brainwashing also consists of symbols, colors, clothing, noises, and groups of people. This symbolism and noise campaigns are thrown in my face multiple times each day to make sure I never forget that I'm being murdered by a process known as "slow kill" or "soft kill."

The largest groups that have been funded involve the state university and a famous medical center I call Pukes Hospital. Now, I am still uncertain as to why these organizations are the most prevalent groups to sponsor my stalking. I have learned that within this state university is the second largest Illuminati cult in America, second to a world-famous theme park in Florida I call Happy Place. Perhaps I am being used as an experiment for the students at the university, or for some military class program.

Another predominant group, just as prevalent, if not equal to, is a women's rights organization. About 70 percent of my stalkers are women, so perhaps I have been falsely accused of violating Marsy's Law or an equivalent. Another group is DARE (Drug Abuse Resistance Education.) That is a whole other chapter on its own. I've also become aware of involvement by retired veterans, persons with disabilities, the National Rifle Association and Harley-Davidson. Lately, even more unsettling, is that I have become bombarded by the marines, army, air force, national guard, and reserves. I literally see uniformed soldiers participating in this stalking game like I'm Osama bin Laden.

Symbols and stickers are used as well. The iconic cartoon mouse head silhouette is the most obvious. Other symbols include a skull, red lips, the American flag, and marathon numbers like 13.1, 26.2, and 0.0. The "slow kill" program is indeed a marathon and constantly throwing these symbols and stickers in my face is how it covertly communicates the sadistic message. The more obvious death signs are having a perpetrator drive by me with a full-size skeleton riding in the passenger seat. Another example is having hearses participate in the vehicular stalking and they even got vehicles to blare their speakers around me with the song, "Murder she Wrote."

A small Puerto Rican flag is a common trigger that is often hung on the mirror of a car. Similar triggers are dream catchers, flowery leis, and fish decals with *Jesus* written in the middle. Seeing these triggers a few times a day would be normal, but I see them at almost every glance, every turn, which makes me feel like an army is constantly following me around. It is disturbing, to say the least, especially combined with the effects of poisoning.

Physically, I feel like a piece of gum that has been chewed by three different people with gingivitis and then stuck to a subway floor to be stepped on by thousands of commuters.

Medically, I've been diagnosed with sinus disease, rhinitis, sinusitis, CIRS, respiratory infections, pneumonia, candida disease, and allergies to just about everything. The CAT scan from ten months ago showed a large cyst in my left sinus with total obstruction of the pathways in both sinuses. The CAT scan of my left shoulder showed that I have a loose bone island, whatever that means. Surgery was scheduled twice but then cancelled by people other than me for reasons I will explain later.

I started to become aware that I was a target of a covert intimidation program during a five-day stay for treatment of pneumonia in Pukes Hospital. I don't remember this episode too well. For four of the five days I was in an induced coma. After the fifth day I was released while still suffering from pneumonia. So, what did the medical staff do to me during those four unconscious days? Certainly not cure my pneumonia. I still feel the congestion in my lungs as I write this story. Pukes Hospital claimed it identified a fractured rib on my left side, which I think the hospital broke intentionally to conceal an implanted RFID (radio frequency identification) device, allowing the bone to heal over it.

Psychologically, I have more labels than a NASCAR stock car. I have been diagnosed with depression, anxiety, psychosis, delusional disorder and paranoid schizophrenia, just to name a few. I have thought about adding Tourette's to the list so I can curse people out and get away with it.

I don't take any medications except for nasal sprays and Benadryl. The psychiatrist tried to pump me full of zombie-causing drugs, but I refused. It's very interesting that the number one side effect of these psychotic meds is suicidal tendencies. Don't forget, "their" main goal is suicide.

My legal background is squeaky clean, except for three fraudulent PFAs submitted by my ex-wife. I have a clean driving record, with just a handful of very old traffic violations. Although I have no criminal record and I'm loved and respected by people who know me, I have been battling through a traumatizing divorce and a profound illness due to mold exposure.

I am a man fighting an invisible war. My health is rapidly declining, I have been blocked from receiving appropriate medical treatment, but my cognitive abilities have peaked to a nearly superhuman level. My intuition and thinking have become so keen that I've been able to stay ahead of the covert intimidation playbook long enough to share my story.

Here is the looming question. See if you can guess the answer. By the end of the book, you will be able to score yourself.
Why is a criminal syndicate spending hundreds of millions of dollars to implement a complex program with the intent of both cruel and unusual punishment and nonjudicial execution?

A. I stumbled onto a classified government secret and became too vocal about how the military uses mold and mycotoxins for biological warfare.

B. I was heinously set up by my Mafia-boss/father-in-law who attacked me at gunpoint and told me he was going to have me killed.

C. I allowed an evil, manipulative woman into my life during a dark period and she just happened to still be married to the sheriff.

D. I managed to upset a powerful mouse and painfully learned its Florida home is not only evil and unforgiving but has nearly unlimited power and influence.

E. All the above.

Chapter 2

The Lutter Lad

I grew up on Shaler Street on the south side of Allentown, Pennsylvania. Our next-door neighbors had keys to our house and in summer we left the doors open at night to let the breeze come through. We were a tight community. My parents, three siblings and I lived in a three-bedroom twin with a front and back yard.

I was the baby of the family. When I was born, my parents were in their late thirties. My older brother was born twelve years earlier and my other brother two years later. My sister is four years older than I am. When I was just six, my bedtime was nine o'clock, which meant I missed out on a lot of family interaction. I remember sitting at the top of the stairs after being sent to bed so I could hear the family having fun downstairs. I wanted to grow up so badly!

Before my brothers left for college, we shared the largest bedroom. I tried to stay awake until they came up to bed so I could eavesdrop on their lively conversations, and then we'd roughhouse and play games until dad would yell, "Knock it off!" When I couldn't fall asleep, they'd tell me fanciful stories like, "Fuzzy alligators are waiting on the floor to eat you if you get out of bed."

I learned a lot from listening to them. I remember wondering why anyone would want to touch tongues with a girl, which they called "making out." I learned how they convinced Mom to let them go to parties. I loved meeting my brothers' girlfriends at the house—

actually. I loved attention from these older girls. They'd sit me on their lap and show me all kinds of affection.

My brother used to take me to get haircuts down the street because he liked one of the hairdressers. I learned a lot by looking down the shirt of this beautiful woman as she leaned over me. I think that's when I knew I wanted a girlfriend.

Krista Brown was my first love and my first kiss—odd, considering we were in kindergarten. I met Krista at the bus stop, and we would hold hands all the way to school. When we got off the bus, we'd lean into each other and kiss on the lips. We were six. The best way I can explain the feeling is "magic."

Maybe you can imagine how devastated I was the day when Krista wasn't at the bus stop. She wasn't in school, either. Nobody bothered to explain why, but I discovered later that Krista and her mom had moved across town. From that point on, I was a hopeless romantic.

After my brothers moved away for college, they would still come home summers to work as lifeguards at the local pools. One year, my brother was named manager, and I got all kinds of special attention when I went to the pool. I got to hang out in the clubhouse and sit on the tower chair with an assortment of attractive, oiled-up women. Maybe these older women in skimpy swimsuits just wanted to impress my brother by pampering me, but I didn't care. At ten, I was cavorting with half-naked women who would let me swim between their legs in the water, put me on their shoulders for chicken fights, or just cuddle me in the water when I was cold—which I was a lot.

When Mom and Dad went away, my brothers sometimes threw parties at the house. Since they were supposed to be babysitting me, I got to join in on some of the fun. These women partygoers were often drinking heavily, which seemed to make them more aggressively affectionate, particularly to me, the harmless little brother.

Because they were nearly the same age, my brothers had a very tight bond, which I would never achieve with them. But they were my role models. I wanted not only to be a part of that brotherly bond but wanted to be just like them.

Being the only girl in the family, My sister had her own bedroom between the other two. My sister and I were close growing up. As a girl, of course, she spent a lot of time on the phone and doing girly things. But when she did have time, we had a lot of fun. Although she was four years older, we'd invent fun games or do holiday decorating together. One of our funniest games we called "Guess What This Is." While one of us was blindfolded, the other one would put all kinds of crazy concoctions on a spoon. The blindfolded victim would taste it and guess what it was. We used things like oil, hot sauce, old coffee grounds, peanut butter, spices of every kind, you name it. We played this a lot until one of us threw up and we got in trouble.

We also played hide-and-seek a lot. We would try—and usually succeed—to scare the hell out of each other by jumping out and screaming. One time, my sister scared me so badly when she jumped out from behind the shower curtain that I began screaming uncontrollably. My flight mechanism kicked into high gear and I leaped down the flight of thirteen stairs without touching a single step. We still don't know how I managed without getting hurt. The racket brought my mom racing into the living room. Once I saw her expression, my sister and I broke out in laughter—the kind where your belly hurts and tears stream down. Another time, we scared each other so badly we ran into each other, knocking us flat on our backs. We always had a good time.

My favorite childhood memories were when the six of us were all together. Christmas was a much-loved time. Each of us would get thirteen presents. Some were silly—like socks or PJs—but each us got the one or two big items we really wanted. I would come down the stairs and see a wall of wrapped gifts stacked so high it blocked the bottom half of the tree. Dad always put four different-colored stickers on the presents and we each had to figure out our own color. Then we'd take turns opening our gifts, holding each one up so Dad could film us with his old-fashioned movie camera. It would take us hours to open our presents. To this day, I still hold each one of those minutes close to my heart.

My parents didn't have the greatest marriage in the world. I recall many arguments and a lot of yelling. Maybe that was why my mom dedicated so much of her life to her children. But I admire the fact that they always worked things out and they're still together after fifty-six years.

My dad didn't make a ton of money and he worked a lot of hours, but he was usually home for dinner every night by six-thirty. He worked for years as a service manager. To this day, I consider him a genius. My brothers, though, experienced that genius more than I did. When they were in Boy Scouts, Dad built a derby racetrack with electronic releases and sounds. He even built the derby cars, which won every race.

During Halloween, Dad would decorate the yard with his inventions. There was a ghost hooked to a wire that floated around the yard controlled by a small gear motor. It had creepy arms with hands that a homemade electronic gadget would open and close. The yard was filled with headstones with monster names on them like "Werewolf" and "Frankenstein." We always got the most trick-or-treaters because our house was the most fun to visit.

Mom was a saint and an amazing mother. She didn't start working until I was in junior high, so she was a stay-at-home mom most of her married life. She raised a household of six on one average salary and still managed to make our childhoods magical. She even helped my brothers with a paper route to help pay for my brother's braces. Somehow, Mom managed to always get us season passes to Dorney Park and Wildwater Kingdom and also took us to the Jersey Shore every year for a family vacation.

Mom grew up with very strict rules. She wasn't really allowed off her front porch while growing up. She earned straight A's in high school and was offered a full scholarship to attend a university in another city. Unfortunately, her father didn't want her to leave home.

The way my mom was raised seems to have influenced her parenting. Her children lived under very strict rules and expectations for their behavior. Mom was never late paying a bill, never got a parking ticket or traffic violation, and never broke a single rule or law. She was a worrywart and a tough taskmaster at home but made up for all the controlling rules with intense love.

She was also superstitious. Our last name, Lutterschmidt, contains thirteen letters. My mother thought the number 13 was unlucky but believed the number 7 was lucky. So, to balance out the bad luck of having thirteen letters in "Lutterschmidt," she gave each of her kids a first name containing seven letters.

I had a few close friends who lived on the same street. The bunch of us would spend summer days creating games and playing football or Wiffle ball in the yard. We'd go on adventures to nearby South Mountain and catch crayfish and salamanders in the creek. In the evening, we'd play flashlight tag or board games on the front porch. We'd build igloos during the winter and have snowball fights, go sledding every chance we could, and keep making up silly games.

I've been blessed with an amazing childhood.

Chapter 3

Identity Issue

Growing up as the baby in the family, with an age chasm between my siblings and me, must have affected my personality. I had a very difficult time finding my own identity. Looking back on that time I see a boy who was self-conscious and lacking in self-esteem and confidence.

I was six when my oldest brother left for college. I was just starting to grow up as my family began to fragment. As a kind of "outsider" because of my age, I was eager to become part of my family, but it was disappearing. My second brother moved away to college when I was eight, causing even more emptiness in my life. I know my brothers hadn't left the family, but I felt like I had lost the opportunity to grow with my family. During this time, my sister was moving through her teenage years. Hanging out with her little brother was not a priority for her, but she was always there for me when I needed her. I am still blessed with an amazing sister.

Ever since I can remember, I had been adored, pampered and babied by every woman who met me, including my brothers' girlfriends, lifeguards, my friends' moms, neighbors and teachers. Strangely, this had little positive impact on my confidence or self-worth.

Throughout grade school, I never had a male teacher—always females—and usually became the "teacher's pet," which became my identity. This brought ridicule and abuse from my peers, most likely out of jealousy. At the time, though, this torment diminished my self-esteem even more. As a result, I found ways to attach myself to teachers. I could usually relate better to these older women than to students because I had grown up with older siblings and their girlfriends. Teachers would give me responsibilities they wouldn't trust other students to fulfill—safety patrol, escorting sick kids to the nurse, special lunch duties, et cetera. My classmates hated me for this attention, and often bullied me because of it. This cruel behavior made me attach myself even more to my teachers, which in turn continued to harden the wall between me and my classmates.

During middle school, my brothers were only home for holidays, my sister was wrapped up in high school life, Mom had developed a career at a bank, and my dad was still working a lot of hours. I was a world-class dork with no clear identity. I didn't know how to style my hair, how to dress, even how to act in most social situations. I did manage to meet my two best childhood friends. Albert had lived in the same neighborhood this whole time, but since he had gone to a different elementary school, I had never met him before. Angel had recently moved into nearby apartments with his mom. For these middle school years, the three of us were inseparable.

School had its cliques, but Albert, Angel and I became our very own group. Still, we meshed well with other groups and all kinds of kids. We made each other laugh so much that others wanted to join our fun. We were all dorks in a way, but we had a great time together. Albert and Angel became my "brothers" and helped me experience the close bond I had always desired.

Since my first kiss in kindergarten, I had been a hopeless romantic, so upon entering junior high all I could think about was having a girlfriend. I had no idea, of course, what that really meant. I was so eager that I asked the prettiest girl in school to go out with me. I wrote a note and had Angel give it to her. "Going out" in junior high just meant being known as a couple. I was so shocked when she said yes that I didn't know what to do. My real brothers had never taught me that lesson. The prettiest girl in school broke up with me a week later, probably because I never really talked to her after giving her that note.

During my first year of junior high school, I had thirteen girlfriends. Twelve of them ended the same way. I was apparently cute enough to catch the girls' attention, but my shyness and lack of confidence gave me the appeal of dry toast. I had no spark.

I remember inviting a girl on a ride called *Journey to the Center of the Earth*. This was popularly known as the "make-out" ride—a slow boat going through dark tunnels punctuated by spooky setups. I had the entire ride to kiss her, but I froze and didn't do anything. Albert and Angel laughed at me for months for that epic fail.

The first girl I ever French kissed was Diana. She was a beautiful but feisty Hispanic girl, certainly not afraid to take control. I really needed someone like her at that time. The kiss occurred in a busy hallway after school. Diana didn't care. I knew the kiss was coming, and I was nervous. Diana grabbed my shirt, pulled me close and stuck her tongue in my mouth. I just tried to copy what she was doing. She told me to relax, gave me a little instruction and we tried again. The kids in the hallway applauded and whistled. I had finally found a shred of confidence.

Diana wasn't just my girlfriend—she became my bodyguard too. If another girl tried to talk to me, she'd get beat up after school. People who spoke badly about me or gave me trouble would get smacked in the face. Diana was a thug, and I loved it. She made up for my lack of confidence.

In high school, I was still winning a position as teacher's pet. Some of my relationships with female teachers even became flirtatious. But as I grew into an attractive young man, I still had serious confidence issues. My physical maturation made it easier to focus on college girls, teachers and older women in general. Those early days at the pool sitting on the smooth, oiled legs of beautiful lifeguards may have shaped my preferences.

In one area I have never lacked confidence—sports. I've played baseball all my life and was acknowledged to have the strongest arm on the team—perhaps in the league. I had a good batting average and started every game. There were times when I would walk up to the plate with unbreakable confidence. I believe these were moments when my true self shone through. Inevitably, every time I believed in myself, I was unstoppable. Most of the time, however, I second-guessed myself too much.

Good grades came easy for me. I never had to study—just paid attention in class. And since I was usually the teacher's pet, I often got a heads-up on tests and occasionally helped create the quizzes. So, getting good grades wasn't a solution to developing confidence.

By the time I graduated from high school, I still had no clear identity. I had no goal other than to get accepted into Kutztown University. At this point, my older brother was getting his PhD, my other brother was on his way to a long teaching career, and my sister was earning her master's degree.

Who the hell was I?

Chapter 4

Id, Ego, or Superego

The summer before I left for college, I was working two jobs—as a cashier at Laneco Foodlane and a waiter at a high-class country club.

Christine, my assistant manager at Laneco, was a gorgeous, petite woman in her thirties. She'd would wear tight, short dresses, and I would constantly get caught staring at her. Before long she was giving me all kinds of special tasks the same way my teachers did. I was attracted to her, but I still lacked confidence in a lot of areas, so I never responded to her seductive comments or body language.

No matter what job I was given, I always seemed to do it well. I was the fastest cashier and delivered great customer service so before long I started to get customers who would intentionally come through my checkout line and tell Christine I was doing a good job.

One day, a woman in her forties gave me a bag of cookies she had baked for me. I opened the bag on my break and along with the cookies—which were kind of dry—I found a note with her phone number. It took me a couple days to work up the courage to call. Eventually, we met at a local park and she confessed her intentions. For the next two months, I became her special friend, discovering I was still attracted to an older woman who took control.

Impressed with my performance on the job, Christine, recommended that I help train employees in a new program to enhance customer service. This would become the steppingstone I needed to find myself. The program was called BARS, and the idea was to acknowledge and recognize good customer service and reward it with positive reinforcement. Suddenly, at just eighteen years old, I was training thirty employees on teamwork and delivering exceptional service. For the first time in my life, I was speaking with confidence, which came from someone believing in me. The main facilitator told me he was going to incorporate some of my original ideas.

Two days each week, I would wait tables at an upscale country club, the kind that costs fifty grand per year to be a member. I wore a black tux with an annoying bow tie. I must have looked like a piece of candy to those rich housewives. While their husbands were playing golf, the blinged-out wives, would get drunk on schnapps and slip fifty-dollar bills down my pocket. They'd keep me chatting at the table and make suggestive remarks. I felt like a prostitute, but I was supposed to play along because these were people of means and my job was to make them happy, so my manager claimed.

I made so much money from tips at the county club that I refused to tell anyone. I felt a little dirty. The cash stuffed into my pockets in one shift would take me forty hours to earn at Laneco, but I continued working at the store because I liked the feeling of success and loved the positive reinforcement.

By the end of August, I left my jobs and headed for Kutztown University, a forty-five-minute drive from home. This would be the first time I'd be completely on my own. I already knew my roommate, Frankie, who I had grown up with me on Shaler Street.

Frankie and I arrived a few days before classes began. Because our moms were so awesome, our room, on a co-ed floor, was loaded up with all the comforts of home. It quickly became known as the "hangout," because it was a resort compared to the other dorm rooms.

Frank took college seriously and studied hard. I figured that with all my success in school I'd be fine, so I did what most college kids do—partied and socialized. I had been confined by strict rules all my life, and now it was time to get a taste of freedom. Of course, I went a little overboard. But the college experience was unfamiliar to me. Instead of having twenty kids in class, I was one of sixty or seventy. I paid attention and took notes, but the professors only covered parts of the material and left it to us to read the rest. I introduced myself to the professors like I had with my high school teachers, but they seemed unimpressed and distracted.

Tests and good grades had always come naturally for me, and I'd never spent hours reading or studying, so for the first two weeks I skimmed through the assignments and reviewed the chapters assigned in my first class. Then we received our first test and I got a big "D" on it. I knew I was in trouble.

Instead of focusing on studying harder, I escaped from the anxiety by just having fun. When I tried to study, our room would be overrun by friends, but I didn't care. For the first time in my life, I was one of the cool kids. But I didn't know how to balance this life with my studies.

After a few short months with terrible grades, I was forced to have a conversation with my parents. I told them that I was having trouble at school and there were way too many distractions. I chose to leave out some details, like my girlfriend Jaime visiting every week, the naked Twister tournaments on our coed floor, the tricycle races in the hallway, the heavy drinking—you know, the fun stuff.

My parents were disappointed but supportive. They suggested I transfer to DeSales University, which was right up the street from their new three-acre dream home. My older brother and my sister had both graduated from DeSales, and our family had developed a close relationship with Father Pete, one of the oblates and professors.

I transferred, and I was now studying in a private, quiet bedroom in my parent's incredible home in a parklike setting. I studied every night and followed a schedule I had worked out with my counselor. I was nailing tests, and my first semester achieved two A's and two B's. I went to the gym with Father Pete before classes and then played basketball with my psychology professor in the afternoon. Father Pete got me a part-time job working in the kitchen of Wills Hall, in which the oblates lived. I only went out on weekends. I had no distractions except for my girlfriend Jaime, who was my first long-term relationship. Jaime and I did everything together, and the connection we shared saved me at a future time.

Things were going well, and I was in a comfort zone. But I still had no end in mind. At this point, I was just going through the motions, but doing it well.

One day, however, Jaime was invited to an ex-boyfriend's house and things took place that I won't describe. I had never gone through a betrayal before, so I started hanging out with other girls and eventually Jaime and I fizzled.

Then I met a guy named Joe who lived by the Laneco I had worked at. He was the first person I'd ever met who suffered from a substance issue. I did pot and beer at parties but never felt a compulsion to get drunk or stoned. I hated the feeling of throwing up or getting the spins.

Joe had a very difficult childhood. He lived with his sister and didn't speak much about his mom or dad. One Friday night, while dancing at a party in a crowded house, Joe pinched a girl's butt. He was just trying to be funny, but she didn't see the humor in it.

I went upstairs to use the bathroom, but right after closing the door heard someone shouting, "Is he in there?" Someone else said, "We'll get him when he comes out."

As I walked out of the bathroom, six seniors pushed me into an adjacent bedroom and slammed me between a bunk bed and the wall. I used the wall to my advantage as I ducked punches and avoided reaching arms. One big guy grabbed my shirt. I pulled his arm fiercely toward me and then threw him onto the lower bunk.

When I was a kid, my sister scared me so badly my "flight mechanism" kicked in. Well, this time my "fight mechanism" accelerated into super-drive. As I threw the guy onto the bunk bed, he held on to my shirt and tore it right off my back. Another guy bear-hugged me from behind. As one of his buddies came toward me to take a swing, I lifted my feet and kicked him hard. He went flying backward and knocked over two dudes behind him. The force of the kick sent me backward as well. The bear-hugging guy hit the wall so hard the drywall cracked, and he released his grip. When I turned to check on him, I was bear-hugged again by a monstrous guy, wrestled down the stairs and flung outside.

I was missing my shirt and a shoe, but I didn't have one scratch on me. Over a hundred people gathered around the ruckus and my fight mechanism gave no signs of subsiding. I had no idea I had been mistaken as the guy who had pinched the girl's butt on the dance floor. I felt that I was just being assaulted.

Joe was nowhere to be found of course. And it turned out that the monster who wrestled me out of the house was the boyfriend of the girl Joe had molested. This big dude then walked up to me and the crowd encircled us as if we were in a cage match.

"Just you this time?" I asked my assailant.

He grunted something.

Then, I said something that won the crowd to my side. Lifting my shoeless foot and pointing at it, I said, "I just want my damn shoe back. You can have the shirt."

The crowd started to laugh and clap.

Never had I ever been a full-blown fistfight. I was always too worried about getting into trouble. So, I had developed skills in avoiding confrontation. But here I was, egging on an older, angry, much larger dude. As I said before, though, I have a freakishly strong arm.

My adversary looked down at me—he was a good two inches taller—then pushed me hard. I pushed him back—harder. Insulted, he wound up and took a swing at me. It seemed to be in slow motion because he started down near his waist and came up and around. I bent backward so his swing just grazed my left cheek.

And then I snapped.

It was a little scary, the feeling of being out of control. It was the kind of mental break I had experienced when my sister jumped out from behind the shower curtain and scared me. The kind of mindless, adrenalin-pumped surge that propelled me down thirteen stairs in a single bound.

My right hook struck him in the stomach. As he crunched down to my level, it was game over. I connected with a vicious left jab followed by a right blow to the head.

The strength of my right arm dropped him to his knees. Before I could even look up, a classmate of mine pulled me away. I had blood all over my bare chest. I looked over at the monster, who was kneeling with strings of blood descending to the ground. Immediately, I felt remorse, and wanted to apologize. I was terrified that I had lost control of myself. Rage had overwhelmed my emotions and I had irrationally responded.

A friend told me I needed to leave, and then took me to get cleaned up at his campus apartment. I was very worried about getting in serious trouble. I'd been doing so well in school—would I be expelled now?

A knock on the door was followed by a male voice: "Open up, this is the police!"

My heart began to race. I was convinced at this moment that I was going to jail.

My classmate opened the door and two officers entered the room. One of them asked for me by name. Seeing the blood on my chest, he focused his flashlight beam on me.

I explained that I had been jumped by a few guys in the house, but I didn't know why. A guy had pushed me, so I pushed back.

"He swung at me, and to be honest, I really don't know what happened after that," I said.

The cop with the flashlight said with a smirk, "You kicked the shit out of him, that's what happened."

Then he said something that calmed me down. "We have statements that he attacked you first." Then he asked me something I was not expecting. "Do you want to press charges?"

I was both shocked and relieved. "Absolutely not," I said.

That Monday, I experienced a new kind of fame as the story must have traveled around the school. (Then again, half the school was probably watching the fight anyway.)

A few days later, I passed my huge assailant in the hallway. He had several stitches over his left eye. I wanted to apologize but couldn't formulate the words quickly enough. We made awkward eye contact and kept walking.

I wasn't even the guy who had pinched his girlfriend, but here I was burdened with guilt.

My friend Joe, who had started the entire affair, called me a few days later. He said later that evening he had woken up in a wooded patch just off campus after blacking out. He couldn't remember anything about that night. It was then that I realized Joe really had a problem

School continued to go well. I started dating a lot of girls and chose not to hang out with Joe for a while. A few weeks later, Joe convinced me to go to a party in Quakertown. We ended up in the middle of nowhere at a dilapidated house. I had a few beers, but noticed the other people were acting strange. I had smoked pot before, but these people seemed to be on a different playing field.

I continued to try to convince Joe to take me back home. He kept walking from the living room, where I was sitting, to a back bedroom. Finally, he came out and said, "Okay, but we have to walk home because no one could drive us."

I dreaded walking home in a cold November drizzle. When we got outside, he stopped alongside a white car, looked inside and said, "Come on, get in. I'll drive you home."

I asked him, "Whose car is this?"

He told me some name that I had never heard before. I knew he was lying, but I just wanted to get home, so I hopped in the car and he started driving.

When we got to a road where we needed to turn, he made a left instead of a right. I told him we were going the wrong way, but he said he needed to leave the car for someone to pick up the following day. He drove another mile and then parked in the parking lot of a closed business.

I asked him again, "Can't you just drop me off first?"

"It's time to go, but wipe off the doors first," he said.

He took his shirt off and started wiping the steering wheel and door handles. Then it struck me that this bastard had just stolen a car! I don't know where he'd gotten the keys, but I was terrified now.

I said, "I'm walking."

I never turned around. It was nearly one-thirty in the morning. I was soaked and freezing when I got to my front door. I didn't know what to do, so woke up my parents and told them what had happened. We all decided to sleep on it.

That morning, Joe called to say that he taken the car to a guy in Philly. I still didn't know for sure if it was a friend's car—not until my mom, who never missed reading the newspaper, read that a car had been stolen in Quakertown and then found in Center City, Philadelphia, with the keys on the dashboard. We didn't know what to make out of it, but one thing for sure, I was never going to hang out with Joe again.

I hung out in my room for the rest of the weekend, trying to get over the anxiety. On Monday, as I came down the stairs to leave for school, I noticed my parents were home from work and sitting on the couch. I also saw Father Pete and my sister, who was supposed to be away at school, sitting on the other couch. I had walked right into an intervention.

My family and Father Pete insisted that I sit down. Then Pete said, "I took care of your classes and you can resume school when you get out of rehab."

I thought, *This is fucking ridiculous!* I had just learned firsthand what it meant to "have a problem," like Joe, and now I was being accused of being an alcoholic, like Joe. I certainly wasn't behaving like him. I had just been around him when he made unwise decisions.

But it was pretty much decided, though, and everything had been arranged. I remember being frustrated and feeling betrayed. I loved and respected my family, so I agreed to treatment, leaving that night for a stint at the Caron Foundation.

The first night was the hardest. I was around alcoholics, heroin addicts, pill poppers and tweakers. As I participated in the groups, I wondered, *Is this really happening?* I was not a drunk. I never did anything more than smoke pot, but here I was, introducing myself as an addict.

I listened to nightmare stories from people in the group. I remember thinking, *Why don't you just stop using?* Why is it so difficult to not drink more than a beer? Why is it so hard to not take a boatload of pills? During those two weeks, however, I learned that some people truly can't control their desire for intoxication or escape. I came out understanding what addiction is and that I was not an addict.

Rehab wasn't all bad. I met a nice, gorgeous girl about my age. She was kind and loving and agreed to treatment because she drank too much in college. Her wealthy parents had forced her to come to Caron Foundation for basically the same behaviors that I had shown at Kutztown University. We connected right off the bat and soon found ways to spend private time together, although it was completely against the rules. During movie time, she would sneak out and walk down to the bottom of a grassy hill. I would wait five minutes and then pretend to use the bathroom but instead rendezvous with her. We'd make love in the grass under the stars, then scramble back before the movie was over.

After my release, being home felt strange for the first week or two. It was Christmastime, so my whole family was home for the holidays. It was unsettling, though, to observe the entire holiday without rum-drenched eggnog, especially knowing that I was to blame.

At last it was time to select classes for the upcoming semester. I was feeling a dangerous anger on top of uncontrollable resentment. I'd been forced to leave school without any say. I'd been getting straight A's at the time. Not only had I been I forced to abandon one of my best semesters, but I also had been compelled to leave school just when I'd become a popular kid for the first time in my life. I had respect and fame. I had girls throwing themselves at me. Every dude wanted to be me—or so I believed.

I suppose pride skewed my decision to not return to school. I was too bitter. I decided to get a job and prove that I didn't need college. So, I assigned myself to work on my résumé. I was very proud of the résumé I created, even though my brother said I was never going to get a decent job without a college degree and would be making minimum wage for the rest of my life. That made me want to prove I could do better than that.

My parents did not support my effort to find a full-time job. The lack of support, however, kindled my commitment. So, I faxed my résumé to twenty different employers who had advertised in the local newspaper. Most of the available positions were entry-level, and I knew I didn't want to sell meatballs in the aisle of a grocery store, so I graciously turned down the opportunities that were offered.

I finally received a call from Dave, a district manager for Kerkins Restaurant. He was looking for assistant managers but was reluctant on the phone to give me an interview because I had no previous management experience. In the small window of time I had over the phone, I managed to make my experience relevant to the position he needed to fill.

The morning of my interview, I ironed the only suit that I owned, which had been bought for several funerals. I didn't have GPS, so I printed off MapQuest instructions for the hour-long drive. Then I headed off for Warminster, a town I had never even heard of before. I combed my wispy hair and walked into the restaurant like I owned the place. I asked for Dave, and the hostess said he'd be right out. I stood in the lobby with my head up and my shoulders back.

An intimidating man came out and shook my hand. I could tell he had already made an assumption about me. Here I was, twenty-one years old but looking sixteen, interviewing for a job where I would be responsible for forty employees and fifty thousand dollars a week in sales.

During the interview, the district manager asked me, "Why do you think you are qualified for this position?"

"Because I can't fail," I said. "I won't fail."

He smirked and asked what I meant by that.

I told him that I had been going to college but didn't know why. I saw students spending thousands of dollars, getting themselves into great debt so they could eventually go out and interview for a job, just like I was doing right then.

"Let me save that money and allow me to jump ahead," I said. "Let me help you make more money." I strategically spoke about my current job, where I was working with the priests at the university.

This meant I was a good Catholic boy. Then I explained how I dealt with the rich, entitled members of the country club. I told Dave that no matter how poorly those members treated me, I always smiled and gave them the very best service.

Dave responded to my honesty and confidence.

I proceeded to tell him about my experience at Laneco. I continued to be myself and only spoke the truth. I explained that I always went above and beyond to help customers. My abilities with cash handling and service had been acknowledged by my manager, Christine, who had asked me to become a lead trainer for a customer service initiative in the company.

Two days later, Dave offered me a salaried management position at thirty-thousand dollars per year with benefits—not bad for 1999. My parents couldn't believe the news at first and thought I was joking. I was now making more money than my mom and earning a higher salary than my brother who had graduated from college. I was ready to start a career and discover just who I was and what I could achieve.

Chapter 5

Michael James Lutterschmidt

In this chapter, I hope to share how my life blossomed so my daughter, Lala, will know the kind of man her father has been all his life.

I became the youngest salaried manager in the history of Kerkins. I was barely of legal age to drink alcohol, but I oversaw forty employees and responsible for an entire restaurant. I only saw my general manager, Ben, during a biweekly management meeting. Other than that, I was on my own to manage the entire restaurant.

The truth is, I made every mistake in the book, but that was how I learned. I made friends with the employees, and when it came time for disciplining certain behaviors, the friendships were hard to keep separate from the business side. But I found my own way.

One of the employees who caused problems was a hostess named Gena Darkino who only worked one or two days a week. For example, she refused to wear a headset to communicate available tables. I used that opportunity to get the busboys more involved instead of making a big deal of Gena's obstinance. Gena was finishing high school with a degree in attitude. We hated each other at first, but over the next several months she began to show me respect and even some affection.

I worked my ass off. The drive to Warminster took me over an hour one way, and I didn't leave the restaurant until one o'clock the next morning, arriving at home just before two. At times I'd stay at someone's house only to wake up and do it all over again the next day.

Eventually, Gena and I started dating. She'll deny it, but she asked me to hang out with her while standing in the kitchen at Kerkins Restaurant. After she graduated, we dated through that summer. The first time I went to pick her up at her parents' house there were four cars in the driveway. I was impressed when I walked up to the beautiful stone home with a huge pool in the backyard.

Gena introduced me to her Italian family, who were having dinner. For some reason, the vibe of her family intimidated the hell out of me. I remember thinking, *Great, I just walked into a Mob family breaking bread.*

Her father, Don, was at the head of the table. He had thick black hair and looked like a character in the Godfather movies. Her mother sat next to him and was oddly soft-spoken, almost as if she were not allowed to speak. Gena's olive-skinned brother and his wife sat next to her mom. He had even thicker black hair than Don and gave me a stern, almost threatening look. His body language seemed like a warning to be nice to his baby sister. Gena's grandfather was at the other end of the table. I swear this picture was right out of a Mafia movie.

I shook everybody's hand, and Gena eagerly pushed me out the door, even though her father had invited me to stay for dinner.

In our early dating days, Gena didn't like to discuss her family. She usually changed the subject or avoided certain questions. I wanted to get to know her, but she was guarded when we spoke about our childhoods. All I knew was that her father owned a construction business.

Running the restaurant became fun and exciting. I have always been a fast learner, so I quickly developed key skills that contributed to my success. Most importantly, the experience provided me with more confidence. After developing and building a cohesive team that demonstrated commitment, I had to be cautious about bringing new blood into the mix.

August quickly rolled around and it was time for Gena to leave for her studies at the Fashion Institute of Technology (FIT) in New York City. We had long conversations about staying together during a long-distance relationship. She was worried about losing what we had started. We started to connect and grow as a couple. During school, she'd come home every weekend to be with me, and I found opportunities to visit her in New York.

I remember driving my convertible Mazda Miata to Manhattan after work one night. The sun was just starting to rise when I got into the city—a truly magical experience. Towering buildings loomed over our heads and the city began to awaken with a hustle and bustle I never knew existed. It was hard to focus on driving. The first time I had come to New York, I pulled up to a construction worker and asked, "Where's Manhattan?" He laughed and replied, "You're in it!"

The distance between us created moments of uncertainty. No matter what drama or arguments arose, we always found ourselves working through them together. She was very attractive, and I knew there were guys around her who she allowed into her life, but I never felt jealously—not often, anyway. On the other hand, I was around many other girls myself and stayed true.

Gena was very insecure, though. She usually assumed the worst and was constantly starting jealous arguments about other girls. I had become a fun and very outgoing guy, which created a level of attraction that she worried about. I was flirtatious by nature, but in my mind the flirting was always innocent. I think her insecurity and lack of confidence were the main reasons she came home every weekend.

FIT allowed only freshmen to reside on campus. When Gena finished her first year, it was her responsibility to find housing. I remember our conversation about it word for word.

We drove to the park near her parents' house, and she asked me a question that would change my life: "Would you be willing to move to New York while I finish school?"

"Hell no!" I replied, then explained I couldn't leave my mom and dad and would be totally lost in the big city.

I thought about it for a few days, however, and I'm still not sure what changed my mind. I called her later that week and I told her our relationship meant so much to me that I really wanted to be there with her. After all, my older brother and my sister had moved away from home and started a career. What was it that was holding me back? Maybe this was an opportunity for me to grow as a person.

Gena was shocked and relieved. Gena and I had grown as a couple the past two years despite being apart so much, but this seemed like the logical next step. I was confident that I could find a job in the Big Apple.

When we revealed our plan, Gena's parents agreed to pay half our rent while she was in school. When I thanked her father, he told me, "I was going to pay for her room and board regardless, and I'm happy she is moving to the city with you."

That weekend, we drove to Brooklyn and looked at three apartments. The last one was in Bay Ridge on Seventy-Second Street, a much nicer section of Brooklyn. There were family-owned shops on the street and the subway was located right on the corner. The third-floor apartment was so small that no matter where we stood, we could see or hear each other, it was clean and far better than the other two units.

After a half-hour of debate, I finally said to Gena, "Okay, let's just do it." We gave each other a kiss, and I believe that moment was the true beginning of our relationship.

My parents took the news surprisingly well. They were, of course, concerned about employment and money issues. So, I updated my résumé and began applying for jobs. Gena's parents helped to buy us a couch and some odds and ends. The rest of our furniture came from hand-me-downs.

Within a couple weeks, I began to receive calls for interviews. My previous job success had stoked my ego—perhaps overstoked it. I'd come to believe that every interview would produce a job offer. I convinced myself that I wasn't being interviewed for a job, but rather I was the one interviewing the company to be worthy of my employment.

After a few interviews, I accepted an assistant general manager position with Kosi Restaurant and Bar in Union Square. I was in my early twenties earning a salary no one back home would believe, and

I was managing a multi-million-dollar restaurant in a trendy section of the center of the universe.

I approached my new position by using the knowledge I had retained from previous successes. Within a few months, I had built a team that would go to battle for me. We were grossing over seventy thousand per week with our open-kitchen concept. Within the first six months, I began to turn the heads of my superiors. I was reliable, trustworthy, and boosting sales. I learned to control labor and food costs while meeting the individual needs of my team.

My role as a leader, backed with the support from an entire team, soon became my identity. Whenever I had a team behind me, I could create magic. Within my first year of employment, I was promoted to training store manager and was responsible for training all new management hired into the company and for initiating a customer service class at our headquarters in Chelsea. I earned the respect of everyone from the president to dishwashers across the company.

During this first year, my career trajectory was amazing, but so was the number of hours I worked every week. This often left Gena home alone. I'd leave for work about two-thirty in the afternoon and wouldn't return until well after three o'clock in the morning.

In the early days, she would try to stay up until I got home smelling like fried onions soaked in a bath of old grease. I would smell so bad that people would get up and move to a different seat on the subway. She'd have a bottle of wine ready and be in a cute little nightie, so I'd pop through the shower as fast as I could only to find her passed out on the sofa.

Gena was very supportive, and I was always there for her. Gena became my rock, my partner. We went back to Pennsylvania often to see our parents. She became part of my family and I became part of hers.

But I had learned that Gena was a very private, guarded person and constantly kept a wall around herself. She suffered from a phobia of crowds, heights, tunnels, bridges, boats, and enclosed spaces. This always made planning a night out very challenging.

Gena's birthday falls on New Year's Eve. For Gena's first birthday with me in New York, I had a fully stocked limo pick us up in front of our apartment and take us to a trendy, upscale restaurant called Theo's for dinner. We felt like movie stars driving around in that limo. After dinner, we were dropped off at Rockefeller Center to see the tree. That night was when Gena and I recognized we truly loved each other.

The Union Square restaurant allowed me to become acquainted with many celebrities. Drew Barrymore would come in every week for a venti two Sweet'N Low iced tea. Britney Spears would occasionally appear with her seven-foot bodyguard. Heather Graham would sometimes have a martini at the bar. Every morning, Spike Lee would stop in and read the newspaper. Steven Spielberg would bring his wife and daughter for dinner, usually ordering the tomato basil mozzarella melt.

After managing the Union Square restaurant for about two years, I was offered a general management position at a different location. I was tempted to turn it down just to stay connected to the restaurant I had nurtured. But it was a ten-thousand-dollar bump in salary, and my first opportunity to be the big boss. Gena focused on the status and money of the new position rather than my emotional equity. I felt very proud to share the good news with my family, but I felt some resentment from both brothers and even my dad when I told them how much I was going to be earning. Nevertheless, they all congratulated me.

My new restaurant was uptown on Eighth Avenue, which had a completely different vibe from the Square. Coming in as general manager presented unanticipated difficulties in forming a bond with the current staff. And now I would have to direct my assistant managers to do what I used to do as a hands-on assistant. My responsibilities went from executing to reporting. Instead of being on the floor with my staff, I was creating budgets, making schedules, preparing for meetings, analyzing cost of goods sold, and running labor reports. I quickly began to miss my role back at Union Square, and I certainly missed seeing Drew Barrymore.

Another year skipped by. I was always hitting budget and getting good customer reviews, but I wasn't getting the superstar recognition like I was at Union Square. Gena was still working on her degree in fashion with a goal to become a buyer. When she started to apply for jobs to gain relevant job experience, she started showing signs of stress. She was facing the real world now, and there was a tremendous amount of competition in her field, especially in New York.

Gena accepted a position as an assistant buyer with Nine West Accessories. Her new job got me thinking about all the unexplored opportunities available in the city. My role at the restaurant had become stagnant, and I disliked always being the dickhead boss. Maybe it was time to look around for something else.

I discovered a newer restaurant company called Heavenly Soups. There was no corporate structure yet, so it was almost a ground-floor opportunity. The twelve locations offered ten different soups every day, each made fresh and delivered daily from a commissary in Chelsea Market. The restaurants had gourmet sandwiches and a salad bar to create whatever the appetite desired. The best part, though, was that they were only open for lunch and early dinner. Every location closed by six in the evening. Most were closed on weekends, which would make my life much more compatible with Gena's.

After gaining some on-the-job experience, I was offered a position as director of training and general manager of one troublesome location, a turn-around proposition. The president told me that after a full year of operation, the restaurant had still not turned a profit. I couldn't resist the challenge, so I accepted.

I spent the next few weeks working harder than anyone else in that store. My prep cooks didn't speak a word of English, so I quickly learned some basics as I worked right alongside them on the production of product. I focused on service by creating fun games. Within my first quarter, we were the third most profitable unit in the chain, our average guest check was the highest in the company, and our number of guests was drastically climbing week to week.

Once again, I had become a superstar and had more time to spend with Gena. Unfortunately, she was very stressed out by the cutthroat people she had to work with every day. I learned all about the cruel, uber-competitive women in the fashion field. I think it was hard for her to fit in, and she started to complain, sometimes even cry at night when I got home.

At this same time, a movie about the dysfunction of the fashion industry, *The Devil Wears Prada*, ironically was being shot next to my restaurant at Rockefeller Center.

After almost five years in the city, Gena was ready to move back to Pennsylvania. We had discussed the idea of moving back to Pennsylvania almost every night for weeks. Most nights, Gena would come home pissed off from something at work or just crying hysterically. The job was draining the spirit out of her.

I was doing well and had created a name for myself, but I had never been afraid to start fresh. It was time to think about us as a couple, and where our relationship was heading. I could not have anticipated the abyss that lay ahead.

Chapter 6

Decision Time

We told our parents about our intentions to move back, and they were all happy about it. After looking at a few houses for rent, we drove back to her parents' house for dinner. I felt that her parents had accepted me as part of their family, perhaps even loved me.

During dinner, Gena's father, Don, surprised us with an idea. "Instead of renting a place," he said, "why don't you look at buying a small starter house? We'll help you with the down payment, and instead of wasting more money on rent, you can make mortgage payments and be earning equity."

My stomach dropped. Gena had been my girlfriend for six years, but I had never thought about marriage. How could we buy a house together with support from Gena's father and not be married? What was I getting myself into? Was this her father's way of telling me to decide about our relationship?

Gena was excited about the idea of buying a home.

"Thank you so much for the generous offer," I said. "I need to think about it because it's such a big decision." In truth, it was the kind of debt I didn't want, especially since I suspected Don might be involved in some illegal activities.

"Gena's going to get my money one day, anyway," Don said. "Why not give the money to her while I'm still alive?"

This notion gave me another concern. Shouldn't his money go to his daughter, not to both Gena and me?

Gena saw me sitting there frozen and without words. She rescued me by saying, "Mike and I will talk about the idea."

I knew I loved Gena, but what did I really know about love, anyway? She was only my second long-term relationship. I had been too preoccupied with my career to think about marriage. How was I supposed to know if Gena was the woman I wanted to spend the rest of my life with?

The next day, I spoke to Don about my misgivings—all but my suspicions about his business dealings. He seemed to understand and quickly produced a handwritten contract stating that if Gena and I broke up, I would have to sign over my rights to the deed. I was relieved, and it gave me some time to think about the idea of marriage. If, for whatever reason a marriage didn't work out, I had the ability to walk away without being in his debt. Whatever I'd have paid into the mortgage I could chalk up as a "Thank you for the opportunity."

We found a cute little corner condo on the outskirts of Doylestown, Pennsylvania. It was a two-story, two-bedroom townhouse. Even the name of the street was cute—Carousel Circle. Her parents helped us furnish the house and it became our own cozy home.

Gena started to apply for jobs in the area, and I continued working in New York. The commute by bus was two hours each direction, a draining and difficult schedule. After a few months, the expense and time took a toll on me, so I started searching for local opportunities.

As I became more familiar with Gena's family, I noticed some odd behaviors that gave me pause. For example, the down payment Don Darkino gave to Gena for our house traveled a very circuitous route. Don first gave thirty grand in cash to Gena's grandfather. In return, her grandfather wrote a check as a gift to Gena. I asked Gena why her father had to deal with cash, especially since it was a lot of money. At the restaurant, it took a large bag to hold ten grand. So why was Don moving thirty thousand dollars in cash instead of electronic transfers, checks, money orders and many available methods?

"Just don't worry about it," Gena answered sternly.

Sometimes Don would ask Gena to run errands and I'd tag along. We'd pull up to various check-cashing business. I'd wait in the car while she took in a dozen or so envelopes. When I asked what this was all about, she'd just tell me, "Don't you worry about it. It's just business for my dad's construction company."

Occasionally, we'd stay on Don's fifty-foot houseboat docked in the Baltimore Harbor. I wondered what the hell her father did to earn money. Maybe his contracting business was so profitable he could afford a big boat in the most expensive harbor in Baltimore.

When her parents took us out for extravagant dinners, Don would periodically leave the table to have phone conversations. Maybe, I thought, he had a construction job going on where workers were pouring concrete on a Saturday night at nine o'clock.

Gena's parents lived in a modest home and drove new but modest cars, but otherwise they lived an extravagant lifestyle and always had an abundance of cash. Clearly the family was hiding behind a middle-class mask to avoid unnecessary attention. I never asked questions, though, and continued to accept Don's kisses on the cheek.

A few weeks passed and I accepted a position as manager of the highest-volume coffee shop in Pennsylvania. The store, in the heart of Newtown, Pennsylvania, was grossing over forty thousand per week in coffee sales, an incredible volume. Within the first few months, the shop was breaking sales records from the previous years. If you ever walk into a coffee shop and they write your name on the cup, know that this idea came from me and my store in Newtown.

Gena took a job with QVC and seemed to enjoy it a lot more than the cutthroat job in New York. Gena and I both had our own careers now, we had our own little house with a mortgage, and we had successfully started a new life in Pennsylvania.

We'd been together for almost six years. I had become a social butterfly over that time, but Gena's phobias kept her from socializing very much. Her ideal night out was going to a quiet restaurant. Food was her passion. She grew up living to eat. I grew up eating to live.

Even with all the restrictions imposed by Gena's many fears, making Gena feel less anxious seemed to be worth the sacrifices.

She had a jealous streak, though. She'd get mad if I glanced at another woman or just spoke to another female. She was insecure to an unhealthy level. But I cared about her, and I appreciated her loyalty. I figured that she deserved the same loyalty from me. We had something special.

That summer, feeling pressure from both sides of the family, I knew it was time to propose. I still had no idea how to do it, so I decided to go the old-school Italian way I'd seen in some old movies. I drove to her parents' house—without Gena, of course. They invited me in, and I asked them for permission to marry their daughter. They seemed very relieved, and Gena's soft-spoken mother helped me pick out a ring.

A few weeks later, it was time for my family's beach vacation in Wildwood, New Jersey. Gena and I arrived a day early so we could have some private time before the family arrived. For dinner, I ordered clams and sneaked an empty shell into my pocket. After eating, I asked Gena to take a walk on the beach. Man, was she stubborn! I planned to propose marriage, but this stubborn woman refused to take a walk with me. She even got upset with my persistence. Finally, though, as the sun was setting, she walked with me in the shallow waves. I had put the engagement ring inside the clam shell, so plucked it from my pocket, kneeled in the sand, looked up at Gena and said, "Look what I just found."

I pretended to pull the clam shell out of the sand and gently placed it in her hand. She looked at me like I was being silly. For a second, I thought she was going to throw it into the water. But then she slowly opened the shell and saw the diamond ring.

Her eyes grew misty and she said, "Yes!" Then she added, "It's about time!"

We laughed and hugged and kissed in the surf as the sun made its final descent, then walked back to our room so she could call everyone she knew with the news.

I fell asleep while she made her calls. Later, when she'd make fun of me for falling asleep that night, I would tell her I was plain exhausted from trying to convince her to take a walk on the beach.

Her parents gave us an amazing wedding. We had over two hundred guests—twenty from my side and rest from her big Italian family. It was an enchanting night, and Gena was the happiest I had ever seen her. My younger brother was best man, and his toast that night still rings in my ears today. He spoke about how behind every good man is a good woman. He said that if there is a tomorrow, everything will be okay. Waking up together and sharing a tomorrow together is what truly matters. He wished Gena and me many, many tomorrows.

As a reader of this story, keep my brother's message in mind, because I am now fighting to be alive tomorrow.

Chapter 7

Leap of Faith

When we got back from our enchanting honeymoon in Mexico, life resumed as normal. She continued working for QVC, and I jumped right back into my role with the coffee shop. The holidays came, and I continued to break more records as a store manager. The local paper interviewed me about why the locals had started calling us the heart of Newtown.

Married life was good. Again, Gena had never been a social person. We never had parties or went out except to eat. Besides family gatherings, it was just the two of us together. I would make some improvements to the house, like putting in a paved patio, fixing the hot tub, installing French doors—just about anything that my wife wanted. If it weren't for my dad showing me how to do plumbing and electrical work, many of these projects never would have happened.

For months, I had been having a conflict with my district manager who seemed to be sabotaging many of my efforts. It's amazing how one individual can make an entire organization toxic. After repeated betrayals and disagreements, I had finally reached my threshold of toleration and resigned.

I remember telling Gena what I had done. She disputed the wisdom of my decision and started an argument, which made matters ten times worse. I was so fed up with the nonsense at work that I didn't find it necessary to defend myself. But Gena felt I'd been impulsive and had no backup plan. She didn't show an ounce of empathy for what I'd been going through. My position was that I had left an amazing career in New York to make her feel better and was disappointed that she would not even try to understand my frustrations in this matter. It really pissed me off.

My heightened emotions probably prevented me from considering the deeper reasons for Gena's attitude. Gena was the product of a difficult childhood, having been sexually abused as a child. I'm not sure who the abuser was on her father's side of the family, but her emotional instability proved to be a continuous difficulty in our relationship. The little bits she told me about her father had led me to believe that he was a narcissistic sociopath—strong words, I know, but perhaps the reason why her mother was so quiet. As a father, Don hadn't been around much, and when he was, he was usually angry. To this day, I blame Gena's numerous phobias on the fears her father instilled in his kids.

I knew enough not to cross Don Darkino. I learned to always show respect so I would remain in his circle of trust for my wife's sake. I knew his business was shady, but it never affected Gena or me, so I just kept my mouth shut.

Gena never gave me many details about her childhood, but her brother, Nick, had been more forthcoming with his wife. Nick and his wife, Jen, had a son named Johny. Their relationships with Don also caused an enormous amount of unnecessary drama. Jen refused to involve Johny in certain family functions. I think she feared Don and didn't want her son exposed to his grandfather's criminal exploits. Once, in a fit of rage, Don tried to strangle his daughter-in-law in a dispute over her refusal to let Johny spend the night with his grandparents. Gena told me that Nick hated his dad and they rarely talked. In fact, if it weren't for Johny, she confided, her brother wouldn't even have a relationship with Don.

The few details Gena told me about growing up in the Darkino household was that her father would often rage about unimportant things like shoes being left in the wrong spot or a sandwich placed on the table upside down. Gena said her father would scream at his kids if they laughed too loud and sometimes chased them around the house with a closed fist. She wouldn't tell me what happened when he caught the kids.

I never forced Gena to discuss uncomfortable emotions. I figured she'd tell me if she needed the help. Having studied psychology in school, I knew that some phobias were very common, like a fear of heights or enclosed spaces. But Gena was unusually afraid of many other things too, like tunnels, bridges, crowds, loud noises, new or strange people, being alone or in the darkness. I believed she had suffered multiple traumas growing up.

Almost any surprise or disruption in our lives would cause a flare-up of fear. After I told her I had quit my job, she literally panicked. Like her father, she screamed at me: "How could you do this to us?" She paced around the room and muttered about how we'd have to tell her father, which itself was frightening, and that we were now doomed to moving into a horrible little apartment, and how our lives were over now. I just sat there on the couch and thought, *She has seriously lost her mind.*

After enduring a half-hour of her direful ranting, I'd had enough and told her to sit down and shut up. I was still going to receive my last paycheck plus a monthly bonus. We had already paid the mortgage for the month and we had funds available for the following month.

"Simmer down and relax," I said. "You know I'll take care of this; I always do. But right now, I need you to stop acting like a lunatic."

After she calmed down, I showed her on paper that we were safe financially. Still, it took another two hours of reassurance before she finally put her arms around me and apologized. I believed her sincerity but wondered if this meltdown was the result of some deep trauma that might require some intensive counseling.

The next day, Gena still tried to convince me to keep my job. Her fears kept flaring up. I know she was afraid to tell her dad I'd quit my job—more afraid of her father's perception, I think, than anything else. In my mind, it wasn't anyone else's business.

Gena's kneejerk outbursts of fear made me question our marriage. Although Gena now said she was behind me, I didn't feel her sincerity. To her, all that mattered was her father's opinion. The depth of her anxiety caused me to question the character and identity of Don Darkino.

I needed to figure out ways to help Gena. So, what was her hidden secret, her trauma? *What the hell did I marry into?* I wondered. I decided to take a couple days to relax and regain my equilibrium. I came up with a game plan to avoid the ugly scene of the previous day. It started with having dinner ready when Gena got home from work. We gave each other a kiss, and I inquired about her day. She asked if I had made any progress on my job search. Instead of answering, I said there were a few questions I needed to ask, and I wanted her to be honest with me. She nodded.

"For as long as you have known me, have I ever not worked?" I asked.

She said no.

"For as long as you've known me, have I ever failed?"

She said no again, adding that I had always gotten promoted.

"Why did you decide to marry me?"

"Well, I loved that you were close to your family," she replied. "And that you're always kind and considerate to my family. You're smart and always seem to succeed one way or another."

Then I asked her why she'd had such an anxiety attack when I told her I'd quit my job.

She started hammering on the money issue again, so I raised a hand to stop her.

"Don't lie to me!" I said. "We're fine with money, and you know I'll have another job in a week or two. So again, where did all that fear come from?"

She stood up from the table, gave me a tearful hug and said she was sorry. She explained that she didn't want her father to worry after giving us the down payment for the house.

"All that matters is that I support us," I said. "I wish I never agreed to take his offer. It's just causing too much stress."

"Yes, I agree," she said. "But I want you to be grateful for his support."

"Of course I'm grateful," I replied. "But if this is going to constantly disrupt our lives, I want nothing to do with it."

She nodded vaguely, then asked again if I had looked for a job.

I shook my head, disappointed that she had reverted to the employment topic again. "I took the day for myself," I said. "I'm really not wanting to talk about anything else right now. I'll take care of us, I promise—and I'll tell you when and where I start a job, nothing more." I hadn't meant to speak so firmly, but I couldn't help it.

She seemed upset, but I think she understood that I was unsettled with the previous day's events. Maybe I suffered from too much pride. Perhaps I just wanted to feel appreciated by my boss. Whatever the reason, I knew it was time to move on.

Chapter 8

Sink or Swim

The next day, I made just one phone call—to Tom Nartin at the insurance company. I knew exactly what I was getting myself into. I knew selling insurance was an all-commission job, and that such a job would rattle Gena's cage. Maybe I was trying to prove a point or to test our marriage. Whatever the reason, I met with Tom that same afternoon and discussed starting a new career in the financial services industry.

Tom and I met for over an hour. He was in his sixties and was a Boy Scout leader. He still used old-school maps and refused to use any kind of technology. He explained that I would need to earn three licenses and pass state exams to be eligible for a sales position. Then I'd need to build a client base on my own to sell various products to individuals, families and business owners. Tom spent some time on the compensation structure too.

While he was presenting to me, I was a bit distracted, thinking, *How am I going to explain to Gena that I'm taking a job with no salary to sell stuff that I have no knowledge of or experience in?*

Maybe it was just ego, but I signed the paperwork that day and went right to the police station to get my fingerprints done, one of the requirements. I decided not to tell Gena until the feds did my background check and I completed a battery of tests from the company and they had accepted me.

About a week later, I was starting a completely different career with no salary right after an epic row with my wife over financial issues. Awesome plan on my part.

That night, when Gena got home from work, I told her about the new job, and that once I was licensed, I could sell every type of insurance and investment product.

"Don't you need a degree to do this job?" she asked.

"Apparently not, since I start on Monday."

She liked that I would be my own boss and could set my own hours. Then came the question she clearly was dreading to ask. Her words came out with fear and uncertainty. "How much will you be paid?"

I explained it was an all-commission position but in the early period I'd have a draw to help us get by. I just had to pass the exams.

"You haven't passed a test in years." she said. "What if you don't pass the exams?"

"Then I don't have a job."

Gena put her head down, trying to control her anxiety. Then she looked up and asked if I really believed that I could do this job.

"I've always succeeded. Why would this be any different?"

"But you don't know anything about it."

"So, I'll learn," I said.

I really thought she'd enter her panic mode at this point, but instead she became supportive. She offered to help me study and started to ask about some of the products. But then she said something that shot burning sparks down my spine.

"Just don't say anything to my dad."

Now I was the one to lose control. I shouted, "What the hell difference does it make? Why does it matter to him what I do or where I work?"

That's when I realized how tired I was of her father coming up whenever we had to make a decision. I truly wished I had never agreed to take his down payment money. I needed to get Don's thirty thousand dollars out of my life.

"I just don't ever want my father to perceive you in a bad way," Gena said, filling the awkward silence with words. "He hates my brother's wife, and it causes a lot of trouble."

"So, because I'm changing jobs he's going to hate me?"

"No," she said. "It's just that a lot of simple things make him worry, and when he worries, he gets involved and tries to control things."

At this point, I knew that if looked up the definition of *narcissistic sociopath*, Don Darkino's big-nosed Mafia face would be the illustration.

"My dad believes that he's always right and he's never wrong," Gena explained. "When he has a negative thought about someone, he never lets it go. Never!"

I started to understand things more clearly, all the events in our recent past, and I became concerned about his criminal activities. I wondered if I had been played somehow. Would he do that to family? I had no idea.

I decided that I couldn't concern myself with the feelings or thoughts of a father-in-law. Why was I even allowing this nonsense into my head? I had a new career, and like every other position I'd ever held, I was going to take it by the balls.

The insurance company office was only three miles down the road in Chalfont. I got there early and went through orientation. My manager, Tom, came over to say hello and gave me a book to study for the Series 6 exam. Passing it would allow me to sell mutual funds and variable products. There were training sessions several times a week, but mainly I just needed to study.

These exams are designed to make you fail. I was told that only 45 percent of candidates passed the necessary state exams. More troubling was that only one person out of one hundred candidates was still in the business after two years.

I sat at my desk, looking at the five-hundred-page textbook, then asked myself, *What the hell am I doing?*

I never studied so hard in my life. I'd get to the office around eight o'clock, study for the entire day, then I go home, eat, and study practice exams until bedtime. For the first time in a long while, self-doubt was eating away my confidence. I tried to keep the words of wisdom in my head from both Tom and my trainer, Gene. They both had said I had something special to offer and that I would pass the test.

Test day arrived and they checked me in by taking my fingerprints and my picture, then giving me an ID before taking me into the test room. I sat at a cubicle and was told I could not speak or leave the computer. I had to empty my pockets and was given a pencil and a piece of scratch paper. The entire process was very intimidating. I logged in and learned that I would have two hours and thirty minutes to complete the 105-question exam. I needed 70 percent correct to pass.

I took a deep breath and clicked the Start button. Right off the bat, the first question was a page long and seemed to include the entire chapter about buying "puts" and "calls." I took my time, read the question twice, and carefully selected the answers I thought were correct. As I continued to click next, the questions got no easier. They were so difficult that I found myself doubting each answer.

Two hours flew by, and I answered the last question. I started to sweat, and my heart pounded. There was no way in hell I had passed this test. I convinced myself that I'd just go get another job and it wasn't really a big deal. I clicked a button that said, "Get my score." An hourglass appeared on a black screen, and the next eight seconds seemed to last a lifetime. I swear I didn't take a breath, blink my eyes or move. I was frozen with fear.

Suddenly, a white screen popped up and read, "78/100, Passed." My heart leaped, and I finally started breathing again. I really had myself convinced that there was no way I passed.

I took my confirmation back to the office, singing songs in the car all the way. I felt like I had just won a battle, and my pride was soaring. I walked through that office holding my paper up, thinking I was going to get some much-needed recognition. Instead, though, a woman named Vicki just said, "Good job." Then she took my confirmation paperwork and handed me the four-hundred-page

Series 63 book. The wind came out of my sails. I went back to my desk, opened to Chapter 1 and sighed.

Joe Capone, the managing director, walked into my cubicle and said hello. This was the first time I had met him. He simply said, "Two more to go."

I approached the Series 63 the same way, studying at the office by day and taking practice tests at night on my couch. A week flew by and then I took the exam. When I finished, refused to review and went right for the score: "76/100, Passed."

I was happy, but my expectations had changed. Passing these exams wasn't a measure of success, I knew, just a ticket to enter the game.

"I'm ready to study for the last one," I told Vicki. She told me the third exam was the easiest one. Perhaps my ego kicked in—anyway, I became a little cocky. I didn't study nearly as hard for this test. I learned a hard lesson on exam day when the white screen popped up and read, "69/100, Failed." I had missed a passing score by one damn question. Fortunately, the life, accident and health exam could be rescheduled again within twenty-four hours, unlike the other two. The next time I was ready. When the white screen popped up, it read: "78/100, Passed."

A few days later, on Thanksgiving Day, I woke up to Gena crying. She looked scared and upset. I couldn't possibly imagine what was going on.

I rubbed my eyes, sat up and asked, "What happened?"

She continued to cry and said, "I just don't know what to do."

"What do you mean? What's wrong?"

Her eyes were red and swollen. "I'm pregnant," she said.

Without any hesitation, I declared, "That's awesome!"

But she was scared that I didn't have a salary, and now she wouldn't be able to work much longer. From now on, I said, life wasn't about me or her anymore—it was about our baby.

In my head, however, I was screaming, Shit! I just left a good-paying salary because of my damn pride and took a job with no guaranteed income just in time to find out we had a baby on the way.

Looking back on it, I think Gena was more concerned with the way I might have responded to the news. I don't think she was expecting me to be so excited. But I was truly happy. I had always wanted to be a father and have my own family.

We made it through the holidays, and Gena decided not to mention anything to her family until the doctor said everything was all right. I think she wanted to make sure I was making money. Nevertheless, she decided to wait a few weeks.

I will never understand the hormonal changes a woman suffers five days out of every month, but for Gena, pregnancy created a whole new monster. Sometimes she seemed possessed by a violent, schizophrenic, bipolar demon. One minute she would cry, the next minute she'd be laughing, and then she'd throw a freaking mug at me. I mostly stayed calm, though, thinking about our baby.

I went back to work with a new level of urgency. I no longer needed to succeed and satisfy my ego—I needed to succeed to support my baby, who would be arriving in seven months.

Chapter 9

Born for Business

My first six months, I worked my ass off. There were days I would get to the office at nine o'clock in the morning and didn't make it home until after nine at night. Unlike my peers, I didn't care where an appointment was located. One night, I would be all the way up north in Jim Thorpe, and the next day I'd find myself in Center City, Philadelphia.

I wanted the most activity possible. If it took two hundred phone calls to make fifteen appointments, then activity was the answer. The more people you talked to, the more opportunities you would find.

My peers, on the other hand, didn't seem to have that attitude. But then, I was in a do-or-die situation. I simply could not fail. I quickly learned why only one out of a hundred agents were still in the business after two years.

I was bringing home a steady income, but I wasn't killing it because I was splitting most of my commissions with a partner, an experienced agent named Wadid. This was common practice akin to an apprenticeship. I didn't look at the arrangement of me giving up 50 percent of a sale. I looked at it as an investment in my education so I could eventually run my own business. Splitting my earnings was an opportunity to earn more money down the road. Nevertheless, my income provided some financial stability after Gena stopped working.

I spent a lot of time getting the house ready for the baby. I turned the second bedroom into a nursery. I painted the room a peaceful yet bold orange, because it was such a happy color. With animal wall coverings, I created a zoo in the room. I made a new litter box room for the cats. It took several days to babyproof the house so Gena's dad could not find any issues to rage against.

Lala was finally born on July 26, 2009. She was a big baby, and despite pushing for two hours, Gena eventually had a C-section. Watching Lala being pulled out of my wife's stomach was traumatizing but watching my little girl wiggle as I cut her umbilical cord changed my life forever. I suddenly understood the meaning of unconditional love.

I had saved some money so I could take two weeks off to be with my new family. Gena was in the hospital for a few days to heal. During that time, I learned how to change diapers and feed Lala, since Gena was unable to breastfeed.

At last, we brought Lala home. At this time, we had two cats in the house, and they were very special to Gena and me. Don seized upon an old superstition and insisted that the cats were going to kill the baby by sucking the air out of her lungs. It didn't matter to him that cats don't have the physiology to suck, he convinced Gena otherwise.

I pointed out that the nursery had a door we could close to keep the cats out, and we could put more monitors and cameras in her room than a casino. But Gena's father possessed tremendous control over Gena, and his method of instilling fear exasperated me. As a result, Gena gave our beloved cats away. I chose not to argue about it—all I really cared about was my little girl.

Gena was in a lot of pain after coming home from the hospital. I took on diaper duty, and we enjoyed sitting on the couch together as we took turns feeding our daughter and holding Lala in our arms. Lala gave me a new purpose in life. Before her, my goal was to simply succeed. Now, my goal was to provide.

That time was magical. Having Lala in our home created a new bond between Gena and me. I wish now it had never ended. After two weeks, however, it was time for me to get back to work. Gena was no longer working, and I was on straight commission. Baby formula was expensive. The medical bills, diapers, and normal costs of living lit a fire under me.

Monday morning came around, and I called into the conference call. I didn't have any activity to report, but when it was my turn to speak, I mentioned my daughter had been born. As all the agents listened, Joe congratulated and asked me to come to his office that morning.

In the background, a voice said, "Oooh, someone is in trouble." I was a bit worried, but I couldn't think of anything I'd done wrong. Even though I had just taken two weeks off, I was still in the top ten for production.

When I walked into Joe's enormous office, he told me to sit down in a soft chair in front his desk. He asked how the baby was, and then he told me, "I went through it six times. After the first baby, a woman becomes a baby factory."

I couldn't believe this man had six kids.

Joe told me that the sales figures I had produced were impressive, and corporate was aware that I was splitting commissions fifty-fifty with Wadid. At first, I thought maybe the extra tracking and paperwork required to split the commissions was creating a problem. But Joe had something else on his mind.

Joe said the president wanted me to conduct a national teleconference with over a thousand new agents across the company to share ideas, teach best practices, and basically explain how I had achieved such success. I was shocked and amazed that I caught the attention of the president. There were over fifty agencies scattered across the country, with a few thousand private offices. I couldn't believe I was singled out among thousands of agents to provide training. I was only six months in the business.

I told Joe I would be honored, and I thanked him for the opportunity.

Joe looked at me and said with a smile, "Don't mess it up." He was a true, full-blooded Italian boss.

The day of the teleconference came, and I delivered a learning experience that I thought was good. But then, who knows?

When I got back to the office, Joe came up and shook my hand. He said he had just spoken with the boss, and then he added, "You nailed it!" Not only did I provide really good ideas to the agents, but the president told him that, based on my ideas, he was going to start creating an agency-wide program along the lines I had recommended.

A few months blew past. My name started to become well-known in the agency. I was approached by a few of the financial planners who had been in the company for their entire lives. Some of the planners wanted me to work with them and team up on sales calls

I started making appointments with wealthy clients and handling investments rather than just insurance. Instead of making a few hundred dollars per application, I was now earning a few thousand each. Even though I was splitting commissions with veteran agents, when you brought in over five hundred thousand dollars in business, my share was still over ten thousand. I was not only making money; I was also shocking the hell out of Gena.

Lala was doing great, and Gena was slowly getting back to normal after her troublesome C-section. I would wake up and have coffee in the hot tub while reporting my success on the nine o'clock conference call, then eat breakfast with my wife and daughter, and finally go out on my appointments. We'd spend our weekends together as a family.

At least once a week, Gena's parents would watch Lala and I'd take Gena to her favorite restaurant. I started to really connect with Gena's brother, Nick, who worked for a bank processing loans. Nick and I started referring business to each other and even had a few guys' nights out. Nick loved to eat, like the rest of his family, and the two of us had fun being obnoxious. The wives didn't like it too much, as we could get kind of rowdy, but both of us had the world by the balls.

My first year as an investment advisor closed with an income over sixty-five thousand dollars. Now remember, I split 80 percent of all my sales, so I looked at the upcoming year with bright eyes since most of my commissions would no longer be split.

I received a prestigious award called the Life Achievers Award. I was awarded the Rookie of the Year Award which led to a promotion within the Agency.

When end of the year rolled around, I had managed to recruit and hire twenty-four successful candidates, which leveraged our agency to win a trophy. My efforts not only made me look like a hero, but Joe was also recognized as the number one managing director in the company.

At the annual agency meeting, I was presented my third award with the company, and this time the etching on the large glass trophy read, "Mike Lutterschmidt, Manager of the Year."

At this point in my life, Gena was comfortable being a stay-at-home mom. Lala was approaching her one-year mark, and my income had soared to well over 150,000 dollars per year. Here I was, with no college degree, no special education or student loans, making more money than my PhD brother or both my parents combined.

My family was proud of me. Gena's parents were grateful for my ability to take care for their daughter and granddaughter. Gena had begun to rely solely on my support, and no longer needed the approval of her father. Life was amazing!

I truly felt unstoppable and thought my success would go on forever.

Chapter 10

The Devil in Disguise

As Lala continued to grow, Gena's paranoia and anxiety increased as well. Even our home became a source of fear.

I loved our little townhouse, a corner unit with a private walkway hidden by towering arborvitaes on either side. We had a small front yard and a patio in the back, which provided a home for our outdoor kitchen and my beloved hot tub. Our bedroom was huge, and Lala had an adorable nursery. I was comfortable there, but Gena no longer felt safe in it.

She started to complain about the neighbors, saying she could hear them arguing. I told her everyone argues now and then, and just about everyone has neighbors. "Remember when we lived in Brooklyn," I reminded her, and we could hear every conversation through the walls. Back then, our own neighbors complained about us being too loud when I got home at three in the morning.

One time she called me hysterically and demanded that I come home where I would find Gena tearfully holding Lala on the couch. She had panicked, believing the neighbors were going to break into our house. I told her there was nothing to worry about in Doylestown.

When we needed the cable TV guy to come out, Gena would demand that I leave work and be home so she wouldn't be alone with the service guy. If FedEx rang the doorbell to deliver a package, Gena would call me frantically, believing someone was trying to break in. Her behavior was affecting my work because at least once a week I had to go home and calm her down. Eventually, Gena insisted that we move, as if a different location would resolve her fears.

At first, I was totally against the idea. I loved our home, especially the hot tub. I believed more than ever that her father and his criminal pursuits were responsible for Gena's problems. I had already given up my cat for Don's irrational notions, and I didn't think it was fair that I should sacrifice my house too. I had put too much effort making that place our home.

Still, I couldn't ignore my wife's deepening fears. If she needed a house away from neighbors to feel safe, then that's what we needed to do. She was the mother of my daughter.

Gena signed with a realtor and started house-shopping online. While I was at work, her father would accompany her to inspect houses for sale. Anytime Don got involved with something, the situation would become needlessly intense and create angst throughout the family. After a month, we finally made an offer on a house that suited Gena, but we were a day too late.

A week later, after dealing with the disappointment from losing the house she really wanted, Gena called me at work interrupting an interview with a job candidate. I answered to make sure everything was fine.

"I found the house," she said excitedly. I told her it wasn't a good time, and she said, "I found the house." She worried that we'd lose this one like the previous house if we didn't make an offer right away. She told me to trust her and let her make the offer. She was sure I'd love the house.

I looked up at the line of candidates waiting to speak with me and told her, "Go ahead, I trust you."

Later that day, Gena told me the offer had been accepted and I needed to meet her right after work to sign papers. I met her at the office, and I signed the paperwork to buy a house I had never seen. I was a little sad to put our home on the market.

Apparently, our home was just as adorable as I had thought—it sold in less than two weeks. Unfortunately, we agreed that the buyer could move into our old home in February, but the new house could not be occupied until June. So, we moved all our stuff into storage, said goodbye to our beloved first home, and proceeded to move in with Gena's parents until the new house was available.

The family living situation was awkward at first, but her parents were very loving. They particularly enjoyed having Lala around all the time, and I really connected with her parents and her brother. I would help with house maintenance and grass cutting, and we'd have tea every night and watch American Idol or make fun of the news.

Her dad was brilliant in his own ways—batshit insane, but intelligent at the same time. He had a wealth of knowledge and proved to be wise in many ways, but I witnessed firsthand the likely source of Gena's many fears. Don had a combustible temper that could flare up at any moment. He would blow up at a convenience store because someone didn't move fast enough. He'd unpredictably argue with his daughter-in-law about her methods of raising his grandson, Johny—one time threatening to spray acid on her face.

I was still getting kisses on the cheek from him—still in his circle of trust. I understood, however, that I'd better stay in that circle or I could become a target for his unforgiving wrath.

Don employed a few Mexicans who would come to the house occasionally and be paid in cash, not a normal way of doing business. He was very hush-hush when discussing business with contacts in person or on the phone. The whiteboard in his basement office listed his current concrete jobs, but the numbers didn't add up to an income that would fund his lavish lifestyle. And he continued to have Gena deliver fat envelopes to check cashing establishments.

One day, when he was particularly angry, I overhead him scream into the phone, "If Cazonaro doesn't give you the money, you know what to do. I want him dead!" Because of his volatile temper, I thought that he might be just blowing off steam. I didn't want him to know I'd heard his entire conversation, so I quietly left the house and drove to a coffee shop until Gena was due home.

Several days later, I read in the newspaper that a man named J. Cazonaro had been shot to death in his own home.

I never told Gena about this, but I don't think it would have surprised her. From that moment on, I became hyper-vigilant when I was with her family and started to piece together the Mafia secrets of Don Darkino's dark life.

Don was making a lot of money from loansharking, I learned. His son, Nick, was deeply involved too. Whenever one of Nick's bank clients got turned down for a loan, Nick would pass along the contact info to Don. Sometimes, Nick would bypass the bank application process completely since he made more money from illegal lending than from bank commissions. When Ralph, the owner of the County Playhouse, was in debt to Don Darkino, I overheard my father-in-law directly threaten his life.

Eventually, I cobbled together more of the story. Ralph and Don had once been friends. When Ralph had trouble paying back his loan, Don orchestrated several large insurance claims on the building with a multi-million-dollar insurance fraud. Ralph was eventually arrested and convicted for the fraud, while Don remained free with millions of dollars in payments from the insurance company.

Speaking of insurance fraud, at the dining room table, Don once bragged to the family about how he had sued a store when a forklift in the aisle struck his knee. I later learned that Don had actually paid the clerk to go along with the deception. Don had torn his ACL playing basketball, and his entire lawsuit was based on false information. The case file is in the county court records, which is how I learned that Don was awarded over a million dollars for this criminal action.

When Don had been more active in the crime family, he and his crew used to buy viatical settlements. They would get someone to sign a beneficiary change from a life insurance policy in trade for cash. Later, the insured would end up having an unfortunate accident. The insurance proceeds would either go into a trust or to a fictitious name. Again, these circumstances made it very clear why Don needed to pay for everything in cash—it made most transactions much harder to trace.

The FBI came to Don's house on several occasions. Gena refused to tell me any of the details, so I assumed the authorities were probably catching up to his illegal activities. Oddly, neither Don nor the rest of the family ever seemed disturbed by these visits.

Imagine my surprise when I discovered that Don was being used as a criminal informant. The FBI agents were his allies. Their job was to keep the information flowing and protect Don from any external threats—which could include me.

Chapter 11

Ignorant Disbelief

Our new, split-level house was located on a parklike three acres with various types of trees and a stream that ran through the front of the property. Previous owners had made a few additions to it and I knew there would be a lot of maintenance to do, but I had always enjoyed hands-on work.

The first issue I discovered was the septic system, which didn't pass inspection. The bank wouldn't approve the loan without plans for a new system. Don worked around this issue by having his contracting business draw up new plans and got the bank to sign off. I didn't know anything about septic systems, and since Don was a contractor, I took his lead on the matter. After the bank signed off, Don told us we didn't need a new system—the tank just needed to be cleaned out. This opened the first door to hell for us.

A bigger issue was that the building inspector found mold in the crawlspace. I had no idea about mold either, but that didn't seem like a big deal to me. I mean, mold is everywhere, right? I loved blue cheese, and penicillin was beneficial, so how bad could a little mold be? I had no idea what I was seeing when I investigated the crawlspace where a fuzzy growth had covered the walls. In truth, the mold allowed the devil to walk right through that opened door to hell.

Don arranged for the seller to remove the mold himself. Again, since Don was a contractor, I believed he knew what he was doing.

I certainly didn't think he would put his daughter or granddaughter in harm's way.

The seller's removal efforts were quite modest—he entered the crawlspace with some bleach and scoured the walls with a scrubbing brush in about a day. When Don said it was all clear, I didn't give it a second thought.

Gena picked paint colors, and her brother and I spent the next few days painting the interior. This proved to be a test of my patience. After I'd spent hours painting the kitchen, Gena decided that she hated the yellow color she had picked out, and I dutifully spent another six hours repainting with a different color. I figured, "Happy wife, happy life."

My brother and his daughter helped paint Lala's room the same orange that we had used in her old room. My niece painted Lala's name with a princess tiara on the wall. Slowly but surely, we started to make our new large home warm and cozy.

There was an aboveground pool off the deck. The way the property slanted downhill made it look like an in-ground pool. Don and I made plans to build a larger deck around the pool and to enclose the pool with an aluminum fence with locking gates. My parents and my younger brother helped with the construction, and in a few weeks the oval-shaped pool was surrounded by a huge deck. My dad and I designed the lighting system and Don had some of his workers help re- landscape the front yard. In a very short period, our home became an enchanting resort.

I was still working many hours, but I was finding great pleasure in making improvements to the property. I turned our oversize, two-car garage into a workshop and pretty much turned it into a business. I had every tool and gadget known to man in there and had a lot of fun making banisters for the stairs, putting in French doors, installing crown molding, and many other projects.

Lala took her first steps in our new home. She was growing up so fast I wanted to get the house put together so I could just enjoy it more.

The last project I tackled before a planned hiatus to enjoy our new life was a second bathroom on the lower level. Don helped to pour a concrete floor and connect the plumbing to the existing septic tank. I knocked down an existing wall to enlarge the new bathroom.

Shortly after taking down that wall, though, I came down with some flu-like symptoms and had to miss a few days of work. I had rarely been ill in the past, but this bug knocked me flat on my back and forced work to halt on the bathroom, leaving bare walls and exposed studs.

I recovered slightly in time for the holidays. We had been using the crawlspace for storage, so I pulled out our decorations, ignoring that this was where the inspector had found mold. Lala loved the decorations and played with the animated characters. After all the decorations were up, however, Lala developed a severe rash. The doctor diagnosed it as eczema and prescribed a cream, but I also noticed she was having severe congestion. This triggered some anxiety, because I was suffering from an onset of new sinus issues as well.

Before long, acute fatigue set in. I was truly wiped out and falling asleep at work. During the middle of each night, Lala would wake up crying. We bought humidifiers to relieve her congestion, but these horrifying symptoms for both of us seemed to be getting worse. Oddly, Gena was not experiencing any discomfort at all except for a stuffy nose. At that time, I didn't see any connection between Lala's symptoms with mine.

Gena finally took Lala to the pediatrician, who diagnosed Lala with enlarged adenoids, which were contributing to her congestion. "This was totally normal", he said. But what was totally abnormal was that I wasn't recovering—I was spiraling downward. I tried to work on the bathroom and fight through the severe congestion, headaches and fatigue. I struggled through work, and my team noticed the decline in my health. I wasn't as sharp as usual, and my sales were starting to suffer.

Finally, my symptoms got so bad that I went to an allergist, who ordered a skin test. The results were shocking. I had developed allergies to just about everything you can be allergic to—trees, pollen, weeds, dust mites, dust, cats, and mold...

This sudden onset of allergies was strange, but at least I had an answer for my physical decline. It was not unusual, my allergist explained, for a man in his thirties to develop allergies. I immediately started taking medication, which provided little relief.

After a few more weeks, Lala and I were still getting progressively worse. I had no idea what to think, so I just kept fighting through the symptoms.

One day, I was supposed to attend a meeting with Ashley, one of my agents. She was able to network her way in and managed to make an appointment with an owner of a restaurant chain. This was a big opportunity, but I was in so much pain I could barely think. Ashley begged me to accompany her anyway, then gave me Adderall tablets which she promised would help. Well, the amphetamines helped so well that Ashley began to give me one or two every day. The fatigue disappeared, but the congestion and headaches worsened.

Increasingly desperate, I started taking large quantities of aspirin, and I abused Afrin to clear my nasal passages. The amphetamines helped me finish the last project in our house, covering up the exposed walls.

It wasn't long, though, before I made my first trip to the emergency room. Gena had started sleeping in Lala's room because our daughter had been waking up every night in tears. Suddenly, I woke up gasping for air. Thick mucus was clogging my sinuses and dripping down my throat, causing me to gag. In a panic, I stumbled into Lala's room and woke up Gena. We raced to the ER in fear.

Mostly, the doctors just observed me and a few hours later my vitals had returned to normal and I was discharged in the same breathless, gagging state. All I knew was that there was a serious problem that went beyond allergies and enlarged adenoids. I needed to get answers.

I found a local doctor and described my symptoms. His opinion was that I was under a lot of stress with work pressures, the move to a new home, and much more. He gave me my very own prescription of Adderall to help me focus at work. A side effects he didn't mention, however, was that Adderall could increase my anxiety.

So, the best medical advice agreed that I suffered from allergies and high stress, and Lala had enlarged adenoids. There was no evidence to support my intuition that we were in danger. Naturally, my anxiety skyrocketed, in no small way fueled by the Adderall. My mission to find answers became a slippery slope.

As with any past problem I had to face, I did some basic research based on our symptoms and the situation, trying to find possible causes for our distress. The information I uncovered was frightening and led to a maze of investigations.

To begin, I had our water checked. We had a well, and I learned that well water could sometimes be overrun with bacteria. There was an active quarry up the street, so something nefarious could be washing into our water supply. This seemed plausible because Lala and I had been diagnosed with bacterial infections. A few hundred dollars later, I was able to check that possibility off the list. Our well water was purer than bottled spring water.

Next, I investigated radon as a cause. I had read that a high level of radon could cause rashes, difficulty sleeping, and breathing issues. After spending another several hundred dollars, the test results showed that our house was clear of radon.

The more possibilities I checked off the list, the more Gena began to think I was crazy. She continued to rely on the diagnosis that Lala had eczema and enlarged adenoids, and I had allergies. Even worse, she began to tell her father about her concerns.

I didn't care what she thought, however. My intuition had never failed me before, and it was telling me that we were in danger. The lack of a credible explanation was maddening.

I was now coasting through work on residual income. I wasn't growing my team, and I no longer possessed the physical or mental stability to be the successful person I had once been. My sole focus was to figure out the cause of our ailments and find a fix before we lost control of our lives.

Apparently, Don spontaneously concluded that I had leaped off the cliff of sanity and started lobbying Gena with warnings about her husband. His usual fatherly behavior toward me stopped and he grew distant and brittle. I remembered how Gena had explained once that when her father developed a perception in his head, he became fixated on it and couldn't ever let it go.

Then one night, I again woke up gasping. My head felt like someone had poured concrete down my sinuses. I rushed to the ER by myself since Gena became cold and heartless towards my declining health. As I lay in the triage room, another possible explanation hit me like a bag of cement.

I had amphetamines in my system and elevated anxiety, so you can imagine how I was perceived by the medical team. When it was determined my condition was not life threatening, I was discharged while still suffering the same intense congestion. At home I logged into my computer and searched for information about the effects of silica dust. Don had just poured a concrete floor on the lower level of our house, and I discovered that the symptoms Lala and I were exhibiting perfectly matched those of silica dust exposure.

I gathered my strength and constructed large dust collectors using industrial house fans boxed in with large HEPA-grade air filters. Then I did something else I thought would help, but which made things one hundred times worse.

I bought the largest industrial house fan available—the kind that could lift a small helicopter—and placed it at one end of the house. Then I opened all the doors and windows at the other end, hoping that whatever dust was lingering in the house would be sucked out.

Gena looked at me like I was the Mad Hatter. Perhaps I was at that time. Nevertheless, I was desperate for some relief, and it was destroying me to hear my daughter wheeze and wake up crying every night.

After a few days of filtering the air in our house, I stop to evaluate the results. Unfortunately, our symptoms got a hundred times worse. Gena, on the other hand, developed a minor sinus infection and modest congestion, but otherwise seemed to be immune to whatever the hell was going on in this house.

My anxiety had now grown to dangerous levels—not just because of my declining health but because Gena, in the same environment, had almost no symptoms. At this point, I had been on a wide range of unproductive antibiotics for my persistent bacterial infections, and the allergy medicine wasn't helping at all.

Gena turned the tables on me by arguing that I needed to let my fears go, a sermon I had frequently preached to her. She began to confide more often in her father, and Don filled her head with his irrational nonsense. Because I was taking amphetamines, they chalked up my obvious physical ailments to a mental disorder caused by amphetamines. I was hell-bent on figuring out the true cause of these ailments before it killed me. I truly believed I was dying.

My next step was to research asbestos. Our home was built during a period when asbestos was being produced. The result of my research was terrifying. I learned that the family members who lived with workers that were exposed to asbestos often got cancer themselves. Contact with the clothing alone provided enough exposure to cause serious health issues.

Gena was totally against having the house tested for asbestos because it was very expensive, but I was insistent. An asbestos inspector came out and conducted a few tests. They took air samples, did tape swabs and removed pieces of insulation from the attic and crawlspace. The air samples came back completely clear, but the asbestos sample they removed from the attic tested positive for asbestos. This caused my Adderall-boosted anxiety to soar through the roof.

That weekend, I spent hundreds of dollars on respirators and gear. I removed all the insulation in the attic and replaced it all with new asbestos-free material. Predictably, this activity made my symptoms progressively worse and I found myself in the ER once again. And all my latest efforts to clean the house produced no health benefits. So much for the asbestos theory.

I decided that some doctor somewhere must have the capacity to figure out this mystery, so I went to a lung specialist, who found nothing. I went to an infectious disease doctor, who found nothing. I went to a holistic doctor, who told me I was eating too many brussels sprouts. She gave me some salts to help me detox. They didn't help.

My job was in jeopardy now. I wasn't sleeping. I was on the computer into the middle of the night. Lala was still coughing and crying. My anxiety was destroying whatever sanity I had left.

I had one more idea to explore. It was the last possibility on my list. I told Gena that I wanted to have our house professionally tested for mold. The symptoms of mold exposure matched exactly what Lala and I were experiencing. I knew the mold found in the crawlspace supposedly was removed, but what did I have to lose at this point but more of my health?

Unfortunately, Gena brought her father into the conversation. Don began to fill our heads with his belief that mold was a scam. He told us that mold remediation companies would tell you mold is dangerous, so you'd spend thousands of dollars on their services. He pleaded with us not to waste our money and promised that the crawlspace mold had been completely removed.

Gena and I started to drift apart. My life had become a living hell.

Chapter 12

No Fun with the Fungi

Gena was completely against having the house tested for mold, largely because Don had convinced her that mold remediation companies were scam artists. To help counter Don's complaint, I found a company that worked directly with the Environmental Protection Agency and only did testing, which eliminated the incentive to distort the results. This made no difference to Gena—she was still against testing.

My decision to ignore the advice of Don and my wife seemed to break those family bonds. Don believed it was proof of a mental disorder and convinced Gena that I was unstable. Worse, he began plotting a way to get rid of me. In his world, this usually meant something beyond arbitration.

The accredited lab did its home inspection the following week. Within a few days, we received the results—our home was "uninhabitable" according to EPA mold contamination standards. The types and high quantities of molds discovered in the structure showed the environment was very dangerous.

I will never forget my wife's reaction to the report—sincere humility. Gena looked in my eyes and said, "I'll never doubt you again." As she tearfully hugged me, I hoped this was true. But her father remained in control despite scientific proof that he'd been wrong. I learned that a narcissist will never admit fault, never apologize, and will go to extreme measures to hide or cover up a mistake.

The problem with our house was that the previous homeowner had poured a concrete front porch that blocked two of the three air vents for the crawlspace. This allowed humidity to build up, causing condensation on the water pipes and damp concrete walls. This produced ideal conditions for large quantities of molds like Aspergillus niger, Cladosporium and Stachybotrys to colonize on the wooden beams, drywall and insulation.

The severe rash that Lala suffered after I removed the decorations from the crawlspace had been caused by mold spores and mycotoxins I had freed from their nurturing habitat. The damnable fungi had also caused our respiratory infections. Now, after talking with experts and conducting my own research, I had become much more knowledgeable.

The previous homeowner had also added a stone finish to the house. But he failed to install a weather barrier, which allowed moisture to seep into the porous stonework. With a little humidity and moisture, spores can grow on anything biodegradable—even the dust fragments that build up in the ducts. Skin cells and bug fragments are like a steak house for hungry mold spores. An HVAC system doesn't resolve this situation—rather, it circulates the already-contaminated air throughout the house.

Don Darkino, of course, was chiefly responsible for this fiasco. He had made an illegal deal with the previous homeowner to clean out the mold without a professional opinion or an accurate test. So, how does a narcissist behave?

After the independent lab results confirmed the mold problem, Don doubled down on his defense, repeating his assertion that many bogus mold contractors he knew lied about mold issues so they could pocket cash from insurance companies.

"How do we know that the lab Mike hired isn't just making up reports?" he blurted out. "I guarantee they get kickbacks from contractors, so they scare people into hiring their buddies."

I didn't have the energy to make a stand.

Gena explained to her father that the lab we used didn't do remediation, so they had no reason to make up test results. And they made no recommendation to remediation companies.

Don slammed his fork down, stood up and yelled, "Don't you think they get paid behind the scenes?"

At that point, Gena knew there was no point arguing.

The test specified that for every square centimeter in our home where air tests were conducted, there existed 72,000 spores of a black mold called Aspergillus niger, 42,000 spores of Cladosporium, and 2,700 of the worst molds, Stachybotrys. My daughter and I had had some serious symptoms that were getting worse, and my intransigent father-in-law refused to acknowledge that I had finally found the cause.

What I didn't know was that Don had set up hidden cameras throughout our house to document my behavior, which he believed was highly erratic. It was true, of course, that I was acting out of character. After all, I was physically ailing totally stressed out by spending thousands of dollars on tests and staying up most nights doing research and building dust collectors. I was going to medical specialists who were dumbfounded, missing a lot of work and watching my income rapidly decline—not to mention the mental and emotional effects of amphetamines.

I had come to expect Don to behave in a way consistent with his deeply rooted paranoia and emotional rigidity. But I never thought he would undermine truth to turn my wife and his family against me.

After an adjuster signed off on the wreckage of my house, it took about two weeks to get a check from the insurance company. There was a five-thousand-dollar limit of liability for mold because it was such a very serious issue and so expensive to locate and eradicate the far-flung spores and mycotoxins, and to locating and fix all the points of water intrusion.

I told Gena that I'd do most of the clean-up work myself so we could save some of the settlement money to pay off hospital bills and other expenses that had piled up. What the hell was I thinking? I was already deathly ill—and now I was going to plunge back into the toxic cloud again. God knows how this was going to turn out.

I installed an exhaust fan to remove the humidity from the crawlspace, since the prior homeowner had closed all the other vents. I also put in a dehumidifier and prayed it would do the trick.

At least doing the work myself saved us some money. Remember my brilliant plan to vacuum out whatever was in the air using that enormous house fan? Well, I ended up pulling out all the toxins from the crawlspace and behind the walls and moving them into the living area where they got deposited onto our furniture, bedding, clothing, and in the ductwork for the HVAC. Before long, I was so sick that I had to leave the house behind and hope I'd have no future exposure.

Don insisted he bring over two of his guys to scrub the beams and walls, remove the insulation and Drylok the entire crawlspace. Unfortunately, they did not set up any negative airflow to collect the micro particles as they worked. Disturbing mold is like setting off a microscopic atomic bomb of mycotoxins and spores. You can never remove all these toxins from furniture or clothing. That is why doctors who understand the danger suggest moving away and leaving everything behind.

Allowing Don's workers to clean up the crawlspace was a disastrous decision. The guys used bleach, which chemically breaks down and mostly turns back into water, which was the main problem in the first place. Even though the cleaned surfaces looked fine after bleaching, the roots of a mold infestation grow deep into the grain of the wood and other materials.

Instead of removing the drywall in the crawlspace, Don told his guys to just paint over it, ignoring what could be growing on the other side. They threw latex paint on top of any mold to "seal" it, but guess what? Latex paint feeds the beast.

The carpets, of course, contained millions of spores and toxins from the ductwork cleaning, so we had them all ripped out and discarded. What a pointless exercise! The removal process was like shaking rugs—all the contamination hiding in the carpets exploded into the atmosphere of the house.

I now understood why the lab that tested our house for mold chose not to be in the remediation business. What a horror story! I was literally decaying the same way that fallen trees in the woods decay as mold gathers on it to break it down and turn it into compost.

Circle-of-life shit. For some reason, my body lost its defense to the effects of mold and I was slowly and painfully turning into compost.

Using what was left from our settlement, Gena got beautiful laminate flooring throughout the house. She got her new cabinets and countertops. I got more ill. Everyone thought that after such a thorough clean-up operation, the issue was over, and I would just bounce back to my normal successful self. The fact is, I got much sicker. At work, while away from home, I'd feel somewhat better. But as soon as I walked into the house, I could instantly feel an itch in my sinuses and lungs.

I started doing more research. One morning, Gena came downstairs while I was in the kitchen with a microscope making slides of my sputum. I'm sure I looked like a paranoid and obsessive fool, but the slides showed bacteria that were linking together—doctors call this biofilm or mycoplasma. This is not a good thing. And my symptoms were worsening. I was losing my vision, smell, and ability to concentrate. I was so fatigued and weak only my amphetamines kept me going. All of this inevitably dissolved my marital relationship—temporarily, I hoped—but to compensate for the lack of physical intimacy, I was indulging in some adult videos on the internet.

Don's hidden cameras caught me at my worst. He gleefully showed his tapes to Gena, a woman so prudish that my listening to Britney Spears would upset her, but more frightfully, I knew he was starting to create a profile for his buddies at the FBI. I could imagine how this profile was shaping up.

In the meantime, I was losing my successful career and going nuts trying to discover why I was still getting sick. The doctors I consulted said I was having another bacterial infection—which I was, but there had to be more to it. I felt like I was dying, but no one would believe me. I was so terrified being in my house that I would sometimes park for hours in random parking lots to avoid more exposure to my toxic home. And if Don had lobbied the FBI to surveil me as a threat to their prize informant—well, that suspicion certainly added to my stress.

One night, while doing more research online, I had a physical and emotional meltdown and shouted for Gena. She ran to me and I broke down into tears, confessing that I was getting much worse and didn't want to die. I hoped she would show some empathy or support because I needed someone at that moment to pick me up and take me away from this hell.

"Michael, you just need to stop this," she said sternly. "You're not dying—there's nothing wrong with the house."

I pulled away, suddenly feeling very alone. If there was nothing wrong, why was Lala constantly complaining that her chest hurt, and she was severely congested? Why did I feel like I was breathing in pepper spray with each breath? I was literally breaking down—decaying—both physically and mentally.

The next day, I told my managing director I needed to step down. I couldn't be supportive to my team, and it wasn't fair to them. This was financially ruinous, but I couldn't go on.

Most nights, I felt like I needed to go to the ER, but I was afraid of building up a medical profile of mental illness without even getting a useful diagnosis in return. My mental well-being was cracking at the core.

I conceived various methods of controlling my exposure to the mold. Even though I could imagine how covert surveillance would likely show a madman doing insane things, I tried to tape and calk around the floorboards so no air would leak from the crawlspace. I sprayed the attic with chemicals that were supposed to seal and smother mold. I installed the best air filters in the HVAC system. I completely replaced the attic ductwork instead of just cleaning them out. I sealed the garage walls and filled gaps in the foundation with cement. I dug a trench under the deck so water would drain away and not puddle by the house.

At this point, Gena and I didn't have a marriage anymore. I was so sick, it became difficult to do anything. The continual deterioration just outright broke my mind. My own mother and father kept telling me it was all in my head. No one believed it was the house—not even the doctors. The frustration of meeting with constant disbelief, derision, even condemnation by everyone in my life was becoming almost more unbearable than the physical and emotional suffering.

To me, it had become perfectly clear that I was going to die if I stayed in our home. And no one believed it.

I begged Gena to move. I suggested that we could temporarily move into an apartment until we sold the house. But she bitterly refused, saying she couldn't move someplace that wasn't safe for Lala. This infuriated me since the house itself wasn't safe for Lala. I tried to persuade her that I could get better and go back to work if we lived somewhere else.

"It's not the house, Mike!" she yelled back. "It's you!"

I could have insisted that we move, or moved out by myself, but I didn't. I allowed myself to become more ill. My confused thinking convinced me that I could still find a way to prove it was mold. Then, maybe I would regain the love and respect that I deserved.

I still didn't fully appreciate how a narcissist criminal like Don Darkino will never admit fault and will undertake extreme measures to protect his warped ego. Don had made up his mind about me, and as Gena had warned, there was no escaping that obsession for either of us.

Chapter 13

A Biological Weapon, Declassified

I continued to study every aspect of mold and fungus to the point that I questioned my own obsessive behavior. I learned the different kinds, how they grow and colonize, which types are more dangerous, and how indoor mold mutates into a hybrid version that is not found outdoors. Also, I learned all the sources of nutrients necessary for molds to grow.

For example, Stachybotrys, the most toxic genus, only grows where there is continuous water exposure. Even if a water leak is fixed, however, an existing colony can continue to spread with just 45 percent humidity. When the spores release into the air, they can land on other nutrient sources, starting whole new colonies. In the right environment, this reproduction cycle is like an alien invasion.

Dust mites, dander, and normal allergens present an all-you-can-eat buffet to these hungry spores. Wood, paper, drywall and even clothing are excellent breeding grounds. So were the Christmas toys kept in a mold-infested crawlspace, which I know caused Lala's severe rash after she handled them. For some reason, though, no one believed mold was the culprit. "Rashes are common," the pediatrician said. Well, so is mold.

I also discovered that certain molds carry mycotoxins that can cause damaging inflammation throughout the body. When mycotoxins get lodged in blood vessels, the physiology of the brain reacts to the exposure, which can lead to depression, anxiety, even early onset of Alzheimer's disease. These mental effects are horrendous, but so are the physical symptoms like muscle and joint pain, headaches, blurred vision, exhaustion and chronic infections of the lungs and sinuses.

I also learned something I wish I'd never read—that the military uses mycotoxins as a biological weapon. In every war since WWI, some form of mycotoxin has been used in combat. Agent orange is the most common, and these weapons are made from common black mold. This heightened my anxiety, which was already at a dangerous level.

I read about schools shutting down because of mold exposure. I studied lawsuits filed by apartment dwellers with landlords who refused to remedy mold problems. I learned that the Bible taught mold was a danger and proposed ways to deal with the contamination. If this danger was known in Bible times, why were medical professionals so blind to the dangers?

I was able to identify a handful of doctors who studied under Dr. Richie Shoemaker, a pioneer mold expert. These few doctors were scattered across the country and specialized in mold illnesses like mine.

Our family savings were dwindling, and I was becoming increasingly discouraged about the future. Then, for the first time, I heard Don Darkino threaten my life.

We were over for dinner one night, and the conversation predictably turned to the house and our struggle to keep up with the bills. Don suddenly lost his temper and shouted that I'd had better pull it together or I was dead. At first, I thought he was expressing concern that stress might kill me. But then he said, "And don't think I don't think about it."

Gena looked straight ahead and didn't say a word. I knew my father-in-law was tied to the Mafia and had influential connections, such as the FBI. I knew he had an explosive temper. But this comment seemed like an open threat, and I lost my appetite. I managed to block it from my mind, though, until future events resurrected the memory of it his threat.

I eventually found an attorney in Maryland who had started representing mold victims after he had become ill from an exposure. He never charged me a nickel while he offered me support and empathy. He even wrote my wife a letter explaining what I was going through, and how his wife had not understood the seriousness of mold exposure either. He wrote that he had asked his wife during the worst part of his illness, "For as long as you have known me, have I ever acted this way before?" His wife had said no and decided to stick by him even though she didn't understand.

I thought the attorney's words would help Gena understand my predicament, since I was acting out of character just like the lawyer. But Gena, like her domineering father, already had surrendered to his view, and like Don, she seemed unable to admit she was wrong.

The attorney advised me to get another test done on the house. If the levels were still high, the test would prove the first remediation attempt hadn't worked. His idea made perfect sense to me. When I explained the concept to my wife, though, it proved to be the last straw. Don Darkino told his daughter to ignore the letter from the attorney, who was only trying to make money. To Don, I was mentally ill, and so he started to expose my behavior and amphetamine use to the Philadelphia office of the FBI.

I took the attorney's advice and got another mold test, which created a monumental squabble. Everyone thought I had lost my damn mind. Doctors refused to see me. My employer thought I'd gone mentally AWOL. My own family thought a psychiatrist was needed. And I found myself on the wrong side of an entire Mafia family. Don not only turned my wife against me but caused me to be investigated and surveilled by the FBI. Who knew what he told the feds?

It turns out, I should have never tried to prove the cause of my illness. I should have just stopped exposing myself to the toxins. Instead, I continued to poison myself nearly to death.

Don already had the FBI creating a dossier on me. What would merit that, I wondered. Was it possible that I had stumbled onto a classified government secret or discovered a military bioweapon?

After a week of waiting, the new test results came back from the lab and showed out home's air still highly contaminated with mold and dangerous levels of both positive and negative bacteria strains. The test was called an ERMI—environmental relative mold index. A dust sample had been collected from different areas of the house and the number of mold spores of each variety had been counted. The mold count from outdoors had been compared to the indoor counts to calculate the ERMI score, which ranged from 1, being no contamination, to 21, being the most dangerous level. Our house had a score of 17.

I was told by the Maryland attorney that a person diagnosed with this illness would continue getting more ill with an ERMI score of 4 or above.

Another shocking discovery involved the types and levels of bacteria that were found. Don had fraudulently manipulated the bank and told us the septic system didn't need to be replaced. The fact was quite different—the system had not been filtering correctly and the ground had been constantly saturated with our waste. It was a muddy mess. Every time I'd cut the grass or walk around the pool, I was covering myself with harmful bacteria from the septic system. Every time I took my daughter into our yard, I was exposing us both to dangerous organisms.

Don was supposed to be a contractor, but I was now convinced his construction firm was just a front because he lacked the basic knowledge necessary to be in the business. His ignorance destroyed my life and was making his granddaughter sick. Yet he couldn't admit to any fault.

Bacteria carries endotoxins, which are just as dangerous as mycotoxins. Don never should have allowed the seller to do his own mold remediation. The bank never would have approved the mortgage if they had known the septic system wasn't going to be replaced. Don, believing his own assessments—or worse yet, perhaps covering up the known truth—caused a lot of harm.

The Maryland attorney gave me the name of the doctor who had helped him through the illness. This doctor was a practicing chiropractor in Maryland who had dedicated her practice, like the attorney, to helping people suffering with mold illness. She and her two children had become ill from their water-damaged apartment.

I was starting to see a common factor here. Many people who had suffered through this terrible illness had dedicated themselves to helping other victims. The problem was that only a handful of doctors acknowledged the illness and were trained to treat it.

I mentioned to Gena that I was going to consult the chiropractor and presented the confirmed results of the ERMI test.

"I've never heard of an ERMI test," she said defiantly. "Doctors tell me mold is everywhere. Of course, the test will show mold."

Sadly, Gena refused to go with me to the chiropractor, which would have helped us both learn about my illness. Don made fun of me going to Maryland, telling Gena that I would never stop looking for a doctor until I got one that agreed with what I believed. I think this was when a smoldering fire of resentment was kindled. My health and well-being were obviously Gena's least concern.

I truly believed I didn't have time left. It didn't matter if Gena believed if physicians couldn't verify the cause of my symptoms. Even if it was all in my head, I thought, Gena should have wanted me to feel better so we could have a future together.

I was also terrified that Lala might start getting worse. Gena's parents predictably had developed a belief that I was inflicting my illness onto my daughter. Don was communicating his theories about me to the FBI, I learned, trying to persuade them that I was a threat to myself and others.

I believed that Lala's constant congestion, sinus infections, night terrors and rashes were likely caused by mold in our home, the presence of which had now been documented by two different lab tests.

Easter morning came two weeks before my doctor's appointment in Maryland. Gena's parents were supposed to meet us at the house so we could all go to Mass. I woke up on the couch that morning choking on thick, rubbery phlegm—more than usual—and totally obstructed airways. I tried to breathe through my mouth, but my throat was filled with glue-like saliva. The harder I tried to breathe, the more phlegm got pulled down into my esophagus, causing me to gag and throw up bile.

Panicked, I walked out the front door and stood on the porch with my head between my knees. I was spitting out globs of mucus when Gena approached me with Lala in her arms.

"Please give me a minute," I said between gasps. "I don't want Lala to see me this way. Take her inside/" I started to purposely snort and hack to clear my head of all the junk. Slime was dripping down my chin, covering the front of my shirt.

Gena refused to move. She just stood there, watching me suffer, then said, "My parents will be here in an hour."

I said again, "Please take her inside."

But Gena just kept standing there. I could see Lala becoming worried. I didn't want her to see me suffer.

Finally, Gena sarcastically said, "Can we not do this today?"

Those words were a pivot point in my life, and I lost all hope that I could avoid my new reality. I didn't want to lose my family, but I had already lost them. In a flash, I recognized that Gena could never be the wife that I needed. At that moment, I gave up trying to keep my family together. I couldn't fight through the physical and emotional distress any longer.

In a rage, I defiantly kicked a chair and it flew across the porch, hitting screen door where Gena was standing. As I stormed toward the door to go inside, I tripped on the chair and my hand hit a light fixture, shattering it. Shards of glass flew everywhere. Gena looked scared, probably thinking that I'd hit the light intentionally. But why would I endanger my daughter?

Gena, of course, told her father about the incident, and he reported to the FBI that I had attacked my wife and daughter by smashing glass in their direction.

I grabbed my keys and left the house that I believed was making me gravely ill. I drove to my parents' house, gagging and spitting out the window the entire time. The entire driver's side of my car was covered in what looked like dried rubber cement. Sobbing and gasping, I walked into their house, flopped on the couch, telling Mom I just couldn't take it anymore.

Unfortunately, my parents also denied I was sick from mold, so I told them I just needed some rest. I fell asleep that morning and I didn't wake up until the middle of the night. One thing I knew for sure—I wasn't going back to that house.

The next day Gena called and said she and Lala were going to her parents' house for a while. I still had a week before my appointment with the chiropractor in Maryland. I used that time to sleep. A few days later, Gena drove out to see me. I begged her to go with me to see the chiropractor.

She just shook her head and said, "Mike, you need help."

"Yes," I said, and this doctor can help us both understand what kind of help I need."

Then Gena said something so cruel I will never forget it. "If you don't get yourself help, Lala will be calling someone else Daddy." She broke my heart that day.

The next day, Gena invited me to her brother's house for a family dinner. She felt it was important for Lala to see us together. I agreed, so I drove over for dinner feeling very self-conscious and uncomfortable. I knew they all thought I had gone nuts, and I really didn't want to face any of them except Lala.

When I walked into Nick's house, Lala yelled out, "Daddy!" I gave her a huge hug and didn't ever want to let go. Before dinner, Gena's brother and I sat in the living room reading the newspaper and pretending that being together was not awkward. Suddenly, I understood the extent of the danger surrounding me.

In the newspaper, I read an article about a man named J. Cazonaro who lived down the street from my house. Cazonaro had been found dead with a gunshot to his head. I recalled the phone conversation about Cazonaro I had overheard at Don's house, which Don didn't know I had heard.

I mentioned the article to Nick and said the murder must have been about money. "Obviously, he didn't pay someone back," I said.

Apparently, Don had been listening because he frantically rushed into the room, asking what we were talking about. Nick said the newspaper had reported a murder.

Don demanded that I repeat what I'd said to Nick.

"He obviously pissed someone off," I replied.

"Yeah, but how do you know it was about money?" Don asked

Okay, hit the brakes, I thought. You're going to betray how much you know and put yourself in peril.

"Of course it was about money," I told Don. "What else would it be? Nothing was stolen."

Don told Nick and me never to speak about this again. We both agreed and dropped the conversation. But I immediately knew that I had made a mistake, and that Don most likely had deduced that I knew more than I should. I was adding more fuel to his desire for me to be dead.

We had a fine dinner, but I was very quiet. Imagine sitting at the same table with a Mafia boss who wants you killed, a fact I couldn't provide but new in my heart to be true.

Chapter 14

Chronic Inflammatory Response Syndrome

My parents tried to discourage me from going to Maryland for my chiropractor appointment, but I was determined. During my consultation, I learned that she partnered with Dr. Bonlie, who was also trained in the treatment of mold disorders. After hearing my story, she said that my symptoms were the worst of all her patients, and she encouraged me to write a book about my experience. You are now holding that book in your hands.

The doctor told me more details about how she and her two boys had developed a terrible illness from mold in her apartment. Most meaningful to me were her words, "Michael, you are not crazy. Many others are suffering just like you from mold illnesses."

The only way to make sure my symptoms were caused by mold, she explained, was to run specific blood tests. If I was a certain genetic haplotype, recovery would be extremely difficult, but I would have some answers. That was my major goal—answers. At that time, I was more fixated on proving I wasn't crazy than restoring my own health. This, of course, was a big mistake.

I had learned the hard way that perception is like a brick wall. Once formed, it takes a bulldozer to remove that wall. The persistence of a formed perception, even when incorrect, makes it nearly impossible to replace it with a true perception.

I drove back to Pennsylvania and shared notes from the appointment with my parents. Both still had doubts about how mold could cause my illness. It just didn't make sense to them that something so ubiquitous in nature could be so dangerous.

The next morning, the chiropractor emailed me the results of my blood tests plus a written diagnosis. She called my illness CIRS, chronic inflammatory response syndrome, commonly attributed to illness deriving from water-damaged buildings. Worse, I had been cursed with a genetic haplotype that made me highly susceptible to this illness and facing a long and difficult recovery, if that was even possible.

Approximately 25 percent of the world population shares this haplotype, but only about 2 percent of us are "triggered" by a dangerously high level of exposure to endotoxins from bacteria or mycotoxins from mold. Since I been heavily exposed, my body's immune system had mutated and no longer recognized these toxins. Normal immune systems would flush out these toxins, but I no longer had this defensive mechanism. The toxins were causing inflammation throughout my body. The thick mucus in my sinuses was due to Morgellons disease and biofilms.

Think about how a pearl is formed. When a grain of sand irritates an oyster, the oyster naturally secretes a substance to protect itself from the irritation. The result is a pearl. Since my body no longer could flush out the irritants, my system formed a thick, glue-like slime over the mold and bacterial spores, sending me on many unsuccessful trips to the ER. Doctors accurately confirmed that I had repeated bacterial infections, but none of them could give me a reason until now.

Here is the actual diagnosis from Dr. Bonlie.

New Paradigm Wellness 30 E Padonia Rd., #305,
Timonium, MD 21093
Phone: (410) 560-7404
Fax: (443) 705-0228
WayneBonlieMD@me.com Date: July 2, 2013

To whom it may concern:

I have seen and examined Michael Lutterschmidt and reviewed his history and prior workup. His case meets the case definition of systemic inflammatory response (SIRS). The cause of his condition is exposure to buildings with water damage. The diagnosis is based on peer-reviewed criteria of genetics, symptoms, and physiologic and neurological parameters.

Mr. Lutterschmidt has exhibited symptoms that include profound fatigue, muscle cramps, pain, nerve pain, loss of strength and coordination, headaches, light sensitivity, red eyes, unexplained shortness of breath, sinus congestion, metallic taste, impaired memory and concentration, weight loss, loss of appetite, disrupted sleep patterns, and frequent urination.

Testing with visual contrast sensitivity (VCS) showed an abnormal deficit that is characteristic of neurotoxicity. Lab testing has shown HLA genetic typing consistent with pattern showing multisusceptible haplotype of 4-3-53. This genetic type prevents the ability to properly clear microbial toxins, endotoxins, mycotoxins, and inflammagens that are commonly found in buildings with water intrusion. Other abnormal labs include MSH, 14 (range 35–81); VEGF, <31 (range 32–86); ADH, 1.7 (range 2.5–3.5); vitamin D 25-OH, 20.6 (range 32–100); TGFb1, 3,480 (range 322–2,382); and C4a 15, 796 (range 0–2,830).

These labs present a pattern that is consistent with the clinical presentation and diagnosis of SIRS while ruling out other diagnosis in which these labs should be normal.

The combination of lab abnormalities, abnormal VCS and HLA typing, is highly accurate and reproducible in identifying SIRS that is related to water-damaged buildings. The likelihood of this happening by chance is less than 1 percent, as presented at the International Society for

Testing and Measurement meeting, Boulder, Colorado, on July 27, 2006.

After examining and interviewing M. Lutterschmidt, I believe that the impact of his illness on his physical and cognitive function is such that he is substantially disabled to the point of being unable to perform his normal work functions or to be gainfully employed in any capacity. With treatment and avoidance of further exposure, he should be expected to make substantial recovery of functional status.

In order to regain and maintain his health, it is essential that Michael Lutterschmidt avoid exposure to buildings with a history of water intrusion, water damage, or water leaks.

Sincerely, Dr. Wayne Bonlie, MD

I was concerned with the vigorous and intense sixteen-step recovery process the chiropractor had specified for me, but I was relieved that I now had a written medical diagnosis to show my wife and her parents to prove that I wasn't insane. I was confident they'd read it understand what I had been going through, perhaps even show some empathy. The mocking and mental illness labels had caused me to become intensely resentful and isolated. If this letter didn't change their perceptions, I knew that I'd lose my little girl.

Chapter 15

Narcissistic, Psychopathic Mafia Scumbag

I walked into the house of my in-laws. Gena and her mom were in the kitchen making dinner, and Lala was coloring at the table. I kissed Gena and decided to wait until the timing was right to share the formal diagnosis.

When Don came to the dinner table, he seemed more disturbed than usual. He sat down across from me, and without any greeting, said to me, "This is what you are going to do. We are going down to court and sign the deed to the house over to me."

Frankly, I couldn't have cared less about this house, which had nearly killed me and made my daughter ill. I just wanted to start my recovery and show my wife the reason I was so sick. But it occurred to me that the mortgage was in my name, so signing over the house without changing the mortgage seemed unwise.

"No," I said, intending to explain concerns about the mortgage as well.

But Don didn't allow me to mutter another word. He started screaming, which scared Lala.

"That's my money!" he screamed, beating his chest as emphasis.

What I had intended to explain was that the deed and the mortgage needed to be addressed together.

He kept screaming and pounding the table. My daughter was now crying, so I stood up and put my arms around her. Then, as I straightened up, I felt a blow to my left temple. I couldn't believe that my father-in-law just punched me.

And then he hit me again on the left side of my head.

I still don't know why he did this, but he didn't knock me out—just made me angry. I walked toward him, and he suddenly looked terrified. For a moment, everything around me became dark, and my peripheral vision blurred.

"Did you just hit me?" I asked in an eerie, calming voice.

Sensing impending violence, Don's wife suddenly leaped between us, which helped remind me of what I was capable of when coerced into "fight" mode. I retreated and kissed my daughter, who was now hysterical, and headed for the door. But I was intercepted by Don, who was now pointing a handgun at me.

"You son of a bitch, I'm going to kill you right now," he yelled.

"At this point," I said with uncharacteristic calmness, "do me the favor."

Waving the gun around, Don said, "Let's walk out to the shed then."

Ignoring him, I moved toward the front door. Don continued to threaten me, shouting that he was going to have "Bofa" kill me, whoever or whatever that meant.

Don followed me outside, continuing to wave the gun around. Gena came running after me, but Don stopped her and yelled, "You choose right now—that scumbag or me!"

Apparently, Gena made her decision because she walked back into the house.

I stood at my car, watching Don rant and then mock me by grabbing his stomach, bending over and pretending to cough.

I drove to my parents' house with a black eye. All I could think about was the diagnosis I had intended to share with the Darkinos to prove I wasn't crazy. The gun pointed in my face made me realize that there was one crazy person in the family, but it wasn't me.

Seeing my bruised eye, my father asked what had happened, and I told them the whole story. I should have called the police, but I didn't. I had a black eye, Don had a gun, and my daughter was old enough to tell authorities what had happened.

My mom convinced me to let it go because she always avoided conflict. "He is just a hothead," Mom said, "so let things blow over."

I took pictures of my black eye for the hell of it and then reclined on the sofa to forget the horrific events. I was too angry to nap—my mind was buzzing with Don's death threats and questions about who the hell "Bofa" was.

The next morning, sheriff's deputy knocked on the door, waking me up. After I opened the door, he asked for me by name and then handed me a certified letter. Inside was a Protection from Abuse (PFA) order from B County Domestics. That bastard Don had called the police and reported that I had threatened the lives of his family. Apparently, he had coerced or intimidated my wife into writing that I had attacked him and threatened to kill everyone in the house.

With criminal cleverness, Don had taken himself to the ER where he claimed I had hit him in the chest. He also got a gun shop to create a fraudulent receipt showing that his handgun was in the shop for service at the time of my attack.

I couldn't believe what was happening. I flew into a rage and was about to drive over to beat the hell out of my father-in-law, but fortunately, my parents reminded me there would be consequences for that—jail time and losing my right to see Lala.

I felt betrayed by my wife. How could she agree to commit this terrible perjury? The event itself was appalling but filing a false police report was outrageous. Now I had to go to court and fight these absurd accusations; otherwise, my daughter would be ripped out of my life. The three-year PFA, if it was approved, would prevent me from any contact with my daughter or my wife. This was my first dose of legal corruption.

Several hours later, I got my second dose. My parents and I were commiserating on the back porch when a car pulled up and stopped. A man and woman introduced themselves as representing crisis intervention, which had received a call that I was going to shoot myself. Don was pulling out all the stops to enrage me, probably hoping that I would do something stupid. I didn't even own a gun!

Following the protocol of a "302," they said, I had two choices. I could commit myself for a voluntary seventy-two-hour evaluation, or if I refused, I would be escorted in handcuffs.

My dad went into a frenzy. I'd never seen him stick up for me the way he did that day. I heard him say, "I'll kill that son of a bitch myself!" The prudent choice, of course, was to bite my tongue and voluntarily comply rather than provide more false impressions for my increasingly meaty dossier.

I entered the hospital not knowing what to expect. As a first step, I was examined by the ER doctor, who checked my black eye and listened patiently to my account of the past day. Then I got undressed and put on a hospital gown and yellow socks before beginning the psych evaluation. The yellow socks, I learned, identify possible risks.

The first three hours were disturbing. I was not allowed to have anything with me, and I was placed in a white room with a bed—no TV, no books, just me and my thoughts. I'm sure I was observed at every step to help determine my mental state. For the next few hours, I lay on the bed, paced the room, asked the reception desk repeatedly what was next, ate meals, answered batteries of questions, visited with a social worker, had a group session, and was interviewed by a psychiatrist.

I couldn't help but wonder at this strange turn of events. Don, the criminal psycho who had threatened me at gunpoint, bruised me with his fists and tried to strangle his daughter-in-law was probably sitting by his pool while Michael James Lutterschmidt, who was seriously ill and attempting to save his family from multiple threats, was in a psych ward.

From the beginning, I suspect Don had been collecting evidence that could be manipulated and falsified to create a compelling portrait of a nut job. He'd hidden cameras and had full computer access to all my accounts, emails and search history because I shared my passwords with Gena. Electronically, he could do anything he wanted in my name. To this day, I still have no idea why my personal email address is under federal investigation.

There was something positive about being in the hospital. I could breathe without getting that itchy, painful irritation in my sinuses and lungs.

I was released nine hours after admission, even though my stay was supposed to be a mandatory seventy-two-hour evaluation. I chalked up the early discharge as a victory. This gave me extra time to find money to retain a lawyer for the PFA hearing.

I called the company's pension department and cashed out what I had in qualified assets. The last of my savings had been spent driving down to Maryland and paying for lab tests. My credit card was well maxed out, so all I had was my pension. I didn't have the time to wait for a mailed check, so I drove the three hours to Harrisburg and picked up the cash in person.

With all my liquid assets in cash, I began to contact attorneys. The problem was that the hearing was in a few days, and most attorneys were unavailable. I received a few referrals and made about twenty-five calls. Eventually, I reached a well-known attorney in Doylestown named Tina, who was able to rearrange her schedule to accommodate the hearing.

When we met, Tina spoke callously and without emotion. "I will need a five-thousand-dollar retainer in order to consider representing you," she stated matter-of-factly.

I paused because this was all the money I had to survive on until I got back on my feet. But I was running out of time, so I agreed and made an appointment for the following day. Then I made a follow-up appointment with the doctor in Maryland to start the difficult recovery process.

The first step was to avoid further exposure, but as the allergist had told me, mold is everywhere. How the hell was I going to avoid exposure to it? But if I didn't avoid further exposure, I would never get better. Think of a bathtub filled with water. If you turn on the faucet and unplug the drain, the tub may never drain all the way. I needed to turn the faucet of exposure nearly off so more toxins would drain out than were coming in.

Second, I would need to take cholesterol medication that contained positively-charged, right-size molecules that would bind to the mycotoxins in my body so they could get flushed out. This was the only way for my body to remove these toxins.

The next step was controversial, requiring me to take the strongest, most intense antibiotic on the market for thirty days. It was so strong that it would turn the whites of my eyes pink and make my urine look like I had drunk Pink Panther piss. This strong drug was needed to kill the Morgellons bug that was reproducing in my respiratory tract. These bugs were the main cause of all those late-night ER visits. Morgellons is almost impossible to remove.

In addition to a thirty-day dose of the uber-antibiotic, I was instructed to eliminate all sugar and gluten from my diet. This meant no cereal, no bread, no carbs. Considering that I was living with my carb-loving parents who were not open to this treatment plan, I was going to have some obstacles.

To prepare for my meeting with the attorney, I pulled together all my paperwork and documented the true events that took place the day Don pulled a gun on me. I printed out the photos of my black eye, and my father wrote a witness statement about my return home and the visit from the crisis center.

My parents traveled with me to Doylestown. We walked into the office and sat in the lobby. The paralegal told me Tina would be right with me. Tina came out and shook my hand. Stern and humorless, Tina got right to the point, which I appreciated considering her hourly rate.

Tina sat down and immediately wanted to see the PFA I had received from the deputy. She read it quickly and asked if any parts were true. I said everything was a lie, including Don's assertion that I had threatened to kidnap Lala and slit Don's throat. Tina asked if I had the five thousand dollars, and I pulled out a stack of twenty-dollar bills, which surprised her.

After she confirmed the amount, she advised me to file for divorce immediately and include a request for custody of Lala. This would start the process in my favor. She wasn't worried about the PFA at all, which was my major concern. There was one thing for sure—Tina was a bulldog.

The next day, we had to return to Doylestown for the nine o'clock hearing. Gena and her entire family were in the hallway talking to a woman lawyer who looked young and inexperienced. Don seemed surprised to see me there with a lawyer. He probably assumed I couldn't afford counsel even if I managed to get out of the psych ward on time.

Tina went right over to Don's attorney, as I observed from a distance. Tina asked the attorney a question, and I saw Gena hold up three fingers, which I assumed meant they were pushing to keep me away from Lala for three years.

Tina shook her head and said so loudly I could hear, "On what grounds? This?" Then she headed toward me as Don yelled at his lawyer and stabbed a finger in her direction.

"Well, they are a lovely bunch," Tina said to me. "You married into a nightmare!"

"It wasn't always like that," I responded.

She told me that Don's attorney was inexperienced and allowing my father-in-law to interfere. "Anyway, that the PFA is all hearsay," she told us. "There's no way it's holding up in court."

In the courtroom, I still didn't know what to expect, but I was confident I had a lawyer who had it under control. At last, after hearing a couple other cases, the judge said, "Don Darkino, Protection from Abuse order."

Don walked up to the judge, who asked if he understood the legal procedure and consequences for withdrawing his claim. This was the first we had heard that he was backing down. I still don't know why he decided to withdraw his claim, but I was ecstatic.

As I watched him walk away from the judge dejected, I recalled something I had said to him just before I walked away from his gun-wielding intimidation. I had muttered, "It was all recorded." I don't know why I bluffed about that—probably because I wished his threats had been recorded. But Don may have believed me, or perhaps he just couldn't take a chance that he'd been recorded.

We left the courtroom, and a security guard asked us if we were okay.

"Why do you ask?" I replied.

He said there was a man across the hallway who was pointing a finger clearly trying to intimidate me.

Tina approached Don's attorney to discuss options. "You can forget about the PFA," she stated bluntly. It's not going to work. We need to discuss visitation schedules until we have a custody hearing later."

Don started to make a spectacle of himself again but finally walked away, his face red with rage. Tina waited until he was out of sight, then asked me what days I wanted visitation. She said, "Right now, it's going to be a fifty-fifty co-parent arrangement."

I decided to go with Wednesday evening through Saturday evening, with Gena having Lala Sunday through Wednesday morning. Tina asked if I would agree to visitation supervised by my parents, which would help get this nightmare over. At the custody hearing, she explained, she was certain we could get rid of the supervision. "Right now, let's just get this in writing and put an end to all the nonsense," she said.

Don had caved in this time, but he was deeply committed to his criminal game, and I was far too preoccupied to even realize he was just getting started.

Chapter 16

Separation and Transition

Having my parents supervise my time with Lala wasn't a problem until I rented an apartment down the street. I wasn't employed yet, but having some personal space had become a necessity. I paid the first month's rent and the security deposit, not realizing how fast Tina's legal bills would add up at $450 per hour. Each email and phone call, every fax was costly. Her bills added up quickly.

The custody hearing wasn't for six weeks, so I had time to enjoy being with Lala. My mom got us passes to Dorney Park and Wildwater Kingdom where we'd go swimming in the wave pool and hop on the kiddie rides in Snoopy Land. We created a lot of happy memories, which I suspected might have to last me for a long time.

My apartment was a large one-bedroom unit with a pool and playground right on the grounds. Gena and her father, of course, freaked out. Don took me to court, claiming the apartment complex didn't have enough security. Gena became fearful of the neighbors in my building, complained about the parking lot, and insisted that I prove my mom was present every time Lala was with me. She had become increasingly paranoid due to her father's risky criminal enterprises and contagious fears. I believed many of these issues were brought up mainly to run up my legal tab.

Fun with my daughter helped alleviate some of the anxiety caused by Gena's family. Lala and I would walk up the Jordan Creek and find treasures, watch movies at the local drive-in and go to our favorite store, Dollar General, for new discoveries. I couldn't spend money on her like the Darkinos could. I couldn't take her out to eat, buy her new clothes or even get her real toys. But the time we shared together was magical. I'm crying right now as I relive so many memories.

While Lala was with her mom, I met with the doctor and explained that I was still experiencing terrible symptoms. The pain was less than in my old house, but whenever I entered a building, I could now instantly detect if there had been water damage. This was my superpower, and I was never wrong.

As an example, after only a few nights in the apartment, I knew there was a water problem. I pointed out to the maintenance guy where I was sure the problem was stemming. After pulling off a panel in the bedroom to access the bathroom plumbing, he discovered a leak with substantial mold growth.

The doctor explained that I had become so sensitive to molds from past exposure that a few breaths in the wrong environment could cause a serious setback. She encouraged me to keep trusting my body and honoring my intuition.

The recovery plan she'd given me was going to be damn near impossible to follow. I needed to be fanatical, she said, about avoiding exposure and taking my cholesterol medication to help counter the buildup of toxins. Every pill was like an empty bus, she explained, and the bus traveled through my system scooping up the toxins and escorting them out of my body.

The doctor reminded me that I had spent two years ignoring my body while staying in my first house. "Learn from those mistakes and never ignore your body again," she advised.

I tried taking the thirty-day mega antibiotics she had recommended. My eyes turned pink as she had promised, and my urine became red. After four days on this medication, I got scary sick—the kind where you can't stand, you can't see straight and you feel like you're going to die. My parents got so worried they threw away the remaining antibiotics, thinking the medicine was causing me to become violently ill.

I learned later that discarding the antibiotics was a huge mistake. I was getting sick because *the antibiotic was working*. As the biofilm and the mycoplasma were breaking up, hidden toxins were now coming free and moving into my bloodstream. My scary sickness was a sign that I was getting better.

Unfortunately, I didn't have the money or the insurance to get another prescription, and I was still suffering from the mycoplasma and Morgellons bugs. Desperate for some income, I got a server job at Outback Steakhouse. I approached my job at Outback with a positive attitude. Well, as positive as I could. The adjustment was much harder than I'd imagined. I had managed a high-volume restaurant and bar in New York, and now I was waiting tables. I had to reinvent myself to stand on the bottom run of the ladder, and my pride got in the way. It was a grind for my coworkers, who had to deal with my lack of enthusiasm, and for me, who had to deal with the chain of command from the bottom up.

For most of that summer, I was still severely suffering from the symptoms of CIRS but enjoying my intermittent times with Lala. I quit the amphetamines because it was clear that my condition required a new way of living.

Soon after moving into the apartment, it became clear that I couldn't afford the rent. I wasn't even paying support or alimony yet, but the cost of my car loan and insurance alone was over five hundred dollars a month. I was forced to leave the apartment and move back in with my parents.

The court hearing for custody occurred just as Lala was about to start school. There was a huge logistical dilemma. I couldn't afford to move closer to her, and Lala needed to go to school Monday through Friday. Because of that, I agreed to see Lala on alternate weekends and visit her for dinner once a week.

This gave Gena a huge advantage on the support calculation since she would now have most of the custodial time. Gena was living with her crime family rent-free and didn't have to pay for a car, insurance, food or clothing.

My support obligation wasn't based on current income but rather on income potential based on previous years. I tried to argue the unfairness of this because my health issues, in fact, limited my potential income. The dialogue between attorneys was expensive. Tina quickly racked up over seven thousand dollars of legal charges I could not pay, so she withdrew her representation, and I was left to defend myself.

I tried to present my medical diagnosis to the court, but Gena's attorney argued that it was from an out-of-state doctor, and the judge threw it out.

"The next time you try to play games," the judge told me abruptly, "you better have a doctor from Pennsylvania."

I was suffering from CIRS, but no one would accept my diagnosis. I finally had a doctor write a letter stating that I was unable to be gainfully employed, but that also didn't matter. In case you're wondering how long this slide to hell would last—well, I was only halfway down.

Besides losing Lala, I now faced crippling support payments. If I failed to make these payments, I could end up in jail. Eventually, I was hired as an investment banker, which earned me just enough to pay for a modest car, insurance and Lala's support.

The truth is, I became overwhelmed with anger and resentment toward the system. At that time, doctors in Pennsylvania did not recognize CIRS as a legitimate illness, which was why I had gone to Maryland in the first place.

To torture me further, Don Darkino dug into the background of Dr. Richie Shoemaker, the doctor who had first discovered CIRS and the relationship between genetics and symptoms. He found that Dr. Shoemaker had lost his medical license for a short period of time due to the miscoding of the super antibiotic that was recommended for the treatment of CIRS. My own research led me to evidence of a military cover-up related to the Shoemaker licensure fiasco. Unfortunately, in court, this information helped discredit my diagnosis.

I kept thinking, *Why can't they just see how sick I am and just try to help me get back on my feet?* I quickly learned that Don had only one goal—to follow through on his death threat, even if by indirect means.

My job at the bank soon fell through because I wasn't physically able to continue the commute of an hour in each direction. How was I supposed to sell financial products when I looked and felt like roadkill all the time? I became as sick as I was in my original house.

My "superpower" led me to suspect that my parents' house was contaminated with mold or water damage. The doctor told me to listen to my body, so I ordered an ERMI test on my parents' house. Within a few days, the report came back with an ERMI score of 14. To avoid damaging exposure, I needed to live in a building with a score of 4 or less.

The house, however, was old but showed no signs of water damage. *How could this be?* I wondered. The ERMI test confirmed high levels of *Stachybotrys*, the most toxic black mold, which requires a constant source of water to flourish.

An idea popped into my head. What if my parents' house wasn't the actual source of the problem? What if the house was being purposely and continuously contaminated with black mold spores? Who and for what reason would some nefarious entity be doing this? Was this just paranoia, or was it possible that the government might be poisoning the house to cover up a secret of some kind?

Later, I will provide proof of the kind of purposeful contamination I suspected.

My parents, of course, refused to believe their house contained mold. They simply disbelieved the lab report, which did not align with their own beliefs. Everyone in my life continued to believe I was insane. I felt like that hillbilly in the woods who saw a real spaceship, but everyone thought he just drank too much moonshine.

I worried that if I didn't find another job, I'd be thrown in jail. I dedicated myself to another job search and was hired by a payroll firm to sell business insurance. For several weeks, I excelled and was given my own team and a territory of seven states. But then, it started again. Within about two hours of sitting at my desk, I began to have agonizing sinus issues. My "superpower" suggested there was an issue with the building—but how could a nine-story office tower be contaminated?

I figured it must be the ductwork. During lunch one day, I went down to the facility room and sneaked a look at the air exchange. I peeked at the filters, which were totally black—in fact, seven months overdue for replacement.

I recalled my doctor telling me that black mold only needed 45 percent humidity to grow. The building ductwork was giving mold spores what they needed. The contaminated ducts and filters were making the recirculated air toxic to my genetically susceptible immune system. Every morning, when I used a disinfectant wipe to clean my desk, it turned black.

I started to notice that a few other people in the office were also getting sinus infections and symptoms of "common colds." Why not everyone? I remembered that only 25 percent of people carry the genes I'm cursed with, and only 2 percent of those poor souls trigger the susceptibility.

If you take two hundred random people, fifty of them will carry this genetic haplotype. But just 2 percent of that group of fifty will trigger this extreme genetic response to a mold exposure. This means that only one out of two hundred people will feel like they need to live in a bubble to be healthy.

How many of those genetically-disposed sufferers—one out of every two hundred—are so persistent that they discover the true cause of their illness? It took me two years to find the answer, which no one would believe anyway. I went to dozens of doctors and spent thousands of dollars on pointless medical consultations and tests.

The idea that other people who were suffering from CIRS would never get a diagnosis was outright scary. Most people like me survive—barely—with false notions of what is really going on. Basically, I believe they are suffering from malpractice.

I became energized with my opportunity to help others—not just me anymore—find their truth and hopefully get the treatment they need. There are a lot of people to help.

As of 2019, the US population was 329 million people. If 25 percent of the population has my genetic haplotype, the country has just over 82 million time bombs ticking away until exposed to black mold. The statistics project that 1.6 million people will move into a mold-infested house or work in a toxic environment exposing them to enough black mold to trigger CIRS.

A national epidemic of this scope would certainly force awareness of the health risk. There is a reason the mold-disclosure documents for home purchases went from one paragraph to a seven-page document. There is a reason insurance companies now require a separate rider to cover mold.

But why do doctors remain ignorant of this health risk? Why did the one doctor who discovered CIRS have to battle fraudulent claims and lose his medical license? Why did the judge in my custody case refuse to acknowledge the illness and lower my support obligation?

Whether you choose to believe me or not, mold is a contributor to countless human illnesses. When someone complains of fibromyalgia, it's mold. When someone gets diagnosed with allergies, it's mold. When someone gets bronchitis or pneumonia, it's mold. It's likely that cancer is simply a fungus.

My research turned up a case like mine in which a surgery resident had been triggered by mold in his home. Eventually, he couldn't work around old textbooks or stay in his house. The smallest amount of exposure made recovery more difficult. Ultimately, he started sleeping in a tent in his yard. Although his wife and two small boys questioned his mental health, they stuck by him, and now he's a well-respected surgeon.

I was envious of that surgeon. He had an understanding and supportive family. More importantly, his story gave me the idea of a tent.

When I had Lala for a weekend, she would sleep in my parents' back bedroom and soon be wheezing and gasping for breath. Her symptoms were so bad my mom gave her cough medicine every time she visited. On some weekends, I took Lala to a hotel, but this infuriated Gena and her father because my parents were not there to supervise. She informed the court of every little thing to prove that I was unstable. It seemed like Gena had become an accomplice to her father's plot against me.

One weekend, Lala and I decided to sleep in a tent inspired by the surgeon's story. It should have been considered innocent fun. After all, most kids get to camp out in the backyard. I did when I was growing up.

To Gena and her father, however, that must have been the last straw. Don started impersonating my own father to make false accusations that I was suicidal. He persuaded the FBI to surveil me more intensively, and as additional intimidation, hired private investigators to follow me everywhere. He had photographs taken covertly of innocent activities that could easily be doctored or taken out of context to suggest I was unstable. Two such photographs were of me sleeping on the front porch and sleeping in a tent in my yard. The campout with Lala also provided Don with an opportunity to make another fraudulent 302 call about child endangerment and mental instability.

Again, I found myself going through a psych evaluation, another negative entry on my profile. And again, I was released early. I soon learned that this second evaluation was a clever effort to build a case against me for use at a judicial panel.

During that year, I was charged three times with contempt of court, and each time I had to stand in front of a judge as Gena's lawyer insisted on a jail sentence. Two of the contempt citations were for support payments that were less than required, and the third was for being over the allowed six thousand dollars in arrears. Each time the judge rejected Gena's request for jail time and allowed me to get caught up, which I always found a way to do. I was sure that if I went to jail, I would not come out alive.

You can imagine, I hope, how my anger continued to simmer. My daughter was being raised by the man who was threatening to kill me and destroying the mental health of his own daughter and granddaughter. Lala was being raised by a known criminal who had charges against him for manslaughter, terroristic threats, harassment and theft of property, not to mention twenty-six traffic violations. In addition, he was uncharged but guilty of other offenses that I knew about—insurance fraud, murder and money laundering. This scumbag was not only killing me but also raising my daughter the same screwed-up way he had raised my wife.

I was forced to quit the payroll company because I couldn't make it through the day without becoming violently ill. This work history, in turn, contributed to my profile of mental illness. I filed for unemployment—legitimately, I believed—but my employer fought the claim, knowing that if it were approved, it would boost its annual unemployment rate.

Once again, I had to attend a hearing during which I brought up one salient fact—my employer had alternative locations in which I could have been placed because of my medical condition, but I was not offered any of those.

At last, a judge ruled in my favor, granting me the unemployment benefit. This hard-fought win bought me some time. I now had a modest income for six months to cover my support obligation and fight my way back to health.

Chapter 17

The Kindness of Others

After I separated from Gena, I started, unfortunately, to rely on the kindness of others. This kindness mostly came from women—too many of them were hook-ups who found me attractive or took pity on me, or both. Lord knows I needed to feel some love.

I met Meredith one day while watching the Eagles game at a local bar and restaurant. When I explained my situation to Meredith, she suggested I try sleeping at her place to alleviate my symptoms. I started by sleeping on her couch and repaid her kindness by doing repairs around the house. I hung a ceiling fan, fixed her bathroom vent and made dinner almost every night. After a few weeks, she fell in love with me, but I was in no condition to have a relationship. I was seriously broken. A short time later, I decided to move back to my parents' house because I didn't want to lead her on.

Then I connected with my old high school girlfriend, Jaime, who was pregnant. The father wanted nothing to do with the baby. I felt bad for Jaime and saw her through the delivery of her baby and those first difficult months as a mother. I went to doctor's appointments with her, helped with her other two kids, made dinners and did stuff around the house. In return, she opened her house to me and helped me get a car by putting it in her name.

A few months in, however, the relationship scared the hell out of me. I missed kissing my daughter good night and was afraid my illness would become a burden to Jaime the way it did to everyone else. The closer I grew to Jaime, the more I started to run away. I know that drifting away was cowardly, and I wish I had another chance to behave differently.

One day, while I was driving down to court in B County, a deer jumped in front of the car. I swerved off the road and totaled the Dodge. Jaime's insurance company didn't cover me as a second driver, so it became a financial burden for her. I felt terrible, but I could barely stay out of jail, I had no place to live that didn't make me ill, I had no auto insurance of my own, and I had no way financially to get out of this nightmare.

Gena, on the other hand, was driving a brand-new car. She didn't have to pay for insurance or car payments. She worked while her mom watched Lala. She was receiving my support payment, which added to her own income. And she was becoming more than comfortable over time as I was falling deeper into despair.

I believed that this was Don Darkino's evolving plan, which also included surveillance intimidation by the FBI. I was sure my entire life was being documented. Don even used Lala's health issues while in my custody to claim I was a threat to my daughter. The stress began to break my sanity. I considered just surrendering, but I wasn't entirely sure to whom or what.

Don's criminal interventions with B County Domestic Relations continued to play out. But no matter how many times I was in contempt of court or defending myself against fraudulent accusations, I always found a way through the abuse. Eventually, though, all the fights started by Don began to break my will. I became even angrier and more frustrated, which led to some bad choices of friends.

I liked to play pool, so I joined a pool league in Northampton to escape the pain. Many of the participants were people suffering with addiction. I think I connected with them because I shared with them a similar kind of suffering.

Before long, I tried methamphetamine. I had used Adderall for a while to counteract fatigue, but the effects of altered amphetamine were ten times more potent. Some of the people in my new pool league were hardened addicts, using anything they could get their hands on. I never wanted to go that far, but this altered amphetamine allowed me to experience bursts of my previous, ambitious self. The drug gave an adrenaline rush, which masked my physical and emotional pain.

I started out doing methamphetamine just once a week during pool league but recapturing my previous self while under the influence led me to crave that sensation more often. I couldn't smoke it or snort it because of my nasal and lung issues from mold exposure. But I had become familiar with intravenous injection by observing the heroin addicts in the league.

Obviously, I wasn't thinking clearly at this time, or I would have understood how damning this behavior would look to the FBI or private investigators documenting my "instability." I fell right into Don's surveillance trap.

Since I was collecting unemployment and I had Lala every other weekend, I went fishing with my new buddies for hours, even days. Sometimes I would be awake for three days at a time and then crash for the next two. I was always clean, though, during my weekends with Lala. Sadly, I started to rely on the drug to function. Everything I did, of course, was being documented.

During this period of escape, I was strategically introduced to another woman, a honey trap, which means an irresistible bait. I will define the meaning of a honey trap in due time. Even now, I am not sure if she had any sincere desire to become part of my life. Nevertheless, the day I met Cracie Wrongway was the day my life was no longer my own.

I was playing pool with my new acquaintances at a bar in Northampton when Cracie walked up to the table and implanted herself in my field of view. She boldly said that she wanted to play. Because I was always drawn to take-charge women, I took note. Cracie was flirtatious—surprisingly so since her husband sat at a table across the bar. My moral compass was fading fast, and I spent the night playing pool with her and talking. Before she left, we exchanged phone numbers.

After a bit of suggestive texting, we decided to spend a day together. At that time, I didn't have money and was sleeping in a goddam tent, but I had told my entire story and explained how broken I was in every possible way. If we hung out together, it would have to be in a free place like a park, or we'd have to do something that didn't cost money.

We met at a park, and I learned something astonishing about Cracie—she was married to the sheriff. I should have ditched her right then, but my judgment was likely impaired by my new recreation. I probably would have latched onto anyone who showed an ounce of kindness.

Cracie explained her own situation, claiming she was unhappy in her marriage, and she and the sheriff had agreed to get a divorce. As I explained the trauma of my divorce and my genetic nightmare with mold, she seemed to really care. Even more importantly, she seemed to believe my story! We connected so well it seemed like a miracle had been gifted to me.

We ended up in her parked van, physically expressing our newly acquired bond. Afterward, I candidly poured out my life to her and explained that I was not in any position to be a partner, and I didn't want to lead her on. I certainly couldn't be involved with a woman who was married to someone in law enforcement, especially the sheriff!

I think it was her persistence that wore me down. Or maybe the fact that she didn't seem to care that I was a broken man sleeping in a tent. There was also the possibility that the entire relationship was one big setup.

Cracie would often come over with her computer, we'd watch a movie in the tent, and she would spend the night. I'm sure the neighbors thought I was nuts. She continued to show me great empathy and affection, which I desperately needed. So much so that I overlooked some obvious warning signs.

I ignored the fact that a year earlier, Cracie had undergone surgical fat reduction and now wanted to divorce a good man while still raising three kids. This was a character flaw I would have detected in my right mind.

Cracie was attentive. She went to medical appointments with me, even helped pay for sinus surgery we hoped would make me feel better. At the time, it didn't occur to me that the surgery might have been staged, which would explain why my deviated septum did not get repaired while I was unconscious.

During our first year together, Cracie invited me and Lala to the beach with her three kids. Of course, Gena and her father did everything they could to prevent it. I had to file an emergency contempt order because Gena and her father did not want Lala to vacation with me. Cracie accompanied me to court that day and watched Gena and Don accuse me of being insane and unfit to be with my daughter.

Fortunately, the judge found no grounds for their accusations, and we left for the beach where we all had an amazing time. I was so grateful for Cracie!

In the past, Lala and I loved to jump the waves at the wave pool. She was always fearless. But when we got down to the water at the beach, Lala wouldn't go near the water. Her grandfather had installed his fears in her, the way he had with Gena. He had told her that if she went into the water, the ocean would suck her out. Teaching respect for the ocean is one thing, but I saw how Gena had been destroyed by his fears. I certainly didn't want my daughter suffering from similar phobias.

Cracie and I became best friends. We laughed all the time. I could be myself around her, and I started to have genuine feelings again. I was still doing a drug to counter my fatigue, unfortunately, and using meth was clouding my already diminished moral compass.

I started to feel bad that Cracie was always footing the bill. I tried to dream up free activities, but she often suggested things that would cost money. It was always her decision to go or do something, which I did not recognize as part of a clever scheme to manipulate me.

I started to find shady ways to keep Cracie from spending so much money. I thought I was doing something good for us, not realizing the long-term negative effects. From time to time, I found a clever way for us to sneak into a movie without paying. I created clever schemes to avoid paying for lunch. This was stupid since she had just divorced a cop. Knowing that I was being watched by Don's goons and the FBI, I must have been out of my damn mind to do this stuff.

Cracie came over one day and told me she wanted to take Lala and me to a huge adventure park in Tampa I'll call Happy Place. I complained about the legal difficulties of getting permission for such a trip, but Cracie said she wanted to go regardless. "Don't worry about the money," she said.

I told Gena that I wanted to take Lala to Happy Place. Gena thought it would be better to take Lala to Happy Place together instead of me taking her with a girlfriend. Then she said, "Lala would enjoy being there with her mom and dad more. Gena convinced me not to argue the case, and we agreed that we would take Lala together one day soon. Truthfully, I still loved my wife. If it weren't for her criminal father's vendetta against me, I would probably still be married. But this manipulative conversation really irked me.

I decided not to fight the battle over a vacation with Lala. Without her, Cracie and I decided to drive all the way to Florida so we could see the East Coast on the way. Cracie and I were amazing together as a couple. I had never had a woman who was both my best friend and my lover. I really thought we had something special—until I decided to make the most idiotic decision a person could ever make.

Still trying to find creative ways to contribute financially, I invented a way to get cases of beer and alcohol without paying. Then I found that I could get food and snacks without spending money as well. Cracie seemed impressed and wondered how I was doing it. Unfortunately, she started to get involved. My messed-up mind was convinced I was doing some good.

We finally arrived in Florida and checked in to Happy Place Resort. Mentally, I just broke down with anger at the world and the pain of losing my little girl to my arch enemy. Maybe my conversation with Gena started me thinking about my family being split up. Perhaps it was the sight of all the little girls around me shouting, "Daddy!" It might have been seeing all the fathers hugging and carrying their little girls. Whatever the reason, I acted out in a way to express how I felt about the legal system that had destroyed my life.

The stupidity started when Cracie and I went to the food court for breakfast. I really don't know what I was thinking, but I chose my food items, walked past the cashier and sat down without paying. Cracie eagerly followed my lead. Having been married to a cop for so long, maybe it was exciting for her to "break bad" for once.

We continued doing this for a few other meals, and my stupidity worsened when we began drinking. Perhaps I was under mind control and the entire trip was a big setup, but when I added Captain Morgan to the recipe, I lost my damn mind. I guess I felt like I didn't care anymore, or maybe I was just screaming for attention.

My Captain Morgan-fueled, idiotic behavior went from eating unpaid food in restaurants to straight-up stealing stupid shit off the shelves. And when I mean "stupid shit," I'm talking about a goddam stuffed animal or a cartoon key chain. Cracie and I got way too drunk, and she started to do the same dumb stuff. I seemed to have lost control.

To this day, I still don't know what got over me. Happy Place has more security and surveillance than Area 51. The technology there is nothing less than the latest military-grade stuff. There are hundreds of thousands of cameras with facial recognition and the ability to scan guest's retinas from five hundred yards away. During our three-day visit, we were probably being recorded as if we were in our own movie. So, why didn't security just approach us and ask what the hell we were doing? But no matter how intoxicated and criminal we appeared, no one ever said anything.

When we left Florida to make our way home, I felt a great deal of remorse. I couldn't believe I had acted like such an idiot. I felt like I had been under some kind of spell. I just chalked up my behavior to my current emotional distress and blamed it mostly on Captain Morgan. The remorse and regret put an end to my creative methods of living off the land. I promised myself I would never act so foolishly again.

I convinced myself that Happy Place wasn't concerned with petty shoplifting. Maybe they had adopted a no-approach policy to avoid making a scene. I figured they wouldn't worry about some food or a stuffed animal. If I did something terrible, I would have been questioned or arrested.

Back in Pennsylvania, Cracie and I decided to move into an apartment together, and I managed to get a job selling health insurance. At last, I had a bit of hope.

Once again, though, my "superpower" kicked into action, and I told Cracie something was wrong with the apartment she wanted to rent. She arranged for the landlord to have a mold inspection, which found a large growth of *Aspergillus niger* in the HVAC system. Cracie called me, crying, because we both loved that apartment.

The landlord agreed to hire professional mold remediation. Shortly after that work was done, we moved into our apartment, and I placed air purifiers in every room.

I was thousands of dollars in arrears for support, but with my new employment, I was able to pay enough to stay out of jail. I was still allowed custody of Lala every other weekend, and we made the best out of the little time we had. We'd go hiking to see waterfalls or go swimming or have picnics together.

Since my separation from Gena had left me with terrible credit and no bank account, I was having my paychecks directly deposited into Cracie's bank account. She helped me get a car, which I paid for but was under her name. She was working as a dispatcher for the Pennsylvania State Police, and I had jumped right into my new sales job. For the first time since getting attacked at gunpoint, I thought my life might get back to normal.

Man, I couldn't have been more wrong.

Chapter 18

Profiling and Staging

At the time, I had absolutely no idea. I'm not even sure when Cracie was viciously turned against me, or if she was complicit from the beginning. What I do know is that an elaborate and covert scheme had been orchestrated, and it was disturbingly obvious that our wild performance at Happy Place had not gone unnoticed. From that point on, I was being surveilled and recorded like *The Truman Show*. A clever, covert operation was unfolding for my eventual demise.

I was starting to find some success again. Unfortunately, I didn't sever ties with my fishing buddies or the pool league, but kept my extracurricular activities away from Cracie, not realizing I was being watched and videotaped by nanocams almost everywhere I drove, slept, shopped and worked.

Profiling is the process of documenting every aspect of a person's life, from urination routines to sleeping patterns. An entire activity tree was being created with data about who I spoke with, who I visited, and all my electronic communications, including social media.

When I cut the grass for my parents or had a great time at the park with Lala, these positive activities were ignored. Only negative things, which could easily be manipulated, were compiled. The individuals who I associated with were being investigated and even coerced into "their" Michael Lutterschmidt targeting plan. Everyone in my life was a possible spy. Let's just say I crossed the wrong mouse.

When I left for work, when I arrived home, what time I went to bed, when and what I ate—all this and more was being recorded and logged by government and military personnel. I would learn later that Happy Place and the DOD had a close working relationship.

Like every job I ever had, I had become a sort of hero in the office because of my high sales volume. The company had a near-monopoly in the health insurance marketplace. It made more money, however, from selling ancillary, high-margin products that could be added to insurance coverage.

The company was so focused on these additional products that sales personnel like me would get threatened with termination if we didn't sell enough of them. The sales process was a nightmare. I looked forward to the day when I didn't have to work there anymore.

Then, one day it happened. I noticed some behavioral changes in Cracie. She had been supportive of the air purifiers I needed to avoid sinus infections, but suddenly they became a big irritant for her. She also became careless with money—extravagant, in fact. She bought a boat on credit and maxed out all her credit cards on unnecessary and overpriced trinkets. This wasn't like her.

Even our relationship changed. She stopped being my best friend, which was very unsettling. Cracie became—or maybe always was—a honey trap. I don't know when or why she turned, but she was now complicit in a covert scheme to murder me.

I was still trying to get a divorce, and I had filed bankruptcy to relieve myself from some of the financial pressure. Gena and I still had the house, which had almost killed me. Jonathon Brice, a colleague from work, showed interest in buying the house, and so I disclosed the mold issue, thinking this would discourage him. However, once Jonathan saw the mini-castle I had built, he really wanted to own it.

The bank agreed to sign off on a short sale agreement, which meant the bank would get exactly what it was owed on the mortgage.

Since Gena was on the deed, the short sale would have helped us both avoid a foreclosure—a win all the way around.

The bank signed, and John signed. All that was left was Gena's signature. Shockingly, someone advised Gena *not* to sign the sale agreement, which caused us both to receive a foreclosure placed on our financial records.

At the time, I thought her father had instructed her not to sign because of some ulterior motive. He had shown his willingness to hurt his own children to achieve his own goals. I just couldn't figure out why she would accept a foreclosure, which obviously hurt her credit.

I realized later that our loan was a Fannie Mae mortgage—a federal loan—and when it became delinquent, the loan got sent down to federal authorities for review. This turned out to be just the beginning of the elaborate scheme.

Over the next few weeks, I got a bad sinus infection and started missing work. Cracie mutated overnight from my caring best friend to a cold-hearted monster. Although I had money coming in every month, Cracie started telling me that I was lazy and refused to work. I was seriously ill for a few weeks, but she told her ex-husband sheriff, my wife and my parents that I was just lying around every day.

I explained to her that I was getting paid regardless of my illness, and my share of the bills was covered every month from the residual income that I worked my ass off to achieve, but she never told people about that fact.

Then Cracie cut the electrical cords on every HEPA air filter in the apartment. She started sleeping at her old house with her ex-husband. At about this same time, just about everyone in my life also started acting suspiciously.

One day, Cracie hauled all my belongings into the yard. I had already had a serious sinus infection, so returning to my parents' contaminated house meant I'd be sleeping in the tent again. Since my paycheck had just been deposited into her account, I went upstairs and grabbed her bank card to get some of my money back.

She yelled at me and said I couldn't drive the car anymore, even though I was making the payments every month.

I grabbed the car keys and her debit card, then drove to the bank where I withdrew the maximum amount allowed—$300 out of the $1,900 that had just been deposited. I was cutting my losses at that point.

After I had left the apartment, she called the police and reported that I had stolen her car and her debit card. The photograph of me withdrawing funds at the bank would be used later as proof of my theft from her card. I had paid for that damn car for over a year, but the payments were all made from her account, so there was no evidence that my paycheck supplied the money. The false accusations—and the negative perceptions about me they created—started to pile up. I really didn't have a clue what was happening.

Clearly, Cracie had been advised or manipulated by a powerful force to turn against me. She had become a honey trap, and I had been lured into it by the alluring bait. A woman who seemed too good to be true wasn't true at all. Unfortunately, it took me too long to figure it out.

It's possible that Cracie had been tracked down and brought in for questioning after the Happy Place fiasco. All our charges were under her name, so she would have been easy to find.

Then again, maybe the trip itself was part of a larger conspiracy plot. I found this theory tantalizing because we left for the trip to Florida just ten days after I'd undergone sinus surgery—a procedure that inexplicably failed to repair my deviated septum. I may never know if the whole thing was staged from the beginning.

Cracie started to tell people that I had manipulated her into spending her money. This made me furious because I was the one who often told her to stop spending. I learned it was all part of this elaborate scheme. Cracie racked up tremendous debt, and then apparently was advised to blame me by name for her bankruptcy in federal courts. My profile was growing fat with lies and manipulation.

I was so emotionally destroyed and physically ill that I couldn't get back into work. Twisting the knife roughly, Gena announced to me that she had decided to take Lala to Happy Place in a couple weeks. I didn't realize then, but Gena had been invited to Happy Place so "they" could gain more information about me and coerce greater involvement in the plot. So much for Gena's suggestion of taking our daughter to Happy Place together.

Since Gena had a fear of flying, she and Lala took a train to Florida. When Gena got back from her all-inclusive trip, she eagerly demonstrated her willingness to be more active in the conspiracy.

The why and who of this plot was mysterious, and it took me way too long to discover several likely and possible explanations. I'll save my conclusions for the last chapter.

I really felt legitimate remorse for the way I had behaved at Happy Place, and frankly for that entire year of my life. I decided to write Happy Place a formal apology letter and offer suggestions for how I could pay them back or make up for my stupidity. I probably over-shared my story, trying to explain how and why my behavior had occurred.

I didn't realize, however, how evil the Happy Place empire was. Naïvely, I thought they would grant me a chance to make amends. I could have never in a million years imagine that this evil empire would use every one of the painful details I shared to destroy me. It turns out I had given them a recipe to brew up some sadistic, cruel and unusual punishment.

The response that I received was from a man with the initials LV who stated that I had a "No Trespass" order against me. LV explain that I would need to write to the security team to lift this order.

I included that Happy Place response here to add to the accuracy and accountability of my dying testimony.

Happy Place Guest Services <guest.services@happyplace.
com>

Dear Mike,

Thank you for contacting us regarding the Happy Place
Resort.

The safety and security of our guests is our number one priority. Keeping that in mind, you will need to send a written letter to request that a trespass be lifted to the following address:

Happy Place Resort Dir of HPR Security PO Box 10, ——

Lake Asto Luego, FL 32——

All requests will only be accepted in writing from the person trespassed. The request will be reviewed by HPR Security Leadership, and a written response will be returned via USPS.

Thank you again for your message.

Sincerely, LV

Guest Experience Services Happy Place Resort

For the sake of keeping my story accurate, here are the apology letters that I wrote to Happy Place, desperately trying to make amends.

First attempt, by email.

How do I begin to apologize and try to make things right? A few years ago, I was fortunate enough to visit Happy Place. Unfortunately, it was during a period of my life when I had given up and hit rock bottom. I refuse to use any excuses. Placing blame has only fed an anger issue, and now that I have a sober mind, I am filled with humility and regret. The way I acted during my visit was completely out of line, and I am so ashamed I allowed the issue to alter my character so badly. I would give anything to take it back. I would give anything to make it right. I would scrub the mouse's toilet with my tongue for the rest of time if I had the chance to amend my behavior. Again, I won't make excuses. No matter what the circumstances life brings, I've painfully realized I can't allow anything to change who I am. I just want to stress how sorry I am, and if there is anything—and I mean any way—that I could try to make things right, please let me know. I would work it off or do community work, whatever it would take. I beat myself up more than anyone or anything else, for this is just one of many apology letters. I have overcome a serious anger issue, I have overcome an addiction issue, and I will never allow myself to give up again. It has only hurt me and everyone around me. I wake up each day, and I have been truly trying to make a positive impact and to make the lives of others better. I'm just sorry it took me too long to get myself together. I am utterly sorry.

Mike Lutterschmidt (Lutterschmidt2@gmail.com)
Phone Number: 6109050542

Second attempt by US Post.

LV,

I appreciate your response. As you do any research, I am hoping to provide you with some details and a brief summary of my situation. Again, no excuses, but I want you to have a clear perception.

In 2012, I was on top of the world. I had an amazing career, had a beautiful wife, and was blessed with my daughter, Lala. I had the respect of the entire community and was a model citizen. Shortly after we moved into a new house, my daughter and I began getting ill. After a short period, my symptoms got so severe that I was missing work. Because of my daughter's symptoms as well, I began to get anxiety over finding a reason. After thousands of dollars and many tests, three different labs confirmed a serious mold contamination.

On a random encounter, I was given an Adderall to see if it would help with the extreme fatigue. It worked so well I developed an addiction to it, which also made my symptoms ten times worse. It got to the point that I had to move out of the house, as I could no longer function. This caused great turmoil among my family, as I appeared insane.

As I became not well enough to work as my illness became worse, my father-in-law attacked me at gunpoint and told me he was going to have me killed. Then the flow of PFAs and 302 calls came rolling in. I filed for divorce, trying to save a relationship with my daughter, but not being able to pay support got me into trouble. Despite the numerous doctor's reports I submitted as evidence, I was threatened to be thrown in jail for contempt time after time. Knowing my father-in-law's involvement in a crime family and seeing him get away with destroying my life, I slowly realized my anger was taking root and developing.

Not having a dime to my name, I began to take things that I needed to survive that I just couldn't afford. Things like nose spray and probiotics. I justified it because I needed it to live. My symptoms began to worsen, and I even tried to sleep in a tent for a few months, as any type of water damage in a house would disable me. As you can imagine, this made me look even crazier. I even tried to build a tiny house on wheels to be my clean room, but since I didn't have money to buy materials, I found myself dumpster-diving. Not having a safe place to stay, I started to associate with people that I would have never associated with before. My Adderall use moved to methamphetamine, and I completely lost my mind. My anger and depression smothered my character, and I began to simply give up. I latched onto anyone who would show me love. Because I am genuinely caring and nice, I found myself living at the kindness of others, mostly women. Because of my state of mind, I just couldn't be a partner, and my issues continued to hurt everyone around me. I guess I had a serious mental break.

One woman in my life decided to go to Happy Place and invited me. I jumped on the opportunity to get away and escape from my life. When I was visiting, seeing all the families together and little girls hugging their fathers brought back painful thoughts. I was so depressed and angry with where I was in my life, I allowed myself to do things I am not proud of. I had no money to contribute to the trip, which made my anger even worse.

To help you understand why I am so sorry, I want to point out some of the things I did that I remember. The woman I was with would have never done these things if I wasn't there. So please do not blame her at all.

At the hotel we stayed in, there was a cafeteria. We ate many meals where I walked past the register without paying. I know that in one of the parks, I ate from a buffet without paying as well. One of the days, I had way too much to drink, and I began to take things from stores. I don't remember exactly what merchandise I took or when, but I just know I did some dumb stuff. I just wasn't in my right mind, and looking back now, I am filled with a shame that I can't live with. I need to find ways to make this right. If I had to guess, I probably owe Happy Place two hundred dollars, which I need to find a way to pay back.

Losing all contact with my daughter was my wake-up call. I'm just not that person, and I am so utterly upset with myself I need to try to make amends. I overcame my addiction issue by cutting the losers out of my life. I overcame my anger issue with the help of counseling and religion. I work as much as I possibly can and still have no means of supporting myself. So, I need your help to find a creative way to make things right. The only thing that I can think of is working it off somehow.

Please know that I truly am sorry. Every day I wake up and try to make someone else's life better. I also made a list of all the wrongs that I did, and my goal is to do whatever it takes to right those wrongs. I will not stop until every wrong is crossed off.

Thank you for taking the time to respond to me, and I am simply grateful for any opportunity to make this right.

Mike Lutterschmidt

Chapter 19

One Last Pursuit of Happiness

Out of the clear blue, a woman from junior high messaged me. After the roller-coaster ride with Cracie, it was nice to have a woman show some interest. Mandy was very attractive, and all the boys had a crush on her back in school. Maybe it was because I was so vulnerable, but over a short time, we found a real connection.

The first night we hung out was magical. We went to a carnival and then sat in the park for hours, talking and kissing under the moonlight. I told her all about my nightmare of a life and what had happened to me after getting exposed to mold. Like the last few women in my recent past, she seemed genuinely concerned.

When we got back to her car, a tire was slashed. When I say I was being followed and harassed everywhere, I truly mean 24/7.

"Have no fear, Mold Man is here," I told her, and we laughed together.

I showed her how to change a tire, and what could have been a highly stressful situation became a shared experience.

Unfortunately, I was still doing stupid shit. Now when I mean stupid shit, I just mean trying to cope with the horrifying fatigue syndrome. My life had been destroyed, and the methamphetamine rush helped mask the constant fatigue and sinus congestion that plagued me. No one really knew about my meth usage—except, of course, the military personnel who were placing nanocams everywhere I went to document my life. I suppose I was being too smart for my own good, and this led to easily manipulated awful perceptions.

Mandy's last boyfriend was in jail for heroin, so I was careful not to bring her around my pool league friends. In my mind, I wasn't an addict—I was just trying to counteract the constant physical distress I was getting from my body's reaction to mycotoxins and mold.

Mandy was understanding. As a CNA at a nursing home, she knew how to deal with my symptoms. She would "cup" my back to work out the glue-like phlegm. I was working through my doctor-prescribed treatment plan too, so I was confused about why my symptoms were getting worse instead of better.

Mandy rented a house owned by her mother, an abusive addict and alcoholic who had virtually abandoned her kids. Mandy relied on her wits for food and money while growing up. Her mom would often bring home addict boyfriends and be with a different guy every week.

Mandy married an abusive dirtbag who had fathered her two daughters. This guy not only hit and abused Mandy, but his behavior was also very traumatizing to his own daughters. The asshole never paid a dime in support after they were divorced, even though Mandy desperately needed the money.

I couldn't help comparing the story of this guy to my own. I was being threatened with jail every month for being a few dollars short in my support obligation to a woman who had everything handed to her on a silver platter. But then, Mandy's ex-husband was not being targeted by powerful forces.

I told Mandy all the details of what I was going through, and it made her think about filing her own court order for support against her ex-husband, but she was terrified of his abusive behavior.

You probably already know what happened when I first entered Mandy's home. Yes, my "superpower" kicked in, and I knew there was some serious water damage in it. I couldn't spend much time without getting sick, but Mandy understood.

She had taken out a loan for a blue Chevy pickup truck for her last boyfriend, who was now in jail. The truck was about to be repossessed, so she suggested that I make the payments of two hundred a month in return for having something to drive. I jumped at the chance. This helped us both out.

When Mandy had an outstanding warrant for overdue parking tickets, I paid the three-hundred-dollar fine for her to remove the warrant. We seemed to share a bond and were always there for each other.

Mandy and I sometimes drove up to the mountains to lie in the back of the truck and make love under the stars. I found myself on the brink of falling in love and happier than I'd been in a long time despite the disabling symptoms. But a covert operation against me was well underway and designed to prevent me from having any long-lasting happiness.

Since I couldn't spend too much time inside her house, we spent a lot of time in the bed of the pickup. There seemed to be an unusually high volume of traffic down her road, which was strange because it was a dead end. We figured the house at the end of the block was probably a drug dealer's. Even during the day, when we were on her front porch, we noticed a lot of traffic. Back then, I didn't understand the profiling process used as intimidation just yet.

Before long, my "superpower" identified where the water damage was coming from. Mandy's kitchen drain was pouring out into her basement, which had a separate entrance outside, so she never went down there. Food debris and water was producing a constant supply of water—and, of course, *Stachybotrys*. Her mother refused to get a plumber to fix the problem, so Mandy decided to find another house for us so we could live together. Since I was driving the truck, I had the brilliant idea of getting a camper that I could sleep in to avoid further exposure in the meantime. Step number one in my treatment plan was to flush out more toxins than I was bringing into my body. Finding a mold-free place to live in the Lehigh Valley with an ERMI of 4 or less is nearly impossible.

Unfortunately, every camper in my price range was waterlogged, moldy, and rusted out. I switched my plan, possibly when in a meth haze, and decided to build my own tiny house on wheels. I bought a hitch and a frame, spent countless hours driving around and picking up materials that might be useful— sheet metal, wood, siding, and pretty much anything I saw lying around. It started to take shape and looked like a tiny house. It was too large to keep in my parent's driveway, so my fishing buddy, Trevor, told me I could park it in his backyard. This was not my best decision, bringing that kind of attention to a house where two heroin addicts lived.

Somehow, Don Darkino got wind of my construction project— probably from an innocent comment from Lala, who had seen my progress—and he told the FBI that I was planning to build a meth lab.

Not only did the FBI know I hung out with dealers and partook in their extracurricular activities—but now they thought I was the next Walt from *Breaking Bad*. I could imagine my dossier by now. I had just stolen goods from Happy Place, filed for bankruptcy and my federal loan was under review. I had a seventeen-thousand-dollar compromise with the IRS because of Gena's ill-advised foreclosure on our home, had recently broken up a sheriff's happy home and supposedly driven his wife into bankruptcy. I was driving another vehicle under a different girl's name. And now undercover cops were driving by a known heroin house while I constructed a meth house on wheels. Could I be any more screwed? You can't.

Meanwhile, Mandy found a three-bedroom house with a nice yard and a basement that was in her price range. The problem wasn't just moving there, but that all her possessions from the house were contaminated by mold. For normal people, it would be no big deal, but for me, it was life or death.

Her house had been severely exposed to black mold for years. It wasn't just the microscopic spores that would cause my severe inflammation; it was the millions of mycotoxins that would break apart and be virtually impossible to remove.

I went to see the house with Mandy, and it was amazing. It had a huge yard, a large basement, a garage, and it was in a nice community. Maybe it was desperation for a real house, stupidity or self-delusion, but when I saw the mold-infested beams in the basement, I decided I could just paint over them. When I saw water damage and furry green growth on garage rafters, I convinced myself I could just avoid that area. Mandy seemed so eager to rid herself of her mother's grasp and eager to start a life, maybe I just didn't want to disappoint her.

I told Mandy the house would be fine. I was excited and nervous, to say the least, but I just prayed to God that he would look out for me and make this whole nightmare work itself out.

The day we moved her stuff, we sprayed down and wiped off the furniture. We vacuumed everything. Lala came that weekend, and we had fun in the laundromat washing every piece of clothing.

Finally, I spent our first few nights in the new house. It was nice to sleep in the same bed with Mandy and not have to make a tent on the truck. I prayed that this time the mold would not affect me.

By the third day, however, I couldn't ignore my body screaming at me. My symptoms were the same or worse than in my old marital house. I didn't want to disappoint Mandy, so I tried to counteract my symptoms every way I could.

I also decided to move the tiny house to our driveway so I could sell the damn thing. The wood studs already had issues, and now the police thought it was a meth lab. I wanted it gone.

A few nights later, Mandy woke me up, crying. I was experiencing the kind of exhaustion that would make you fall asleep at the wheel. Mandy told me that her older brother had just committed suicide. I didn't even know how to act.

What made this situation a hundred times worse was that Mandy had already lost a sibling to suicide years ago. Now she was the last child alive from her mother, who was a messed-up woman. Mandy really needed me that night, but I couldn't keep my eyes open no matter how hard I tried. I suggested we get some sleep and deal with it in the morning.

I wish I could go back in time and punch myself in the face. That night shattered whatever magic we had shared. She had to call her best friend, who came and spent the night with her. She should have been able to rely on me, but I couldn't even rely on myself at this point.

Someone knew just when to throw the honey trap back in the mix. Cracie began to infiltrate my life and cause even more problems. I had already figured out that Cracie was the person who'd slashed Mandy's tire that first night. At first, I thought Cracie was just being jealous, but she was the one who broke up with me and threw me out. Suddenly she was calling and texting Mandy. Was this an intentional part of the plan to destroy me?

I didn't know it then, but Cracie was being paid to cause turmoil for Mandy and me. We started seeing her parking up the street, stalking us and randomly driving by the house. She'd text Mandy all kinds of nasty stuff about me, trying to break us up.

One day, Mandy was so angry she called the Pennsylvania State Police, where Cracie worked and told an officer that Cracie Wrongway was stalking her and possibly using police equipment to access private information on Mandy. It turns out Mandy was right—Cracie was fired for unauthorized use of equipment. So, add that to my dossier. I was held responsible for getting a Sheriff's wife fired from State Police, even though I had nothing to do with it at all.

At about this time, my residual income was running out, and I needed money. Pam, an acquaintance of mine who just happened to distribute some things, told me she had been pulled over the day before, and her car was impounded. She was freaking out because she'd left a bundle of cash and a stash of drugs stuffed into the seat. Since she didn't have a valid license or the cash to get her car back, she was worried they'd find her stash and she'd be arrested.

I can't remember where I got the idea, but I proposed that if I went to the lot and retrieved the stash, I could keep the cash. She agreed. I told Mandy all about my plan, and for some reason, she wanted to go with me.

I got the keys from Pam and drove to the lot about one in the morning. We parked a mile down the road and entered the cornfield behind the lot. As soon as I jumped the fence, I'm sure a surveillance camera captured my image. When I opened the door to Pam's car, the damn alarm went off and I panicked. Frantically I searched the seat, finding a black bag but no cash.

I raced back to the fence and leaped into the cornfield where we ran like hell. At our vehicle, I opened the bag and found a bundle of heroin packets, a white rock of meth and a bunch of pills I didn't recognize. The next day, I told Pam the whole story, and she was greatly appreciative. But I had not gotten the money and undoubtedly had been seen breaking into an impound lot and probably driving to a drug dealer's house.

I needed the cash because it was likely I was going to be charged with contempt again for falling short on my support and alimony payments. This was a vicious cycle. How could a normal guy survive this domestic court abuse even without having a devastating illness? Either Pam lied about the money or the impound guys had already found it and padded their own pockets.

After Cracie got fired from the state police department, the texts and other harassment got worse. I lasted a few months in the house with Mandy, but my symptoms became disabling to the point of madness. I found myself frequently sitting outside, and for the first time since my marital home, I noticed someone lingering in the shadows. I even detected the glimmer from a lens and a small green light. When I'd try to investigate, no one was there.

Today, I realize the culprits were well-trained military personnel, so of course, it was covert. At that time, I never could have imagined that I was under surveillance. Why would I be so important?

I was so bored most of the time and spent a lot of time on my phone. I laughed at all the weird scams and games that were going on. "Escorts" on Craigslist advertised for business and solicited credit card numbers. I responded to a few, and when it came time to supply my card number, I responded with a "Not on your life!" message.

Nevertheless, I started playing some of these games. The more games I played, the more game links were sent to my phone. Then I started getting many spam messages and bad websites popping up.

Cracie told Mandy that I was looking for women on Craigslist and had some of my innocent exchanges to illustrate her news. I tried to explain to Mandy, "I just thought it was funny to read what some of these idiots post and advertise." I'm not sure if Mandy believed me—she was very insecure—but it was true.

I started to suspect that some of the posts and games I interacted with might have been created by the FBI to track and flag sex offenders. It turned out that when I responded, "Go screw yourselves," I was really talking to FBI agents overseen by our friendly NSA.

Over time, the relationship between Mandy and I started to fall apart. I was not only sick as hell and couldn't spend much time in the house, but Cracie's slander had destroyed that magic we once shared. The day finally came when Mandy said, "Mike, you're not a bad guy, but—"

I didn't need to hear the rest. I could only be thankful that she had stayed with me for so long and had never betrayed me like so many others.

Chapter 20

Staging for Suicide

It felt like whiplash. Cracie went from being cruel and intentionally evil to showing me love and affection. As soon as Mandy and I broke up, Cracie swooped in. She told me I could park my tiny-house-on-wheels project in her ex-husband's driveway. Why didn't I see this as a setup at that time? Don Darkino had already told authorities I was building a freaking meth lab, and now it was parked at a sheriff's house.

Cracie would invite me over to her husband Clark's house when he wasn't home—likely she was staging entrapment. Naturally, I walked right into a cop's house, where cameras had been set up to record my actions. When I went into the cop's bathroom, I was being recorded. Since no one was home, Cracie told me to go into her daughter's room to find a "movie" for us to watch. Now I understand why—I was being recorded in yet another room.

Cracie asked me to go with her to Sanibel Island in Florida. As before, she said, "Don't worry about the money." She wanted me to get away from the stress, she told me. I had no money, and support was due in a few weeks, so yes, I was under stress and agreed.

The narrative that I was helping create through my recorded actions was that I had left Mandy to go on a vacation with another woman. Cracie was obviously just playing an assigned role in this unfolding drama. But I saw through her kindness and empathy. I just didn't care anymore. I had surrendered.

Unfortunately, I made another monumental mistake. I started to wonder if my illness, or perhaps all the harassment I was enduring, was somehow impairing my judgement. Maybe, I thought, that was the plan!

I needed to pick up my clothes from Mandy's house. I had asked Cracie to wait in the car, but Cracie had been advised differently. Mandy was waiting outside when we pulled up, and instead of remaining in the car, Cracie got out and followed me. I turned and told Cracie to go away. Then, as I turned back, Mandy started hitting me. In fact, she beat the shit out of me.

I was always the guy who didn't retaliate when he got insulted or slapped around by a woman. I was the guy who had done nothing but show love to women. As Mandy swung her arms to slap me, I just stood there and took the shots. I didn't put my arms up, and I didn't say a word.

Cracie stepped between us and tried to hold Mandy back. I put my hands behind my back and took Mandy's wrath. I ended up with a torn shirt and scrapes on my cheek and neck. Cracie had known what was going to happen before it did. I know this because she had called 911 before getting out of the car. Within a few minutes, the police arrived.

At first, I thought Cracie had called 911 to get payback for Mandy getting her fired from her job. I learned that the call was just a small step in an unfolding operation.

Seeing marks of violence on me, the officer insisted on filing a report. Even though I didn't want to press charges, it was out of my hands. From Mandy's perspective, I had charged her with assault, and I later discovered, this was the intended outcome. Now even more enraged, Mandy was more willing to slander me and add even more false information to an already incriminating profile with a claim of domestic terrorism.

In the aftermath, Mandy told authorities that I had stolen from her credit card. The truth is, when we split up, I gave her one thousand dollars to help her out, and I paid off a TV and dehumidifier I had leased. Mandy had given her permission to use her card on the application, which required a credit card. Mandy still had the TV, and I had a receipt proving I had paid for the items, but proof and evidence apparently don't matter if you have no opportunity to present your case.

Then I saw a Facebook post from Mandy's mother that really insulted me. I wish I had not responded to her so angrily on Messenger, which is highly monitored by the very people who were plotting against me. I should have kept quiet, but instead, I angrily wrote that it was her fault two out of her three kids had committed suicide. I was speaking the truth, but that comment was very insensitive. I can imagine how I must have been perceived by other members of her women's rights group. I just wanted Mandy's mother to understand that she should do whatever it took to be there for her last remaining child. But again, my confused actions certainly created false perceptions of me, which could be easily manipulated.

I was learning that otherwise well-intentioned organizations— women's rights groups, neighborhood watch organizations, vigilante police radio clubs, you name it—can be coerced into participating unwittingly in campaigns of harassment and intimidation. The natural passions, commitment, and even hate can be manipulated into hostile actions against an innocent person by false charges and misunderstood behavior.

I'm certain that some, perhaps many, of the "pawns" and perps engaged in gangstalking me are not hired conspirators but passionate members of these groups who have been led to believe that I am evil incarnate—a menace both to society and their particular hot button issue. Couple that with a vigilante mindset, fueled by a belief that law enforcement is not doing enough, and you have legions of people in search of targets for their zealous revenge or nonjudicial punishment.

In Sanibel, I wasn't much fun for Cracie to be around. From posts on my phone, I had just learned that two of my pool league friends—Ed Gunn and Bryan Deisner—had passed away in Rita's house with heroin in their systems. I was sad, but never imagined that their deaths had anything to do with me.

As I was processing the shocking news, Cracie rushed up to me. I can't explain how my intuition works, but I had a feeling that Cracie had been instructed to keep me from learning about the death of my two acquaintances. She wasn't subtle about it. She grabbed the phone from me and threw it into the sea. I just sat there and watched my phone sink into the surf. I didn't care enough anymore to react.

I learned later that there was a clandestine reason why Cracie asked me to go to Sanibel. My two buddies had already died, and Cracie had been instructed to take me away so private investigators could begin coercing fraudulent testimonies about how I had distributed the heroin that killed them. The vacation in Florida was just a cover story for my diversion.

The night after flinging my phone into the deep blue, Cracie flipped out and told me I couldn't stay in our hotel room. She threw a tantrum—"staged" one is a better word—trying to make me so angry I'd publicly do something stupid that would attract the police. Cracie's goal was to cause a domestic dispute, which would have brought the police. Since we were in Florida, home of Happy Place, I can only imagine who was behind Cracie's manipulated behavior.

Fortunately, this time I didn't fall for the trap. Even though I knew something weird was going on, I still had no knowledge about the elaborate conspiracy that was in play.

When I didn't react to Cracie's violent outburst as expected, Cracie eventually calmed down. The next day, while sitting in the passenger seat as we drove to a Florida campsite, I started weeping like a child. I was thinking about my daughter and how I missed her. Instead of showing sympathy, Cracie laughed cynically, mocking me.

She started texting someone as she drove, probably asking her handlers what she should do next. I grabbed her phone and threw it out the window, returning the favor of throwing my phone into the ocean. We were passing a rest stop, so she pulled in and said she was going to call the police and claim that I'd hit her.

At that point, I knew I needed to get the hell away from this woman for good.

Cracie walked into the rest stop, and I got one bag of clothes out of the trunk and started walking. I didn't know where I was or how I was going to get back home. I had a hundred and sixty bucks in my wallet and was frankly amazed that the fear and uncertainty didn't drop me to my knees right there on the side of the road.

I just started walking along a busy highway when Cracie drove onto the shoulder beside me.

"Just get in," she said. "At least help me look for my phone."

Without looking at her, I said, "I don't know you. I don't want to know you, so leave me alone."

"Come on," she insisted.

I continued to walk, looking straight ahead. She raced off, and I felt a strange uneasiness come over me. I had no idea where I was going—kind of like the past few years of my life.

About a mile down the highway, I passed over a large bridge with vehicles flying by at over eighty miles an hour three feet away. On the other side, a guy in a truck pulled over and offered me a lift. When he asked where I was going, I looked down at the floor and tried to formulate my words.

"I need to get back to Pennsylvania somehow," I answered.

Fortunately, there was an airport a few miles away, and he dropped me off there. I put twenty dollars of my cash in a pocket for an emergency reserve but couldn't find a flight cheaper than one hundred eighty bucks, and that was just to Philadelphia.

I paced up and down the airport checking each airline for a flight back to PA. I was getting a surge of anxiety because I couldn't find a flight cheap enough. At the last counter, I approached the agent with genuine tears in my eyes. The woman seemed genuinely concerned. I was going to ask her about buses, which might be cheaper, but before I spoke, the woman asked me, "Where do you need to get to?"

"I need to get back home to Allentown, Pennsylvania," I said, "but I only have a hundred forty bucks."

This wonderful woman went into her purse and pulled out a credit card. "It's okay," she said, "I'll pay the difference so you can at least make it to Philadelphia."

Her kind nature triggered something inside me and made me want to call Don Darkino and resolve things somehow for my daughter's sake.

The entire flight, I thought about calling the Darkinos. If they truly understood or knew why I had to leave that house and take the time to consider the blood work I never was able to show them, maybe things could be civil again.

From an airport phone, I dialed Don's home number, and he picked up, recognizing my voice immediately. "Where are you?" he demanded.

Why would Don ask where I was unless he was looking for me? I wondered. His henchmen followed me everywhere I went. In fact, Cracie had told me her ex-husband, the sheriff, had reported that private investigators had come to his house looking for me. Maybe Don was responsible for the deaths of Ed Gunn and Bryan Deisner, possibly to frame me for drug dealing.

I just told Don that I was out of town, but I was calling to tell him I'd always considered him to be like a father to me. I just wanted to try to explain what I was dealing with medically every day.

He said I needed help and hung up, so I immediately called again. I wanted to ask him if we could talk man-to-man since I was in Philly, so could he just give me a minute.

This time, Jane answered and said, "If you call again, we'll call the police." I felt kicked in the gut. I'd had serious panic attacks before, but this one really shook my soul.

Everything in the airport was blurry, and the sounds echoed. The fluorescent lights were blindingly distorted, causing the mirage of a white tunnel. My heart was pounding. I noticed a cop standing by the sliding door. As I approached, I dropped like a sack of potatoes.

The officer came running over and then called in the first responders, who arrived within minutes in an ambulance. On the ride to the hospital, the paramedics calmed my breathing and slowed my heart rate. I arrived at the ER, and my vitals came back clear. I was obviously an emotional wreck.

The ER doctor asked if I felt like hurting myself or others, and I just broke down in tears, saying with complete honesty, "I don't know what to do anymore."

I was sent for yet another psych evaluation. Sitting in the waiting area of the psych unit, I was able to compose myself enough to begin speaking rationally. I peed in a cup and had a completely clean drug screen. Eventually, I walked out of the University of Pennsylvania Hospital in downtown Philadelphia. I had tried so hard to regain some normalcy in my life, but I was utterly lost.

Meanwhile, Cracie wasn't letting up. She called Gena and told her I was a heroin addict, and Lala was in danger.

I had just enough money for a bus ticket to Allentown. My cell phone was in Davy Jones's locker, so I couldn't call my parents to say I was coming home. As I walked up their driveway, I noticed my brother's truck on the street but didn't think anything of it.

I silently walked in the back door unnoticed as he was telling my parents, "You need to leave now. Get on the plane and go." He certainly didn't mean for me to hear that.

When my brother noticed me in the doorway, he looked like a deer in headlights. I asked them what was going on.

"Nothing. What's up?" he said.

I didn't buy that, so I asked again, "Really, what's going on?"

My brother made a lame excuse for why he needed to leave right away and how he'd be in touch soon. After he left, it took about an hour of intense interrogation to learn that my siblings had bought plane tickets for mom and dad to go see my brother in Texas and then fly to Oregon to see my sister.

"That's awesome!" I said, then asked when they'd be back.

They didn't know because they had one-way tickets.

That hurt.

A few days later, my parents left for Texas, locked the door behind them, and left me homeless without a resource to my name.

They even locked their damn car door, which was parked in the driveway. I felt abandoned and betrayed by everyone, even my family.

The handlers who were controlling the conspiracy to make me suffer had persuaded Cracie to turn against me and had done the same thing with my younger brother and his wife. They had convinced him that I was a heroin addict, and my parents were enabling me. Complete bullshit, by the way, since I never touched heroin.

Even though my family had taken me to the brink of suicide, in my heart, I believe my siblings had been manipulated into thinking their actions would help me in the long run.

That night, I slept on the back porch alone, cold and hungry. I had no phone, no money and no one to turn to for help.

The next day, out of the blue, Rita drove by the house. Now, Rita was a woman I met playing pool. I was often at her house, and it was at her house that my two buddies had died with heroin in their system. I jumped at the opportunity to sit in her warm car and have some food at her place. When she kept helping me out and giving me free stuff, I fell right into another honey trap.

I thought it was very odd when she insisted on going to a strip club with a friend of hers. That wasn't my scene—I'd never paid to see naked women. Shortly after we arrived, I saw two well-dressed women sitting at a table and a stubby man standing in the back. Their furtive glances tipped me off that they were stalking me. Rita's friend boldly approached the guy, who was openly recording us on his cell phone, and told him to leave us alone—but it was already too late. One picture of me in that club would add another seamy detail to the fraudulent Lutterschmidt profile.

At this point, the covert plan started to become overt. Vehicular stalking kicked into action. One day, as Rita and I were in the car, I started pointing out the stalkers to her amazement. We drove to the mountains, the woods and all over the Lehigh Valley, and I kept identifying the people and the cars who were around to intimidate me.

At a ski lodge, I confronted a woman stalker and angrily asked, "What are you doing?"

Refusing to make eye contact, she quietly said she was just going skiing. Amazing, I thought, since the slopes were closed, and she was wearing jeans and heals.

I called the police at a store parking lot in Northampton and complained that two trucks were following me. The cop questioned the two men in the truck, but they said they were just getting dog food. Amazing, I thought, since the car had a Maryland license plate, the driver carried a Maryland driver's license, and they followed me all the way from Allentown. From Allentown to Northampton, they had twenty-seven different stores at which they could have bought dog food at.

Once again, though, I was not only being stalked, but being played for a fool. While Rita was witnessing the cruel madness unfolding around me, she was a well-coached pawn in this evil conspiracy. Since I had no cell phone, Rita did give me an old one to use. I'm sure now that it was wired up to electronic surveillance.

When I wasn't staying at Rita's, I was sleeping in a tent on the back porch. I made a few outreach calls, and one of my superiors from the insurance company ordered me a pizza one night because I told him I was homeless. His kindness would continue.

A few days after my parents had left, a woman came up to the porch where I was sitting and handed me a certified letter containing another PFA, this one claiming that I was a heroin addict and suicidal. If left to stand, this would remove my daughter from my life for three years, and I'd be denied any contact with Gena or her parents.

I was devastated. As I read through the PFA, dumbfounded by the cruel lies, I heard applause. The timing could not have been coincidental. On a porch two houses away, a handful of women watching me had started loudly clapping and laughing. The delivery of the PFA clearly had been staged like a scene in a movie.

As I continued to sit on my parents' porch, the flow of traffic down the quiet street was much greater than normal. I even saw drones fly overhead, which was particularly disturbing. Who the hell was I to attract this kind of expensive attention? As I ducked behind the brick wall of the porch, I witnessed a car stop on the street and heard someone ask, "Where is he?"

At that point, I knew I was screwed.

I walked to the local bowling lanes to get away. Halfway there, a cop pulled up, lights flashing. He asked if I was all right and if I had ID.

"What did I do?" I asked.

The cop said the department had received a call that a guy was lying on the ground unconscious. What the hell? I gave him my ID and he let me go. As he drove away, numerous cars and trucks passed as if watching my every move. Where had they come from?

At the bowling alley, the shit didn't stop. People entering made it obvious they were looking for me. I got so nervous I went into the kitchen, out the back door and down a fire escape into the parking lot of an adjacent Home Depot.

In the parking lot, cars literally raced up to me as if chasing, so I hid behind a dumpster. I started trying to reach people I knew on Messenger. The first person who responded was Tracey, an old high school friend I hadn't talked to in ten years. I told her I needed help and asked if she could pick me up in the Home Depot lot. She must have thought I was nuts—I even thought I might be—and wondered if she would really come to get me.

She did. I jumped in her back seat and asked if we could please go to her house, and then I'd explain everything—which I did. *If I were her*, I thought, *would I even let this guy with such a wild, paranoid story into my house?*

Exhausted, I fell asleep on her couch. When I woke up, we had breakfast, and then I did the only thing I could think of doing at that time. I called crisis intervention and told them I needed help. Then I walked to the park to take attention away from my friend's house. An ambulance met me there. So back to the loony bin for me.

Since I had admitted myself, I had the luxury of signing myself out as well. After two days, I did just that so I could try to figure out what was going on. I also needed to find a job and a place to live.

I left the hospital with a list of nearby shelters and recovery houses. It was nearly seven o'clock in the evening when I stepped outside and my phone was dead. The hospital was at least ten miles from my parents' back porch, where all I had was a leaky tent and a phone charger.

I walked up to Schoenersville Road and reviewed the bus schedule. I didn't have a nickel, and the bus wasn't running at that time of night anyway, so I just kept on walking.

When it became totally dark, they almost had pushed me to the limit. In the middle of a huge, empty parking lot surrounded by massive, dark buildings that were obviously closed, I dropped to my knees in despair.

In the distance, cars slowly drove by with a creepy intent. They turned their headlights on and off, as if telling me they knew where I was and would never leave me alone, and then drove on.

I laid down, looked up at the stars, and as I started crying, a feeling came over me that I never felt before—and never wish to feel again. I didn't want to live anymore—I just wanted the pain to stop. I felt so alone and abandoned I couldn't even move.

I've mentioned a few times that angels had appeared to help me at times when I needed them the most. The truck driver in Florida who pulled over and gave me a lift at a very desperate time was an angel. The woman at the airport who paid exactly what I needed to make it back to Pennsylvania was an angel. With those memories stirring in my mind, something moved me to never give up. I was hoping that another angel might find me.

I stood up, surrounded by darkness and sinister headlights eerily circling around me. I took a deep breath and started walking. At one of the buildings, a light was on, and a guy was sitting in a parked car eating a sandwich. I asked if I could use his phone, but I didn't know anyone's number—which I'm sure sounded stupid. I really didn't know whom to call, anyway.

The man noticed that I had a hospital bracelet on my wrist and asked if I was all right. I explained that I needed to get back to my parents' house but was completely stuck. He said he'd take me home, but his work shift was about to start in a few minutes.

I had found my angel that night. The man suddenly put down his sandwich and told me to wait a minute. He walked into the building, and within five minutes returned. His boss had let him clock in so "I can take you home right now," he told me. Not only was he being kind, but so was his boss, who had never even met me.

That evening, I believed that I had seen the ground floor of hell rapidly approaching before an angel rescued me. But believe it or not, I still had a way to go before I bottomed out.

Chapter 21

The Will to Survive

I grew up going to Mass every Sunday, but over the years, my time in church became limited to holidays and special occasions. I lost my spirituality. That morning was the first time in many years that I sincerely prayed to God. This time I asked for just one thing, "Please give me the strength to fight through this evil so I may once again rise to the person you created."

God doesn't give anyone courage—he provides opportunities to be courageous. God doesn't just give someone success—he provides the opportunity to become successful. He doesn't step in to save anyone, but he provides us with what we need to save ourselves. Although I was beaten down and near suicide, giving up was not in my nature.

I took the phone off the charger and started to look for jobs. I didn't have a car, had no money and was faced with another do-or-die situation. Maybe the handlers thought that if I didn't allow pain to push me into suicide, I'd be forced to steal food or money. They were waiting for me to slip up.

I responded to a few posts on Craigslist for general labor jobs and got an offer with a small landscaping business. The owner had a dump truck getting repaired down the street from my parents' house and asked if I had a Class-C license and knew how to drive a stick shift so I could deliver it to him. I didn't have the license but fortunately knew how to drive a stick. Unfortunately, I had no idea how to drive a dump truck, but I always believed I could do anything.

I ignored the question of why a stranger with a business to lose took the chance of me picking up and driving a hundred-thousand-dollar truck without the proper license or experience. Maybe he was another angel. He told me to bring the truck to his house in the morning, and we would go to the job site together.

My next task was finding shelter within walking distance of my new employer since I had no transportation. I found a halfway house in Quakertown and convinced the woman who ran it to give me the last bed in her house, which was shared by seven recovering addicts. The rent was a hundred dollars per week, and I quickly did the math. Eight guys paying that amount came to $3,200 per month—not bad for the woman, even if she had a mortgage.

My first day at work seemed to be all set up, and I was feeling hopeful. But the phone Rita had given me was recording all my calls and conversations, though I didn't know it at the time. Everywhere I went, that little device was doing its duty.

I started thinking about how to get some food. As I plugged the phone into the charger, I heard a car pull up. I saw Rita sitting in the driver's seat talking on her phone, but as I walked over to see her, she quickly hung up—nothing suspicious at that time, but now I'm sure she was getting instructions from her handler.

She offered to buy me a meal. What was I supposed to do, go the whole day without eating and then start a labor-intensive job the next morning? It seemed like Rita was being a true friend.

We went to McDonald's and then back to her house to hang out—and I was lured into another trap. Rita influenced me with free "party favors." I was already a broken mess and adequately influenced psychologically, to give in. I figured it would help me get through the day. I ended up wide awake all night.

The next morning, I went to pick up the truck. I had driven a five-speed stick on my Mazda Miata, but this baby had a ten-speed transmission with reverse in an unfamiliar position. I managed to work my way through it after a few nerve-wracking trial runs around the block. At last, I headed for the highway to Quakertown. The only issue I had was when I drove down a smaller road and didn't realize how far out the passenger-side mirror extended from the truck. I managed to take out a few limbs off some trees.

When I pulled up to the business owner's house, he was waiting for me outside. He looked around the truck to make sure it was all right and laughed when he pulled small branches off the mirror. I spent the day pouring stone and using a tamping machine to level out the ground for the patio. I built a form and poured concrete for the steps. His confidence in me felt good.

I still have no idea how I was attacked. I didn't understand the technology that was used. But on the job, I became severely congested with chest pains. *Just the usual symptoms*, I thought. I managed to work through the nine-hour day, but I felt awful and was having severe chest pain.

Nevertheless, I had to meet the woman who ran the halfway house. Two guys were sitting on the front step as I walked up, so I introduced myself, and they asked me if I was the new guy. I smiled and said, "I hope so."

I met the woman, and she was very kind and sincere. She asked me for my boss's telephone number to make sure that I was working, informed me about the rules and then showed me to my room. I ate dinner with the guys, who were of different ages. Everyone had a story.

I did the dishes, and then I took a much-needed shower. As I scrubbed the dirt off my body from the good day of work, I couldn't help but notice the mold growing around the calking on the tub. I looked up at the ceiling vent, and it had accumulated a thick coating of dust, and my brain started to analyze all the issues. I just kept telling myself, "It is a place to sleep, eat, and get back on my feet." I came down from my shower, and the eight of us held a meeting and read from the Alcoholics Anonymous book.

After the meeting, the pain in my chest became unbearable. I laid down on the couch and tried to snort the thick, glue-like mucus out of my chest, desperately trying to get relief. Imagine trying to keep this sound down in a crowded house. My chest felt like concrete had been poured into my lungs. The feeling was like the extreme congestion I used to get while in the mold-contaminated house, but the cement-filled-lungs symptom was extremely painful and suffocating. The pain became so bad one of the older guys insisted I go to the ER.

I was dropped off at Pukes Hospital in Quakertown, which was a prevalent priming and stalking hub, by one of the guys. As soon as I checked in, I landed on the ground floor of hell. Satan himself was waiting for me to arrive. I explained the chest pain, and the ER staff took blood, vitals and a few x-rays.

Two hours later, a doctor entered the room and explained the results. I was diagnosed with pneumonia, a broken rib on the left side—and, of course, methamphetamine was found in my system. I was hooked up to multiple intravenous fluids and told they were antibiotics.

I didn't wake up until four days later. The doctors or nurses would not disclose to me why they medically induced a four-day coma. And how did I ever get the fractured rib they had found? Nothing made sense. When I woke up, I was alarmed at how callous and rude the doctor and nurses were to me. They treated me like I was a convicted felon. I figured their cold manner was prompted by their belief that I had drugs in my system, which meant I was an addict.

I had no idea that the Department of Defense had just spent the last three days surgically implanting body area networking throughout my body for human experimentation purposes. With these devices implanted, the handlers could now use remote neural monitoring to document my heart rate, blood pressure and changes in metabolism. More disturbingly, the cochlear and retinal implants they gave me allowed them to hear through my ears and see through my eyes.

Welcome to my hell.

After I woke up, I started to check the messages on my phone. Since I had just slept through the last four days, I had missed calls from my boss wondering what the hell had happened to me. I also had a message from the halfway house lady who informed me that I was no longer welcome there because I had amphetamine in my system.

I wonder who called her with that news?

My overwhelming feeling of abandonment fueled resentment to everyone in my life. I started to send emails to B County Courthouse, Gena's attorney, and "Honey Trap" Cracie Wrongway. I don't even remember what I wrote. I just remember the feelings I was trying to express. My ramblings, of course, labeled me as more of a threat to myself and others.

I also started to post on social media, exposing my current situation. I took pictures of the three intravenous tubes, which made it look like I was wired up for a science fiction movie.

My cry for attention on social media brought me three visitors. First was a girl I hired back when I was with the insurance company. She woke me up with flowers and a card and said she wanted to show her support. I had been an amazing manager, she told me. Her kindness helped elevate my emotional state.

Jonathan Brice also came to see me. To this day, I'm not sure how or why he was involved in my targeting. I don't think he knew either. We had become close friends while selling health insurance. I still don't understand why he moved into my house without permission. My last visitor was Jaime, my high school sweetheart. She saw my posts and was genuinely concerned for my well-being. Why I didn't marry this girl astonishes me.

I was discharged from the hospital the day after being released from the coma, and strangely the doctor told me I still had pneumonia. In other words, I was still suffering from the same illness that I went into the hospital for. Clearly, the morphine drip they had me on was intended to covertly hide pain from the invasive surgery to install all kinds of technology into me without my permission or knowledge.

Jaime picked me up and took me to her sister's house for convalescence. Her sister was very nice and had three kids and an ex-husband. I helped around the house and tried not to be in the way.

Over the next couple of weeks, Jackie and I became close friends. One night, Jaime took me back to her house, and I made dinner for her and the kids. That evening, I fell asleep at Jaime's house and never went back to Jackie's again.

I was a mess the first time Jaime opened up her life to me. This time, I had been completely and utterly destroyed by a covert program that was orchestrating my execution. I had descended so close to hell I had convinced myself there was no way of climbing back out.

Chapter 22

Stairway to Neverland

I truly did not handle my emotional trauma well and started spending more time with the wrong crowd, all of which was staged and recorded, though I didn't know that at the time.

My circle of friends expanded to include my friends' associates as well. I hung out for a while with a woman in Bethlehem, who was a known distributor of everything bad, and I spent a night in Northampton with a different female dealer. I was a mess and helping them to create a toxic dossier. It wasn't too long before authorities discovered my social networking activity, which made me appear, I'm sure, like the kingpin of some large drug operation.

Before long, I met a guy named Jared, a gay fellow who was the son of a big dealer in Bethlehem. He was abusing more than I was. I never wanted to use heroin. I just wanted to feel glimpses of my old productive self, and amphetamines really helped.

Jarred found creative ways to fund his habit. I would come over to his mom's house, and I would watch him open credit cards under various names and write bad checks. It was stupid, I know, but I let him use my computer a few times. Everything, of course, was set up like *The Truman Show*.

One day I noticed that my computer had been stolen from my parents' back porch. I think Jared took it, and I have no idea what he did with all the passwords that were saved in my browser. Perhaps that's why my old email account is still under federal investigation.

I was convinced that I had no hope and that my life was over, which made me reckless. Nothing seemed to matter anymore. A bunch of us would spend our nights dumpster-diving. When Best Buy threw away their floor-model TVs with cut electrical cords, we grabbed them, and I did the repairs. We figured out when Bed, Bath & Beyond would discard expired products. We haunted Craigslist and picked up crazy stuff people would throw away. We'd sell this crap and then repeat the pattern. I was a long way from managing an upscale bar and restaurant in Manhattan or being a nationally known well-respected manager of an insurance company.

Cracie was still being used as a honey trap. She'd coerce me to stay with her in hotel rooms. She would strategically leave out bottles of alcohol so cameras could capture the incriminating pictures. Most of my recollection and intuition didn't come until it was already too late. In a hotel room one night, Cracie must have slipped me some type of truth serum. I poured out all the events of my life, sobbing like a schoolgirl. Looking back on that event, I can remember talking out loud, but I didn't feel like I was talking to Cracie, but rather to an audience who was listening to my speech. My intuition told me those sound bites were edited to manipulate perceptions even more.

I was back and forth from being at Jaime's house or idiotically falling for Cracie's honey-trap nonsense. My parents eventually returned home, so I acquired a third option. The goal was for me to either be dead or locked up by the time they returned; however, angels were still on my shoulder.

There were some sections of Craigslist that I found downright humorous. So I'd reply and mess around with these clowns. I was getting ads from porn sites, and I tried to mess with them as well. I'm sure the FBI didn't find my behavior as amusing as I did. Julian Assange exposed many of the FBI's entrapment secrets, such as using sex sites to catch sex offenders. I was just having fun, but perceptions are hard to change once the foundation is laid.

Then a major disaster struck. Gena and the B County Domestic Relations, prompted by Happy Place or DOD—maybe both—began a process to incarcerate me. An extradition process was already in place to send me to Florida for a trial.

This was about the time I became truly aware that I was the victim of organized stalking. It had finally become obvious I was being followed and harassed and anywhere—I mean, *everywhere*—I went. Every time I went into the bathroom, even at a friend's home, nanocams were recording my extracurricular activities. The body area networking implanted in me during my hospital stay for pneumonia was providing data to my handlers. They knew everything about me.

It suddenly occurred to me that I was also being slowly poisoned, and amphetamines had become a cover for the poison. Cameras and mics had been installed throughout my parents' house. My entire profile had been shared without my knowledge to domestic relations, and the image of me portrayed in it turned my ex-wife against me.

It's true that methamphetamine use can interfere with your moral compass and make you desire intimacy. I had way too many intimate partners. I can only imagine how my *Truman Show* tapes played to my unseen audience. Because I had several partners doesn't mean I deserved to be executed. I was a faithful partner to Gena for our entire marriage.

I never imagined the dating and sex sites I played on were run by the FBI. I'd spend hours playing games on them, not knowing the NSA was looking over my shoulder and didn't understand I was just goofing around. Combined with the other false but incriminating information in my profile, I had apparently become a domestic threat.

The truth is, during much of that time, I was out of my damn mind. One of those innocent dating sites required a photo. I don't know what I was thinking, but I uploaded a picture of Lala and me— probably because I wanted people to know I was a single, proud dad. But clearly, I was looking for love in all the wrong places. Many of the innocent dating sites sell personal data to other bad sites, and I am left only to imagine how these criminals manipulated those events.

At my parents' house, a lot of mail accumulated. Desperately looking for help in order to survive, I had filed for SSDI based on

Dr. Bonlie's written diagnosis. I got a letter from the SSDI attorney stating the firm could no longer represent me for my disability claim and refused to give me any further information as to why. This made me think more deeply into the whole mycotoxin conspiracy. Maybe filing for government assistance based on a government secret about the military using mold and mycotoxins as biological weapons might not have been the best decision. *Oops*.

I also got a notice from the court ordering me to attend a contempt hearing in ten days for falling short on my support payment. Previously, the court had told me I wouldn't have to make payments because of my pending application for SSDI. Now I understood that this statement was a clever deception to get me incarcerated.

I decided to lie low for a few days to calm down. The following week, I went to court and was immediately held in contempt by the judge. He did, however, give me thirty days to come up with the eighteen hundred dollars I needed to stay out of jail. But by that deadline, I would also have to show proof of employment or I would be incarcerated for six months. Deep down, I knew if I went to jail, I would not come out alive.

Technically, I still had my contract to sell health insurance, which was proof of employment, so I just needed to find the money. Even if I sold some policies, I wouldn't see any of those commissions for at least two months. I needed another angel, and my mind flashed on a candidate—Pete, a superior of mine at the insurance company, who had always been a friend. Pete gave me six hundred dollars in cash to help save me—a gift, not a loan.

I sold some tools and other crap at a thrift shop, which meant I was still eight hundred dollars short. For the next two weeks, I went on Craigslist and picked up any job I could. I got forty bucks to remove a cast-iron stove and ten bucks for taking three hundred pounds of junk to the scrapyard. I was nickel and diming but making up some ground.

Finally, a guy from Easton contacted me about the trailer I had built the defunct tiny home on. He offered six hundred dollars but had a busy work schedule and couldn't meet for a few weeks.

I cut off the house part from the trailer and donated the shed-like construction to a rod and gun club, where they used it for a chicken coop. I still laugh at the irony of it all because I was building it to have a clean room to sleep in, and now it will be filled with chicken shit.

I was running out of time, so I told him I'd meet him after he got off work in downtown Easton at two-thirty the next morning. This was the night before the hearing. If I didn't get the cash from this transaction, I'd be in jail the next day.

Mandy loaned me her truck. I drove this goddam trailer to Easton, arriving just past two o'clock in the morning. All the cops were out looking for drunk drivers. I drove to his work parking lot but couldn't find the address the buyer had given me. I repeatedly called him, but he didn't answer. A panic attack was building. When two-thirty passed, I considered just running away—maybe to Bolivia, like Butch Cassidy and the Sundance Kid.

Two cop cars pulled into the lot and parked right behind me. I was sure they were preparing to question me, but the cops never got out of their squads. At 2:50 a.m., I decided to make one more call before I accepted my fate. The guy picked up on the second ring and told me he was on his way. He directed me to a small garage around the block.

With the six hundred from the trailer, I was still short eighty bucks. Fortunately, the Bank of Mom came through. In court the next day, the first thing I did was make the payment. When my case was called, Gena's attorney told the court I was a drug addict and spent about ten minutes performing a character assassination. When my opportunity to speak came, I gave the judge a receipt payment of my entire obligation and handed him a letter from my employer stating I was still contracted to sell health insurance—proof of employment.

Gena's attorney presented six different arguments for why I should be put in jail for this petty offense. While she outlined her reasoning, I watched an officer put on gloves and take his cuffs off his belt, as if my fate had already been decided. Even in court, everything appeared to be staged.

Based on the attorney's statements about me, the judge ordered me to waive my HIPAA rights, which guaranteed the privacy of my health information, and sign over my medical records to Gena's attorney. Outrageous as this demand was, I nevertheless complied so I wouldn't be held in contempt again.

Then the court reporter announced that there had been a calculation error. I was still short on my obligation, she said. What the hell was going on? And why was everyone against me?

It turns out the calculation was correct, and the judge condescendingly told me I was free to go. I felt a disturbing tension in the courtroom when I walked out. I suspected that Happy Place or some other conspirators had plans for me to get incarcerated so I could be extradited to Florida, but I had frustrated their attempts.

When I stepped out of the courthouse, I noticed a strange mass of familiar vehicles passing by. I was vaguely familiar with the concept and rules of gangstalking, which had nearly driven me to suicide once before, but still had no idea what it was all about.

During the drive home, I had no idea why there were so many shiny, black pickup trucks everywhere I looked. One was always behind me, in front of me, passing me, and pulling up next to me. The feeling I got seeing these trucks lurking around was eerie and unsettling. Finally, I pulled into a shopping center to see if they'd follow me into the parking lot. Sure enough, trucks and vans followed me in and parked, the drivers simply sitting in their vehicles and staring at me.

As I resumed my trip, the stalking just didn't stop. About two miles from home, I noticed a police car parked on the side of the road. I pulled off and approached him as he was standing next to his squad. I started to explain that I was being followed, but he interrupted me by listening to a message in his earpiece and then jumping in his car and speeding off. Maybe he had he been called to a crime in progress? My intuition, however, tells me that someone called into his headset and told him to leave me there without help while getting psychological warfare from the parade of cars following me.

My parents contacted the B County Public Assistance Office to request an attorney to help me. I needed to lower my support obligation to avoid future efforts to throw me in jail. Also, I needed to get divorced, regain visitation rights with Lala and prevent all the fraudulent PFAs I'd been getting. I was assigned a lawyer named Steve Moore.

I gave Moore evidence proving that every PFA I had received was fraudulent. I gave him medical documentation showing support should be lowered, and the six thousand dollars in arrears should be adjusted.

My first order of business was to restore my right to speak to Lala. After speaking with Gena's attorney, Moore advised me that Gena and her father demanded I attend rehab before they would consider communication with my daughter. I was pissed off, to say the least. I cannot begin to describe the overwhelming exhaustion I get from the constant bacterial and fungal infections. Using amphetamines were necessary to keep me alive and upright.

Swallowing hard, though, I agreed to enter rehab to give myself a shot at having a relationship with my daughter. The rehab facility was a dirty old building in Reading. Can you guess what happened? My superpower kicked into high gear, which meant the building had water damage. After just two nights, I got another agonizing sinus infection.

I spoke to the rehab nurse, and she confirmed that I had a bacterial infection. I was practically immune to antibiotics at this point, so the version she gave me did no good at all. But the staff was helpful, arranging a transfer to a renovated facility in the mountains.

The next day, I was transported to the White Bear rehab facility on top of Blue Mountain, which looked like a ski lodge. Fourteen of us were housed there for group therapy, both men and women. I was the only one there voluntarily. Everyone had an interesting story about how they had landed at White Bear.

I could tell that when they had renovated the facility, they hadn't remediated for mold. The building was located on the side of a mountain, which meant all the runoff water was collecting against the foundation. I had trouble sleeping and would wake up with terrible headaches and chest pain. I had learned that complaining about my rare disorder only made matters worse, so I fought through my symptoms.

During a group meeting on the fourth day, the head counselor really pissed me off. We were going around the room and telling our stories. My turn came, but when I started to describe how Don had pulled a gun on me and threatened my life, the counselor interrupted and told the group that I had an ego problem.

Looking back, I know he was trying to help me, but I got very frustrated. Here I was, truthfully telling my story, and suddenly the counselor set out to shatter my pride and ego so I would stop blaming everyone else for my problems.

"Look, I'm here voluntarily," I said, "and I don't need to sit here and get abused. I get enough abuse out in the real world. I came here simply to get my daughter back from a damn crime family who is trying to murder me."

The counselor said something next that really hit home, and I still use his words today. He told me, "If you spot it, you got it."

I think about this concept every day. Does calling my ex-father-in-law a narcissistic psychopath mean I'm a narcissistic psychopath too? I've said that Cracie Wrongway is bipolar. Since I spot that condition in her, does that mean I'm bipolar too? It's overwhelming to consider this because I spot all kinds of conditions and flaws in people. Does that mean I have all the issues I can identify? Holy shit!

Anyhow, I passed up telling the rest of my story, perhaps as a pout. Later that afternoon, I felt intensely anxious. Not normal anxiety, but an "induced" anxiety, which I was now starting to identify.

I recalled feeling like I was under some kind of spell while I was at Happy Place and acting like a complete jackass. I began suspecting that mind-control technology could have been at play there. When my parents were coerced into leaving their house, it was after the structure was wired up like a movie set for the recording of all my actions. When I chemically induced myself with alcohol or methamphetamine, perhaps I was making this mind control and stimulation technology even more effective.

But who cares so much about me? Today, we have evil empires trafficking kids and hiring pedophiles. We have churches undergoing huge pedophile conspiracies, and judges parading around at home in pink bunny outfits and dancing in heels. We've had a president who used a cigar as a toy on one of his staff members. Am I really worth being the focus of someone's filmmaking? What was I being set up for? Why were people around me being manipulated?

During those instances at Happy Place and my parents' house, I couldn't differentiate chemical influence from this wild mind-control technology. While I was White Bear, however, I was removed from any chemical influence, plus I finally cleared out some of my anger issues through group therapy.

Thinking clearly at last, I could feel the onset of something very strange. Only now do I fully understand it, but at that time, I started to see that the vehicular gangstalking I'd been experiencing was going to do something terrible to my parents. It became even more clear to me how Don Darkino was setting me up, and if I stayed at White Bear any longer, I wouldn't be able to defend myself. My urge to leave rehab became irresistible, as if an outside force was pulling me to leave immediately.

Thinking rationally, though, the decision made little sense. I had no other place to stay that didn't make me sick. I was staying in a resort with movies, ping-pong, group activities, all while getting some much-needed therapeutic release. The food was good, and some of the women were attractive. Also, this was my ticket for getting my daughter back.

I learned later that I was experiencing technical mind control, not to be confused with psychological mind control.

An example of psychological mind control is when a person is left homeless, destitute and hungry, so he accepts food and shelter from a drug dealer who offers free drugs. An example from my life would be when Cracie swooped in because my relationship with another woman was falling apart and invited me on a free vacation.

On the other hand, when a person is surgically wired up like a goddam robot so satellites and computers can influence that person's brain, that's technical mind control.

That fourth night at White Bear, the urge to depart became so intense that I went to the front desk and told them I was leaving. The facility did everything in their power to prevent me from leaving. First, they refused to return my personal belongings. When I reminded them I was there voluntarily, they told me that I couldn't make any phone calls.

I actually had to have a friendly patient, with phone privileges, call Cracie and tell her I was going to start walking down the mountain. Finally, I was convinced to speak with the head counselor over the phone before I left. He practically begged me to stay, and at the time, I didn't know why he cared. Only now do I appreciate that if I failed to complete the program, he knew I was going to be nonjudicially executed by the government.

Why didn't he just tell me the truth? Why couldn't he just say that my life depended on me staying? That probably would have trumped the mind control that was influencing me. Regardless, his last effort was to explain that if I left, I'd never be allowed back for treatment. Considering I didn't believe I was an addict, I shrugged off that threat and simply said, "Thank you for your time."

The last effort at White Bear to save me was a phone call from the sheriff, Clark Wrongway. From the first day I met Clark, I considered him to be one of the nicest, most genuine and most respectable men I had ever met. I felt terrible for how his ex-wife Cracie had treated him. I felt worse when I became a guy who was involved with Cracie. Neverthelsss, Clark tried to convince me to stay in rehab.

"I know you probably don't want to hear this," he told me, "but staying is for your best interest." I wish I'd been smart enough to have understood the hidden message he was trying to communicate, which was: *If I didn't stay, you're going to be killed.* But I blew him off.

I asked Clark if Cracie was going to pick me up, and he said he didn't know. He told me she had been hysterically crying in the shower ever since I had called her.

I wondered, *Why the hell is she crying? Because she knew I was going to be murdered? Did she really have feelings for me?*

I put on my jacket, exchanged hugs and headed down the mountain in the snow. I walked a few miles, and it was enchantingly quiet and peaceful marching through the white-covered hills. My only light was from the moon reflecting off the snow.

As I was passing a row of houses, I saw a bicycle leaning on a mailbox. I was tempted to take that bike and make my trip much easier, but I had promised my group at White Bear that I would never break a rule or a law again. Maybe the bike was placed there to tempt me.

About three hours into my journey, a passing truck stopped, and the driver asked me if I needed a lift. I couldn't help remembering the angel who had helped me in Florida. I hopped in, and the same conversation I'd had in Florida played out. He asked me where I was going. I looked down at my bag and quietly said, "I need to get back to Allentown."

He let me use his phone to call Cracie, who picked up right away and said she'd been driving around looking for me. The driver said he'd drop me off at a truck stop down the road, and I gave Cracie directions.

She picked me up in the yellow Ford that I had basically paid for. We talked for a while, but I could just tell she wasn't the same person I once knew. I told her I need to ignore this bullcrap, get a job, and fight the corruption from the ex-wife to get my daughter back. I dropped her off at Clark's house, and she agreed to let me drive the car so I could search for a job. Why in the world was I still trusting this woman after everything she'd done to me?

The next day, I went to Jaime's house and explained my situation. I trusted her perspective on everything. Right away, she said I was an idiot for driving the yellow car or having anything to do with Cracie. In my heart, I knew she was right.

Unfortunately, the day I left White Bear to walk down that mountain was the day I slid into a covert, extrajudicial execution.

Chapter 23

Targeted Individual

Attorney Steven Moore was the only attorney offered to us by the Public Assistance Office. Too late, my intuition prompted me to do some research on him. It wasn't hard to figure out he was another pawn in the intimidation conspiracy. Two years, and seventeen thousand dollars after he took on my case, Moore hadn't done a damn thing to help me.

Research turned up information supporting my beliefs. Steven Moore, an employee of the United States government, had been disbarred in 2002 for taking funds from a client without providing services. This was my experience with him, as well. He'd been a judge advocate in the military and had lived most of his life in Florida, home state of Happy Place—both highly suspicious, in my view.

I had given Steven Moore all my files and evidence, which proved that every PFA was fraudulent, and I deserved a reduction in support and alimony payments. Moore made no effort to use this documentation to my benefit because he was not assigned to help me, but rather to drain my financial resources and manipulate me into permanently losing custody of my daughter.

When I described to Moore how organized stalking was being used to intimidate and harass me, he admitted that there was such a program, but that the intended targets were terrorists, murderers and sex offenders. He asked if I fit any of those descriptions, and I said no. I thought to myself, Not being a murderer or a sex offender, however, doesn't mean that you haven't been framed and classified as one.

I managed to get a job at 1360 House Restaurant near Jaime's house. I continued to drive Cracie's yellow car since I had made payments on it for over a year. But the truth was that Cracie let me drive the car so that false perceptions would be documented about how I was selfishly using women. I was driving Cracie's car while staying with Jaime, and occasionally driving Mandy's truck too. So, the perception that was cleverly created made it appear like I was using women. The targeting process depended on amassing numerous details that precisely fit together to present a persuasive, bullet-proof narrative.

I had made the payments on the yellow Ford, but my paycheck was deposited into Cracie's account, so I had no receipts. I had paid two hundred a month to drive Mandy's truck, but I gave her cash, so I had no evidence. When Jaime helped me get a car by putting it in her name, I made the payments until the deer incident wrecked the car. Truthfully, I had voluntarily contributed to the gathering and damning Lutterschmidt profile every time I had behaved exactly as the controllers expected I would.

The goals of the targeting were to destroy my credibility by having me committed or incarcerated, ruin me financially, and manipulate me to commit suicide. Since I hadn't killed myself yet and had successfully escaped incarceration numerous times, clever tactics were being planned for my demise.

I quickly concluded that the program chiefs were using a domestic abuse law to legally execute me. They pressed Cracie to fraudulently blame her bankruptcy on me and continue her entrapment efforts. They invited Gena to Happy Place to coerce her collaboration. They pressured Gena not to sign the short sale agreement, causing us both into foreclosure because the federal loan was only in my name. Gena and her father received expert advice about filing fraudulent PFAs. When Mandy and I split up, Cracie lured me on a holiday, making it look like I was just using her to get away.

Now I can understand how I fell for these traps, and I can identify every one of the setups and lies. But at the time, I was too mentally and emotionally spent to see it happening.

In domestic abuse cases, the problem with legislation like Marsy's Law is that a man is not granted the right to launch a defense. If a judicial panel obtains evidence from multiple women, the guilty verdict can be made without considering the man's story. This decision, unfortunately, can lead to a form of extrajudicial execution. When a person does not have the right to defend themselves, it allows for unchecked manipulation, falsification of evidence and criminal misconduct.

The main reason for writing this story is to show the world that I am being executed without the right to defend myself.

Happy Place wealth, influence and power were covertly and criminally used to take me down. On top of purchased, falsified testimonies, electronic harassment provided unbearable intimidation and evil perceptions. My personal Gmail account was placed under federal investigation for unknown reasons. Fictional personal profiles under my name began appearing on dating sites stating that I was gay. I was being followed everywhere I went. And I had lost my little girl.

The first two days at my new server job went great, providing a bit of relief from the anxiety of my support obligation. This obligation is not based on income but on income potential. The Darkino attorney proved that I used to make over one hundred fifty thousand a year, so that level of income was my potential. My medical history was considered irrelevant because many of the diagnoses were from out-of-state doctors.

On my third day in the restaurant, I experienced my first dose of employment sabotage. All new servers were required to take a server test to determine our knowledge of the menu. Out of the twenty questions, I missed four items from the ingredients. The female manager scoring the test also took points off for writing "lettuce" and not "crisp lettuce" for one answer. I was told I couldn't continue working until I got a better score. This manager had undergone an extreme attitude shift since the previous day. Previously, she had been warm and welcoming, but she now seemed anxious and curt.

I asked to see the other servers' tests to see how they were graded, but the manager refused and said, "Just come back tomorrow and retake the test." As I left the restaurant, another server told me that two men had come into the restaurant earlier with a folder and had spoken to the manager. The server didn't see what was in the file, but she heard one of the men say, "Mike Lutterschmidt." I thanked her for telling me, but I didn't really know what it all meant.

The next day, an hour before I was scheduled to retake the test, the manager told me they no longer had a position open. This was my first experience with employment sabotage. A new stage of targeting was just getting started.

That night, I sat on Jaime's front deck. She lived in a trailer park that had only two access points from the main road. There was little reason for too many non-resident cars to be driving on that road. As I sat on Jaime's front deck, however, I notice an unusually high number of cars passing the house. I was learning that the intent was to prompt paranoid-sound complaints or a physical attack on the perps. I did neither, but the visible evidence of this gangstalking created a crushing anxiety.

The next day, I found a nearby telemarketing job selling business credit reports. I hated telemarketing, but the job came with a small hourly rate plus quarterly commissions, and I could start the following Monday. I had modest success despite some agonizing sinus issues. But the stalking and psychological warfare continued to distract me.

Late in my first week, I saw two well-groomed men with impressive tans enter the office. I had now been primed to recognize such activity and suspected it was about me. After they left, my manager started to act very stiffly and nervously with me. The attitude shift tipped me off that the two men had probably presented a false but incriminating story about me to the manager, just as in the restaurant. Before long, the word seemed to pass to other employees because they started behaving coolly as well.

I just tried to push through my days. I started to hang out with a few people from work who remained friendly, and once or twice a week, we went to a bar after work. I became tight with a girl named Viola, who stuck up for me whenever negative comments were made.

I eventually lasted a few months in this job, the whole time enduring the obvious stalking and harassment. I started to point out the stalking perps to Viola, knowing that I sounded paranoid. Viola told me she was hesitant to talk about it for fear of sounding crazy, but she had been stalked as well. Finally, some more proof of this evil shit. Because of our common experience, Viola and I started to hang out but didn't take it any further. I knew that adding another woman to my "harem" would create an even worse profile of me, particularly since Viola openly spoke about recreationally using some substances.

While I was with Viola after work one day, Cracie called, and I put her on speakerphone. She said she wanted the yellow car back. I decided it was time to take Jaime's advice and cut all ties with Cracie, but something was odd about her request. At first, Cracie said she'd pick up the car, but then she was interrupted by a male voice in the background. After a brief silence, she said, "No, you need to drive the car back to Clark's house, or I'm calling the cops."

Viola was with me. "Damn, that bitch is crazy," she whispered.

My intuition told me it was a setup, so I called AAA and had the car towed to Clark's house, which I still find funny today. When Cracie discovered I had not personally delivered the car, she was furious.

Viola said, "What the fuck is wrong with this bitch? She got the car back. What else does she want?"

This failed setup was confirmed the following day. After work, Viola took me to see another coworker who had called in sick that day. We got to her house in Allentown, and the coworker wasn't sick at all. She was high as a kite. We sat on her back porch for a few minutes, and then the coworker invited us inside.

As we stood up, my intuition held me back. I just froze, overcome with a sense of impending danger. I noticed that a fire truck had pulled up to the side of the house where I was standing by the open door. Suddenly, I saw a SWAT team jump from the truck with guns drawn. I immediately started walking toward Viola's car away from the house, scared to death. Then Viola calmly joined me in her car and asked what was wrong. I told her about the SWAT team, but she had no idea what I was talking about. When I turned to point them out, the SWAT team had vanished.

I was very confused and disturbed, so I asked her about the coworker. After some questioning, Viola explained that the father of her coworker's baby had been charged with distributing heroin a few months ago.

I flashed back to Cracie slandering me to Gena with lies that I was a heroin addict, and then a fraudulent PFA filed about the same thing in a court of law. These lies were responsible for Lala being ripped from my life since I could not defend myself. I also vividly recalled that two people I had associated with died from poisoned heroin in Rita's house.

Clearly, I was being set up for another heroin charge—guilt by association. I had been given a warning, a vision of what might have been set up to occur if I had walked into that house. Was a SWAT team standing by to barge in and discover me with a guy who was already charged with distribution? I can't know for sure. Who knew what had been staged? Perhaps, because of angels on my shoulder, I am still free to speculate and document what happened.

A few days later, I quit my telemarketing job. My manager had turned against me, and many of the staffers had become hostile. My work history was becoming more concerning.

The constant gangstalking prompted me to get answers to certain questions. Since Cracie had been fired from the State Police, I decided to start at the police station off Airport Road. I walked in and asked to speak to an officer. A young man appeared, and I tried to explain what I was experiencing. His expression betrayed a concern for my mental health. He told me, "Unless you have been physically attacked, there is nothing we can do."

Having come up empty, I headed for the Allentown courthouse. As I was staring blankly at the front desk, trying to summon the courage to ask for advice, I saw a woman and man descending a nearby stairway. I overheard the woman tell the man, "Well, since he left rehab early, we just signed off on the documents."

No joke! The coincidental nature of this remark made me think it must have been staged. But my trip to the courthouse was so randomly scheduled, I couldn't think of how.

Seeing me at the bottom of the stairs, the man said in a quiet voice to the woman, "Shh, I think that's him."

What the hell was I supposed to think? If this was a random, highly coincidental comment about my leaving White Bear, it was certainly ominous. What documents had been signed?

When I asked the officer at the front desk who I should consult about stalking and harassment, he told me to start with the crisis intervention office, which was down the hall. As I waited to speak to someone there, I paced back and forth in the window-lined hallway and was shocked by what I observed across the street.

Just fifteen minutes earlier, I had spoken to a young, uniformed officer at the State Police station. Now, the same young officer was wearing street clothes outside the courthouse and talking to two men in black suits. My stomach tightened with anxiety. Right after I left the station, this officer must have been called and then instructed to meet these two men.

Directly across from the courthouse was the local headquarters for the Federal Bureau of Investigation. What the hell was going on?

A woman from crisis intervention finally called me into the office. The circumstances had made me very disturbed. I tried to explain the stalking and employment tampering, but I couldn't formulate my words coherently. The woman obviously decided I was mentally unstable and advised me to voluntarily commit myself to a mental health clinic so I could get some help. I was not going to do that again! I angrily left the office with no clear plan of what to do next.

The next day, I decided to face the situation head-on. At the library, using the Pennsylvania Docket app, I printed out Don

Darkino's charges for manslaughter, terroristic threats, harassment, disorderly conduct, theft of property, and about twenty-seven traffic violations. I also printed out my court response to the first PFA, which was filed when Don was trying to cover up the fact that he had attacked me and threatened to have me killed.

Then I went to my parents' house and put on a suit, telling them I had an interview. If I had told them my true intention—to confront the FBI—it would have unleashed a shitstorm of stress and complex questions.

At the FBI building, I asked to speak to an agent. Amazingly, the agent assigned to this task had gone to high school with my younger brother. I took him through the litany of unsettling and criminal offenses I had suffered and then asked if I had been accused of anything that would cause the government to perpetrate these tactics, or if I could somehow find out why this was happening.

The agent assured me the FBI didn't have enough funding to just follow me around. "If the FBI wanted to get information about you, we'd just come and ask you." I wasn't one of their concerns, he said.

I was anticipating these answers, of course. So, I handed him my file on Don Darkino, explaining how my father-in-law had threatened my life and coerced my wife into filing fraudulent PFAs. I sincerely explained that I was worried for my safety.

The agent said he would investigate Darkino, but even if he found anything, I would not be entitled to know if any action was taken.

So, what was I to do? The proper channels were of no help at all.

I had no choice but to find another job so I could pay support and keep my butt out of jail. I went to a career fair at the Lehigh Valley Mall and found a job at a casino. With all the cameras and security systems there, I concluded, that venue might help keep stalkers away. I also believed that if I was being investigated for anything, the thorough fingerprint and background checks would prevent me from being offered the job, and I could possibly discover why I was being stalked.

Amazingly, all the checks came back clear, and I was hired as a food and beverage supervisor with a salary and benefits. My support payments were set up to be garnished, and once again, I began to have hope.

I was pretty much staying at my parents' house again. Jaime had a baby girl now and two teenagers to worry about, so it was too much to have me around. I also didn't want stalkers to cause her any grief.

I met a nice girl named Megan, who worked days babysitting a bunch of kids and then worked part-time at a grocery store. I enjoyed helping her babysit, which, of course, made me miss my own daughter. After watching how great I was with the kids, she couldn't believe my ex-wife would keep my daughter away from me—until I told her my horror story.

As I started job training, I noticed another trainee constantly watching me, which made me uncomfortable. Also, a new general manager had just been hired. I didn't think much of it at the time, but employment sabotage was already underway.

I jumped into my role, and everyone said I was the best supervisor they'd had in a long time. Back in my element, I did whatever I could to help my servers and bartenders.

The first attempt to sabotage my job was conducted by the new woman who had become general manager of food and beverage. In a meeting, she reprimanded me for—of all things—helping my bar staff make drinks when they were overloaded. I needed to supervise rather than help them work through a rush, she said.

Although I was reprimanded for doing what I believed was right, I no longer had the luxury of pride. I needed to keep this job. Even though the bartenders appreciated my help, I had to follow instructions and not provide assistance anymore. Being a good boy for a change—a compliant employee—probably irritated my handlers, who were expecting different behavior.

My symptoms were progressing, but I just chalked it up to the increasing mold susceptibility and fought through the pain. Megan would let me use her mother's oxygen tank for some relief. The stalking and vehicular harassment became more intense to the point that Megan and her son witnessed the harassment as well. One night, her son and I drove us around in his lifted Ford truck as I pointed out some of the young stalkers. It was fun intimidating them for a change.

While sleeping at her house one night while Megan was working, I experienced just how elaborate this targeting program was and the extent of its technology. I woke up with a strange tingling in my ear. This was the only time they tried to induce mental illness by projecting a hologram of a green skeleton arm so big it covered the entire ceiling. Slowly, the arm reached down and started to open its bony hand. As it got closer to my face, the hand appeared to be reaching down to grab me. I was mesmerized by it, but as soon as the hand got to my face, it disappeared.

I assume the hologram was intended to frighten me or question my sanity, but instead, I loved it. I wanted them to do it again. But imagine if I reported to a psychologist that I had seen a skeleton hand trying to grab me. It is no coincidence that 80 percent of all surviving targeted individuals in this country end up getting diagnosed with schizophrenia, which is basically seeing and hearing stuff that isn't real. When you obtain third-party witnesses, however, the handlers take drastic and cruel actions to hide their crimes.

So, here was "their" dilemma. I learned to accept life and live with my symptoms. I wasn't trying to mask my pain anymore. Since I was no longer using amphetamines to push forward or hanging around bad influences, my handlers had to come up with new and creative tactics to reach their goals.

One day at the casino, the stalking became so obnoxious that I called Anthony, another supervisor, over to observe a guest. I said this woman playing a slot machine was one of many stalkers and explained what I was going through. As we continued to gaze at the woman, she began to get flustered. Finally, she glanced over at us, got up from her machine, and power-walked out the door.

"That was weird," Anthony said.

The program's handlers cannot tolerate witnesses. Once people start to recognize the harassment, they simply turn up the intensity, believing they are invincible. The night we drove the slot machine lady out of the casino, I woke up with a huge lump on my left buttocks. Megan said there seemed to be a small hole in the middle of it. This swelling was the size of a baseball, and as hard as one too. I tried to work that day, but I couldn't even walk.

I was terrified that I'd been injected with something in my sleep. I left work and visited a doctor who said he'd never seen anything like it—there was no buildup of fluid inside, which would have been typical. He thought it was a methicillin-resistant Staphylococcus aureus infection (MRSA) and gave me an antibiotic. I mentioned that I'd become immune to most antibiotics, but he just looked at me like I was nuts.

Even though I needed a friend, I stopped hanging out with Megan and her kids because I didn't want them to get caught in the crossfire of my targeting. But Megan and her son can testify to the stalking they witnessed. To this day, I wonder if I was injected with something like HIV, even though I've been found clean several times.

After receiving the MRSA diagnosis, I returned to work with the doctor's note. The perpetual wave of stalkers coming into the casino really made me question why I was so important to merit such attention. I again confirmed with state, local and federal authorities that I did not have any arrest warrants. I knew that I had passed a federal background check before getting my casino job, which should have given me some peace of mind. So why were all these people following me?

I started to analyze the numbers. Hundreds of people seemed to be around me just for the sake of getting in my head, forcing me to tell others that I was being followed. Assume one hundred stalkers, to make it easy. Also, assume that each person was hired to be a stalker with a salary of fifty thousand dollars a year. In one year, that calculates to five million dollars on salaries. This does not include the gas, food, vehicles and other expenses—or the technology, vehicles and salaries of administrative people who were planning and orchestrating the program.

I asked myself again—why was I so important?

Chapter 24

Empowered Individual

In targeting individuals, handlers put false ideas into targets' heads to keep them guessing about how, why and when the targeting occurs. The idea behind this covert torture is to make a person insane, bankrupt, discredited and/or suicidal in an undetectable manner. The term for this is *gaslighting*, which is:

> A form of psychological manipulation that seeks to sow seeds of doubt in a targeted individual or in members of a targeted group, making them question their own memory, perception, and sanity.

When trying to figure out who was behind my targeting, my first suspect was Don Darkino, a Mafia boss, FBI informant and narcissistic psychopath with a violent temper who had threatened to kill me in front of his daughter, who was also my wife. I had inside knowledge of some of his crimes, so I was a potential threat to him. But he was not alone in my mind.

I also think he may have been responsible for killing a woman who lived next door to my trusted friend, Jaime, and was planning to frame me for the crime. One day, this woman suddenly disappeared. Her name, Polly Prim, and her story were spread all over the news, and a statewide investigation began.

My first experience with gaslighting really messed with my head. I reflected on an overheard phone call in which Don ordered a hit on J. Cazonaro, who was murdered a few days later. I thought about the way he behaved when we read about the murder of J. Cazonaro in the paper.

Unfortunately, I made the mistake of discussing my thoughts about Don Darkino with just about everyone, which made me sound paranoid and unstable. As we know, however, a major goal of targeting is to create the credible perception of mental illness in the victim. I fell for their traps early on.

The casino I worked at had State Police right on the grounds. One day, I went to the security desk, and I asked to speak to the head of security. I explained that I was being stalked on the casino floor, which was preventing me from doing my job. I asked to speak with the State Police on site.

Security walked me to the police station where I explained that I believed my ex-father-in-law was setting me up. I told most of the story revealed in these pages, including his death threats. Then I mentioned Polly Prim, which raised some eyebrows. I was staying at a house next door to Polly's, I said, and it seemed way too coincidental that the girl next door to me had vanished. Don Darkino, I said, may have had something to do with Polly's disappearance to frame me.

The trooper brought up Don's mug shot on the computer, and I verified his identity. Then, he said something that shook me to my core, "You don't have any PFA filed on record," he told me, "and if I were you, I'd go see my daughter."

I knew, of course, that there were PFAs on record, and if I went to see my daughter would be arrested and likely extradited to Florida, maybe even assassinated. I also knew that the Trooper didn't realize that I was a human lie detector.

I immediately understood that a state trooper at my place of employment was trying to coerce me into violating a PFA, which would result in my incarceration. What the hell was going on? I knew Don had connections and some old military buddies, but I didn't think he had the funds and clout to pull off such an extravagant program.

I tried my best to keep working and do a good job. One day, my bartenders were overwhelmed with drink orders. I decided to simply clear some glasses, which would help them get caught up. I never jumped behind the bar to help, which my manager had warned me against. But a few hours later, my boss called me into her office, and I was reprimanded again for helping the bartenders. I had to sign a formal written warning this time, which told me something was askew.

During a concert several nights later, a server informed me that two women wanted to take us home that evening. Without even looking at the women, I laughed and told him I was not in the mood. The last thing I needed was to bring another woman into my nightmare of a life. I can't remember exactly how it happened, but one of the women, Lori, slipped me her number. We eventually hung out together while I was still working at the casino.

After making my report to State Police regarding on-site stalking, I was called in to answer questions about Polly Prim. The detective asked how I knew her, and I said, "I didn't know her at all."

He asked why I had mentioned her disappearance to the State Police, so I explained my experience with Don Darkino, and my suspicions. The detective took my information, but I could tell he shrugged it all off. A few days later, the news reported that Polly Prim's body had been found buried in the backyard of one of her coworkers.

This is how gaslighting and targeting mess with a person's mind. I understood what was being orchestrated around me, but those targeting activities were meant only for me to see. When other people became aware of those activities, the targeting actions intensified. The fact that Polly Prim's body had been found, and her death appeared to be unrelated to Don Darkino, just proved to everyone that I was paranoid—also part of the plan.

After I made the report to my security team and State Police about the harassment, I guess it was time for them to get rid of me. The fact that I was pointing out perps to other supervisors, and they themselves started to see odd activity, it was time for them to terminate my employment.

One day, a female supervisor was speaking with two girls and a guy at the bar. I just stood there to see if she needed any assistance. The fact was, I was good at my job, and I knew it just pissed off my handlers. The customers asked to speak to another supervisor, and since I was right there, I introduced myself. The two women said they had been asked to leave because they were refused additional alcohol service. In a casino, if a person is cut off for drinking too much, they're required to leave the casino floor so they can't blame the casino for allowing them to lose money while intoxicated.

I explained the policy to the customers, and one of the women began crying. Her father had just passed away, she said, and they just wanted to sit at the bar. Her tears seemed genuine. But I supported my coworker and politely requested that they leave. With genuine sympathy, I escorted them into the vestibule.

Later, security informed me on the headset that I had a personal phone call at the desk. This was odd because I was carrying my personal phone and an iPhone provided by the casino. Who the hell was calling me at work?

The two girls I had kicked off the floor asked if I wanted to hang out with them after work. It occurred to me that all incoming conversations were being recorded, and fraternization with customers was against policy. I declined, of course. That same evening, the person who was hired with me filed a complaint that I had cursed at him over the headset. The next day, my boss told me that I could not return to work. The reason? I was not meeting management expectations, and I had left the casino floor with two female customers.

I knew that the targeting program was behind this. Clearly, the two women had collaborated in my wrongful termination. But what was I supposed to do? Pennsylvania had a no-fault termination policy, which meant employers couldn't terminate employees without cause, which was provided by the vague statement that I wasn't meeting expectations.

I realized that nothing in my life was a coincidence. Every event, every scenario and every situation was a well-orchestrated plot to destroy my life.

The day I was fired, Cracie drove to my parents' house and tried to convince me to live with her for a few weeks to stabilize my mental equilibrium. What a trap. First, Cracie reinforced in my mind that I was mentally ill, and second, if I took time off, I'd go to jail for not paying support.

Everything in my life seemed to be playing out on one big stage. Even though I didn't see the entire picture, I was able to recognize the bullshit, so I walked away and didn't look back. I was done feeling sorry for myself. I had let myself wallow in misery for too long. Instead of giving up, I got motivated.

I got a job at a large warehouse—not a great job, but I'd earn enough money to keep me out of jail. With my casino income, I had earned enough money to buy an old Ford Ranger and insurance, so at least I had transportation. Unfortunately, I started to get sick again at my parents' house. I started missing a lot of work and was still experiencing employment sabotage.

I had been hired as a picker, but when I arrived, I was shifted to a sorter position. Pickers walked around the warehouse gathering items to fulfill orders. Sorters stood in one spot and sorted items into carts and slots. My handlers had called ahead, I believe, and arranged for me to be a sorter, which would be easier to sabotage—which they did.

My job was to take an item, scan it to get a letter, then place the item in the slot with the corresponding letter. This wasn't brain surgery. Every cart I completed gave my manager grief because there were several mistakes. Do you really believe I can't match two letters? One day during our lunch break, I marked the floor where the wheels of the cart were setting to see if the cart would be moved when I returned. Sure enough, the cart was moved three inches over to the right. During lunch, no one would be lingering around my station, and it was very clear someone was getting paid to sabotage my work. So, there I was, once responsible for a multi-million-dollar restaurant in one career, managing millions of dollars in a second career, and now perceived as a mindless slug who couldn't even do a simple warehouse job.

After a few weeks, I quit. A full forty-hour workweek barely covered my support payments to keep me out of jail. My symptoms were in full-scale bloom again. And I had to sell my beat-up Ford Ranger to stay current on my support obligation for one month. This was an intentionally vicious cycle, but I refused to give up.

During this emotional time, I really needed a companion, so Lori and I started to hang out. She liked to go fishing, camping, and do other things I liked to do. She was ten years older than me, and her maturity provided much-needed stability to my life.

I eventually wrangled an interview to manage a restaurant and bar called Big Foody's. As I sat at the bar waiting for my interview, a customer entered and sat right next to me. When he started tapping on his phone, I felt pressure build up in my head, and then pain stabbed through my left sinus cavity.

To distract from the pain, I walked to a server who was rolling silverware at a table and asked her if I could help. She was shocked that I offered. I simply refused to give in to the attacks.

I was hired on the spot with a higher salary than the casino had paid. Although I didn't fully comprehend the campaign of intimidation, I was smart enough to realize I'd become a target. The new job gave me a surge of empowerment, and I started emailing everyone that I could think of with my story—local authorities, the FBI, my senator and governor, NBC, FOX, ABC, CNN, *The Morning Call*, WFMZ, and *Time*. I included lawyers and human rights groups as well. I probably said the wrong things with the wrong tone and the wrong words. I may have sounded like a madman on a rant. Predictably, I suppose, my efforts only made things worse.

Though I was hesitant to start another relationship, I accepted a key to Lori's apartment. Something was telling me I had met Lori for a reason. As an LPN, she was very nurturing and seemed to care about me.

Soon after I started my job at Big Foody's, Mandy came into the bar with a very well-dressed woman. I gave Mandy a hug and apologized for the way our relationship had ended, and that Cracie had been coerced to break us up. The woman Mandy was with kept whispering in her ear, and Mandy seemed edgy as she nodded at her friend's comments. My intuition told me they were not here by coincidence.

We chatted for a couple of minutes with unsipped drinks in front of them. Eventually, I went back to work, but when they were ready to leave, they asked the bartender for the check and requested that I come over to speak with them. Their drinks had not been consumed.

Mandy's friend said that since they were not going to have their drinks, could I just take the drinks off the bill. If you have ever worked in a restaurant or bar, you know that "voids" need to be limited and fully explained because they are so often abused by staffers.

Immediately, I knew that I was being tricked. I suspected it was an act of revenge by a women's rights group that perhaps had been fed bogus but inflammatory information about me by my handlers. If I had voided those drinks, this woman probably would have called the owner with some lies about my voiding the drinks, and I would be out on my rear.

I had reason to suspect women. Think about my story so far. Gena filed fraudulent PFAs against me and had refused to sign a short sale, causing my federal loan to go into default. I had behaved like an idiot at Happy Place with a cop's wife. Cracie had blamed her bankruptcy on me and entrapped me numerous times. Mandy had been turned against me. A female manager at the 1360 House terminated me after two days. The casino fired me after two women called the security desk to ask me out.

The perpetrators in all these incidents were women. I knew that some women's rights organizations, like neighborhood watch committees and other "watchdog" groups, could have members who were militant and susceptible to alerts about dangerous and unsavory persons. In fact, participation in campaigns of intimidation and harassment can be coerced from entire communities, organizations, even authorities through manipulation, slander and falsified records.

I knew Cracie was a honey trap. She stupidly told Jaime that mold was being put in my vehicles to poison me. She also directly let slip these other facts:

- I was put on a watch list.

- I was being targeted by the military (DOD).

- Poison was being put in my car.

- She was used as a honey trap.

- Cameras and microphones were placed in Clark's house.

- She had worn a wire.

- She was told to blame her bankruptcy on me.

- She was directed to tell Gena I was a heroin addict.

- She was coerced into tell Gena that Lala was in danger.

- She was told to take me to Florida.

- She was ordered to break up Mandy and me.

- I would become homeless.

- I would never see my daughter again.

Work was going well, support payments were being made and I was living with Lori in Bethlehem. I had enough money left over to buy a blue Ford Ranger. I didn't have any credit, so I went to a "buy here, pay here" car lot. I loved my truck and was proud of myself for starting to get back on my feet after violently hitting the ground floor of hell. With all things considered, I had to question why the hell I was still getting so extremely targeted. I ran the numbers before in my head and really couldn't figure out why the hell I was still this important. I still had no criminal record, I was obviously working and doing well, and I cut all ties with anyone I used to associate with while in that dark period of my life. I was not doing anything wrong, but I was still being stalked, harassed and poisoned.

Despite my harsh words about attorney Steven Moore, he was able to convince Gena to let me speak to Lala every night. In my twenty-minute calls, I asked her about school, played some fun riddle games, and told her how badly I missed her.

Gena never said a word to me, and she always seemed over-eager to get Lala off the phone. Now, this gaslighting thing always kept me guessing. Then one day, we had a productive conversation. I couldn't understand why she was so against allowing me to see my daughter. I finally got her to consider dropping the ridiculous PFA, and she said she'd talk to me later that night.

Well, I assume that Don convinced her otherwise. Gena never called me back, and the idea of dropping the PFA was no longer an option. I spoke with Lala for a few weeks, and the pain of not being able to see her really got to me.

One night, I broke down and made a huge mistake. I told her to never forget that she had seen her grandfather pull a gun on me. I explained I couldn't see her because Grandpa wanted me out of her life. I admit, telling this to an eight-year-old was not a good decision, but my pain at that moment was unbearable.

After I told Lala never to forget those awful events, I was told I could never speak to her again.

Still, I was not about to give up. At this point, I realized many people in my life had been coerced to play along with this cruel program. The genius behind it was that no one would ever witness me being provoked, but cameras and microphones would record how I responded.

I was doing so well at work, the owners wanted me to take over a new restaurant. The location wasn't as busy as South Fourth Street, but my boss knew my experience and drive would help make it successful.

Perhaps because of my refusal to surrender, the targeting became much more elaborate and extravagant. The more I succeeded, despite the constant physical and psychological attempts to disrupt my life, the more my self-esteem grew. To communicate with all my perps and their handlers, I made a sign with this statement for the back of my truck:

Slander me, I shine! Stalk me, I gain fame!

Fire me, I get promoted! Poison me, I become immune!

Implant me, I enhance wisdom! Take me down, never!

After pasting this on my truck, I started to get stalked by the bumper sticker: "Smash Egos and Break Necks." Their relentless persistence may have been due to the fact I was implanted with body area networking, cochlear and retinal implants. I think there was no way in hell they would let me survive long enough to expose their handiwork. The handlers, I hoped, knew they had met their match, and now it was all about damage control.

Chapter 25

Desperate Damage Control

I had instant success at my new location. Once again, I had an entire team behind me, and I was back to being my best while still stuck in the grasp of hell. Within the first few weeks, the restaurant had a 30 percent increase in sales. Ironically, much of this increase was due to all the perps and stalkers who came to harass me.

I wasn't afraid to educate the staff about the program and recruit them into my support system. I created signals to point out stalkers and trained the bartenders to get names and addresses from stalker driver's licenses or credit cards. A few of these people were private investigators, policemen, detectives and undercover federal agents. Some had been arrested a few weeks earlier for possession of narcotics. We concluded that they were coerced into cooperating as part of a plea bargain.

The big question was, why were all these people stalking me? An FBI agent had assured me that the agency didn't have the money to follow me around. Then who was funding the program?

The handlers quickly caught onto our game. Perps started to use prepaid credit cards, which did not list a name. No matter what adjustments they made, however, I found new ways to expose them. One way was to strictly enforce the Liquor Control Board laws and make everyone show ID no matter how old they appeared to be.

The handlers, of course, could not allow an entire team of people to witness their targeting campaign. I was supposed to appear mentally ill and allow the harassment to negatively disrupt my life. Instead, I was sarcastically thanking stalkers for their business and using their sabotage attempts to make me a stronger manager.

As a counterattack, efforts were made to get me in trouble with the Pennsylvania state liquor control laws. Stalkers started sneaking in with expired licenses or fake IDs, which could get our liquor license suspended. Then we started to get many people trying to buy beer after legal closing time. I had to put the entire team on high alert. Next, a health department inspection was ordered for the restaurant based on false accusations. The inspector said we were the cleanest restaurant he had ever inspected. These attempts at harassment just made me stronger and created a stronger bond with my team.

During most of my shifts, stalkers sat at the bar and interacted with their phones. That's what people do in today's world, so it didn't seem very sinister. People sometimes asked if they could plug their cords into the outlet behind the bar. At one point, there were so many connected cords I had to make a rule against it. It was an electrical liability, I explained, but having so many cell phones waving around freaked me out. I had no idea at the time how cell phones could be used to induce and elevate my symptoms.

I often saw my parents' Vietnamese neighbor lurking around the dry cleaner's shop by my restaurant. This dude always gave me the creeps. Since I got sick so often at my parents' house, I wondered if this neighbor had been coerced into attacking me using some kind of electronic weapon. When I finally learned about the power of weaponized cell phones, the possibility seemed more likely, but I could never prove his involvement.

At this point in my targeting, I was investigating everything and questioning everyone's intentions. A girl I met playing pool asked me to text her my number, so I did along with my name. I wanted to save her phone number so I could check out anything suspicious. I saved her number under a guy's name. If Lori saw a girl's number on my phone, she might misunderstand.

I never spoke with this girl after that night, and the entire encounter was completely innocent. But a manipulated characterization of it was communicated back to Lori, who could not believe that such a message could have been part of a targeting campaign.

It turns out that a third-party spy was at the pool hall that night to cause another disruption in my life. Remember, a target individual is under 24/7 surveillance and is stalked by the entire community at large. Naturally, Lori got upset and assumed the worst. Instead of breaking me down, however, this harassment was making me stronger.

The handlers progressed from having restaurant guests conduct harassment to coercing employees to join the effort. They really stepped up their game, sparing no expense.

I was still getting primed and stalked by vehicles. I observed a yellow Penske box truck everywhere I went and felt constant pressure in my head. I imagined some type of radiation gun or directed-energy weapon aimed at me from the back of these trucks.

One night, after getting home to Lori's after three in the morning, I was unwinding on the front step when I saw a yellow Penske truck drive up the alley. This activity so early in the morning was suspicious, so I walked over to investigate the truck when it stopped. I knew that the intent of this constant priming and stalking is to get a target so upset he reacts violently.

As I walked up to the truck, the driver got out looking very scared. He was dropping steak rolls off at the pizza place, he said. I introduced myself and told him I managed a Big Foody's and would be interested in comparing prices. He gave me a card, and as I turned around, a police car drove by the alley.

I'm sure the handlers had spent the past week priming me with a yellow box truck twenty times a day to provoke a violent response in the alley. You must admire the persistence.

I saw this same driver on other nights after our confrontation. On each of those evenings, he was driving a personal vehicle. It became clear that he was not a pawn in the program. Some non-participants also drive yellow box trucks. These handlers were putting innocent people in danger from targeted and primed individuals like me.

During my next management meeting, the staff was told that the owners of Big Foody's had hired an outside consultant to help grow the business. Right off the bat, I knew this was a ruse tied to my intimidation campaign. I knew the owners were way too proud to let some outside "expert" tell them how to run their business. And the owners were too cheap to fix a damn bread mixer—they'd never spend money on a consultant.

That night at work, I noticed one of those creepy white vans—you know, the child-molester kind with no windows. I knew something was odd about it. I didn't see it park, but I got an urge to harass the harassers. I made a deal with a group of guys at the bar. I offered to buy them a pitcher of beer if they'd go out and bang on the white van. These guys probably would have done it without the beer.

Outside, the five guys walked up to the van and started pounding on it and yelling, "Come out! What are you doing in there?"

The back door of the van open and two frightened, twentyish guys jumped out. I was laughing so hard I started crying. What made things even worse for the handlers was that my entire team saw it happen, which confirmed that the program and the surveillance was real.

One of the stalkers looked at his phone, probably reading texted instructions to come into the restaurant and pretend innocence. When they ordered drinks, of course, I asked for their IDs and smiled rather arrogantly. What could they do? I was not surprised to find that the driver's licenses were from the Sunshine State of Florida. After one beer each, they cashed out.

I waved to them and said, "Thank you for your business." My mistake was in taunting them so arrogantly. The program was about to show me just how much power, influence and money I was up against.

Inez Yadura—not the prettiest woman—was their easiest target for coercion. She was a full-time cashier and had several kids at home. What kind of mother would quit her job on the spot? A mother who was offered enough money to do something criminal, like make a false charge of sexual harassment against me.

Inez claimed that I had put my hands on her shoulders and touched her inappropriately. When my boss asked her where this had happened, she asked which location had a camera blind spot. When she was told of a specific place that a camera could not see, she replied, "That's where it happened." At this point, my boss didn't even ask to see the statements from other employees. The matter was dismissed, and Inez quit her job.

I worked with a woman named Dena Marcelo, a kind of grown-up tomboy who had been coerced into entrapping me with some serious drugs. Dena invited me to take a break with her and go to a festival that was being held across the street. Although Dena and I were on good terms, I could tell by her behavior that something was up.

At the event, we rode the twister, ate some french fries and went back to work that night. After work, she asked me for a ride home. It was common for me to drive an employee home, so I agreed. When we got to her apartment, she invited me in for a beer. Since I had to use the bathroom, I said yes.

She had a one-room apartment with a shared bathroom, which I used before entering her room. As I tried to quickly finish my beer, I detected the beginning of her entrapment ploy. She pulled out a large Ziploc bag filled with tiny baggies of pre-bagged methamphetamine. At first, I thought it was a joke. There were hundreds of baggies with little white rocks in them.

Based on experience with my old acquaintances, I quickly estimated that there were about two hundred little baggies, each containing a half gram of meth. Each baggie could be sold on the street for about a hundred bucks. So, Dena, who was working part-time at $7.50 per hour, was sitting on $20,000 worth of product.

She asked me if I could help her sell it. I assumed there were cameras and mics capturing my every move, in addition to implants in my ears and eyes. I was pissed at Dena for trying to set me up. Possession of this many narcotics would put me away for twenty years.

I played along about how we could get rid of the bag. As a test of her reaction, I told her I wanted two hundred dollars out of the deal—a ridiculously low commission. She just nodded and said that was fine, which told me she had no idea about the value of the drugs in that bag.

The next day, I wrote a letter to the Allentown Police Department with a copy to my boss. Dena was quickly terminated. The fact that I walked away from that elaborate plot pissed off this powerful force even more.

During my next two days off, I went camping with Lori. The vehicular stalking was intense, and the looks I got from drivers in their new trucks were obnoxious and angry. When Lori and I stopped for gas, a guy walked up to us and asked if we had any pills we could sell him. Seriously, these people were so desperate to get me, the program was no longer even covert. Lori had not been primed the way I had been all day long, so many of these events appeared to be random. But she would tell you the truth—a guy walked right up to us and asked if we'd sell him some pills.

The handlers eventually were able to influence my assistant manager, Ana Shamey. I'm not sure what lies they told to gain her participation, or what incentive they offered, but Ana played out a series of events that would lead to the end of my employment. She hired a delivery driver, who went AWOL on a busy night, so I had to take over delivery duties. During that entire night of driving, squad cars tried to cut me off and get me into an accident. What authority could get the Allentown Police to act like a bunch of criminals?

One delivery was at the Red Roof Inn. When I knocked, an attractive woman opened the door wearing just a towel and asked if I wanted to stay for a while. I didn't fall for the bait, of course, but this kind of shit only happens in the movies. Was my life a movie? The next day, Ana assured me the delivery guy would be in for work that evening, so I didn't bother to cover his shift. I did have a written warning ready for him to sign, however, for not showing up the previous night.

Sure enough, five o'clock rolled around, and the delivery guy never showed up. I wasn't going to have a repeat disaster, so I called

Lori to see if she could help. She had just spent the day working her normal job, but she agreed to step in.

One of her first deliveries was to the towel lady's room at the Red Roof. She called me because no one answered the door. Clearly, the handlers had not anticipated Lori's involvement, so their plan—whatever it was—had to be shut down.

The handlers were infuriated that I kept rejecting their bait. Considering they had exposed their tactics so badly, they desperately needed to destroy my team's support and ability to testify to the program they were executing.

Ana Shamey was directed to have our daytime pizza maker, Julio, write a nasty letter to our boss complaining that no one was doing their job and the restaurant was dirty. I found this exasperating since the health inspector had just reported that our restaurant was the cleanest he had ever seen, and our sales were higher than ever. I showed Julio's letter to my team, and the whole night shift was upset.

The nighttime pizza guy—"Hooty," we called him—said, "That couldn't have been Julio. He would never do something like that. If he had a problem, he'd have told us instead of trying to throw us all under the bus."

I wish I had grasped it sooner, but Ana was instructed to coerce Julio into writing that letter to provoke my rage. I had fallen for the trap. I had sent an email to my boss with an extremely angry tone telling him I was going to be making some changes if certain employees were unhappy with their job.

Lori drove me to the store that day to pick up my paycheck. When I left, Ana followed me to Lori's car. Lori witnessed the entire following conversation as she was sitting in the car.

Ana asked me what was wrong.

"I want to know who told Julio to write that bullshit to cause trouble," I exclaimed.

At first, Ana played dumb and then said, "I'm sorry, I have to worry about my kids." Was this a defensive response indicating that her family had been threatened?

My response was, "I have a daughter too. What does that have to do with writing some bullshit to the boss?"

I got in the car, and Lori drove away. An hour later, my boss called me and said Ana had filed a complaint claiming that I had screamed at her in the parking lot and she was now afraid to work with me.

I couldn't believe this was happening. Another woman was telling more lies and causing me more grief. I kept thinking about her remark that she had to worry about her children. She used to bring them to the restaurant, and we played tag and had a lot of fun. Then a disturbing realization hit me. A complex plot had been unfolding for a long time. It began when I was banned from seeing my daughter and couldn't even talk to her on the phone. Then my email account went under federal investigation— for what? The last time I was in front of the masters in court to get Gena to let me see my daughter, the master asked Gena if she'd consider supervised visitation. When I asked about why I would need supervision, the master had said, "You definitely need supervision."

I suddenly saw an extravagant but cohesive program that involved the entire community at large, including authorities. These were not random tactics to harass me, but instead was being set up as a pedophile. The entire scenario made so much sense I immediately got sick to my stomach.

In any event, Ana Shamey's charge that she was afraid to work with me gave my boss no option but to let me go. Lori was there the entire time and heard the conversation. Not once did I ever raise my voice or say anything threatening. Lori wanted to beat the hell out of Ana for being such a liar, but it wouldn't have done any good.

That night, I went to Monocacy, a beautiful park down the road. It's the peaceful, magical place where much of this story had been written. I walked down a small path where there is an entrance to a cave. I sat in front of the opening, as if the spirits of the past were trying to communicate with me. I stared into the darkness and asked for help. I didn't hear anything, but I was able to let my anger go and accept what I had to do next—look for another job. The story of my life.

On my way back, I noticed a hand towel neatly draped on a branch. It had not been there when I was walking in. On the towel was a snowman with the phrase, "Everyone deserves a meltdown."

It's very disturbing to know with certainty that you are under constant 24/7 surveillance and that countless people are attacking you with psychological warfare. Again, however, I refused to give up.

I found two job opportunities. One was an all-commission sales job to estimate and sell contracts to fix water-damage issues. I was already an expert, and I knew I could use this opportunity to help save other people from the dangers of mold and water-damaged buildings. But I was terrified about putting myself at risk again in damaged buildings.

I decided to take the second job driving a bus for Best Coach. I would be transporting mentally ill and disabled persons around the Lehigh Valley. The job didn't pay so well, but I knew that driving around all day would make it hard for the handlers to sabotage my job or target my health and sanity with electronic devices. Well, I couldn't have been more wrong.

Chapter 26

Cruel and Unusual Punishment

Bus drivers must pass a drug screen to be hired and then pass random drug testing to stay employed. I was working sixty-five hours a week, so obviously, I wasn't an addict, even though undercover cops and federal agents continually harassed me. I believed I was being investigated for some stuff that was worse than drugs. I suppose the fact that I didn't give up and got another job, really started to get on "their" nerves.

I was on the road thirteen hours a day, driving hundreds of miles. I witnessed hundreds, maybe thousands, of stalking vehicles. The most prevalent were black-and-white pickup trucks. However, I also saw an abundance of Mercedes, Jeeps and Range Rovers.

In addition to the trucks, I was primed with the same symbols continuously. State University, Pukes Hospital and Happy Place were the most prevalent brands. I knew I was in serious trouble when I started to see Army, Marines and Air Force symbols. What had I done to make the military want to execute me?

In the all-black Suburban government vehicles, most of the drivers were women. They would pull out in front of me, cut me off, or jam their brakes in front of me. On one trip, I had a full bus of mentally and physically disabled passengers, and these women drivers were trying to cause an accident, which shows some heartlessness for the safety of the passengers.

I tried everything to ignore the constant psychological attacks. After a few days of trucks swarming me at every location, I began to see Mercedes and Discovery vehicles at every turn as well. Imagine trying to follow the GPS while evil people are trying to make you swerve or brake. How much money was being wasted on trying to break my mind? And why?

In addition to the vehicles, I saw a priming symbol at every turn as well. I saw the red lips, which I assumed represented women's rights. I saw the blue and yellow equals symbol (=) and the rainbow symbol for gay pride. A small Puerto Rican flag and a dream catcher hanging in the mirror were popular priming symbols. The point was to make sure I saw these symbols and cars everywhere, so I'd be aware of and overwhelmed by the stalking.

For people not being stalked or primed, three black trucks stopped at a red light were just a random coincidence. Until sensitized to these vehicles, they were virtually unseen by other folks. The unstalked drivers would never recognize that I was surrounded by a Mercedes in front of me, alongside me, and behind me.

This whole program was both stupid and ingenious. Before long, I was seeing numerous FedEx trucks, box vans and white vans. Even post-office workers tried to pull in front of me, making me swerve. You can imagine why I had been diagnosed as mentally ill. I understand too. Having a target categorized as paranoid or schizophrenic is a main goal of the program.

By this time, I'd been conditioned to notice everything, even driver hand signals. I noted that 70 percent of the priming vehicles were driven by women and that bright-yellow shirts had been introduced into my program. I observed that the perps had begun to wear skintight jeans. The most frequent state license plates were Florida and New York. Normal people might notice one or two Vacation Club stickers on a trip, but I'd see scores of them. I often saw twenty Happy Place mouse symbols per hour. White and black pickups are very common but having two or three around you always is disturbing.

To make this priming even more frightening, my conditioning caused me to see and understand license plate messages. I saw black "DARE" license plates all day long. Yes, I had used methamphetamines for a time, but couldn't these idiots see I was driving a bus that required federally mandated drug screens?

I saw "KLL" on license plates so often it couldn't have been a coincidence. I learned that this meant I was being killed. "KLC" meant I was being killed with cancer. Then I started seeing even more disturbing messages that I didn't even want to think about—"KSX" and "KIDY." The conditioning process put those messages into my mind dozens of times every hour. Eventually, I started to figure them out.

Parents and passengers started writing into the company, thanking me for being so kind and helpful. For each written compliment received, the company gave me a gift card for five bucks. I was thrilled with the free coffee it paid for, but even more excited to compile them as proof for the judge that would be ruling on my visitation privileges with Lala.

I still was not allowed to speak to Lala. I was getting praise for taking such good care of other people's kids, but I couldn't have a conversation with my own child. If I sent Lala a birthday card, I could be sent to jail. Everyone was saying how wonderful I was, but my wife had been coerced to say that she was afraid of me, and so was Ana Shamey, my own assistant manager at Big Foody's. It was very clear to me now that they were using the same plays with different people. Were they just following some sadistic playbook?

Since I was having success in my job despite the targeting activity, the handlers stepped up their game. One day on the bus, I picked up a guy in a wheelchair along with his young nurse. The entire trip, the guy talked to me about assorted things. Then he asked me to write down his phone number so we could get together and watch sports sometime. He wouldn't let up on this. He and the nurse were the only passengers, so there were no witnesses to his persistence.

For a moment, I thought about switching on the camera, so I had some proof, but I didn't. I figured that would play into the whole paranoia plot. When I pulled up to his drop-off, I finally gave in and wrote his name and number down on the company-run list. For the rest of the day, I kept thinking about how my other jobs had been sabotaged, and often by a woman.

That night, when I returned the bus, I decided to write an incident report about how the passenger wouldn't stop asking me to take his number. As my reason for writing the report, I stated, "In the event a fraudulent claim is made to the company about asking for a nurse's telephone number, I am writing this statement to protect myself."

My intuition was perfect! The man in the wheelchair had given me the number for the nurse, and a claim was filed with the company claiming that I was hitting on his nurse and asking for her number. If I hadn't written that report, I would have been fired or suspended for sexual harassment. I'm not sure if the guy was refused future service from the company, but I never saw him again.

While on the road for thirteen hours a day, I made a painful discovery about these vehicular surges. The army of vehicles was not just to drive me crazy—some of the vehicles were equipped with directed-energy weapons, radiation guns and sprayers connected to the tailpipes that could blow out mists of bioweapons.

One day, while following a black truck. I saw the driver's hand rise and press a button on his visor. Immediately, a stream of fluid shot out from the tailpipe. It looked almost like a stream of water from a squirt gun. I thought this must have been a malfunction of some kind because the driver, apparently detecting the issue, quickly turned the wrong way down a one-way road. Whatever chemical had been discharged from that truck, my busload of passengers was in harm's way—not just me.

I continued to build up my email distribution list of contacts to alert about new developments in my targeting. Unfortunately, many of the local cops, FBI personnel, the morning-call newspaper and others blocked me after a while, but that didn't stop me from publicizing the evil torture I was enduring.

One night while I was home with Lori, we saw flashing lights through the kitchen window. Outside, a vehicle had been pulled over by the police on Linden Street. It seemed like a routine stop. But then six other squads and two unmarked cars arrived, which seemed excessive for a traffic stop. The driver was pulled from his car, violently choking and gagging. *Probably smoking pot*, I thought. But the guy didn't stop coughing, and he was putting his head to his knees in pain. I remembered how I thought I was sprayed at the Dollar Store, an episode I related earlier. I had bent down to my knees too and was coughing. I even told Lori that eight cars for one guy was very strange.

I watched several officers flipping through the pages of a document. It was too far away to see what the document was and left to speculate with my newly acquired magical intuition. Oddly, the police never searched the car, the guy never stopped coughing, and an hour later, the cops just let the guy leave.

I remembered a black truck that had squirted liquid from the rear and then suddenly turned the wrong way down a one-way street. I thought about how Cracie had mentioned that I was being poisoned and about my own pain from those agonizing sinus issues. I also thought about all the priming vehicles I witnessed every day, and how my bartenders and I had confirmed that we had undercover federal agents sitting at the bar.

What if this pulled-over vehicle was equipped with a bioweapon that was instructed to spray out something harmful when he drove by our apartment? What if that spray mechanism had malfunctioned, causing the bioweapon to seep into his vehicle and set off a violent coughing attack? What if the document the police were reading gave this guy the executive authority to spray the chemical, which was why they let him leave?

I will never know the truth, but this driver had been pulled over near my domicile and surrounded by eight police cars—an overpowering show of force—and I knew that coincidences no longer existed in my life.

I am not technical enough to understand the surveillance technology they were using, but somehow, they knew that I was suspecting the use of bioweapons. While driving the next day, I became aware of a physical reaction on my left side. My head ached, and my left sinus down to my lung was smothered in a gluey silicone-like substance that was so irritating I could barely stand it. I used straws and spoons to scrape out this gluey gel, reaching up to my sinuses through the back of my throat. You can just imagine how this made me look. This scraping gave me enough relief to get through the day.

The sudden onset of this thick, suffocating glue started about the same time that trucks and vans began surrounding my bus, so I wondered if those vehicles were poisoning me. The drivers, scores of them, would boldly point their cell phones at me while driving, and shortly thereafter, I would get an instant tingling in my left temple, which seemed to precipitate the production of the gluey gel that was so agonizing.

I believe the handlers wanted me to know I was being attacked by cell phones. How could I communicate my concerns, though, without looking like a paranoid fool?

Since I was pushing through and doing well, these criminals once again stepped up their game by adjusting the dashcam on my bus to the highest level of sensitivity. The dashcam was meant to record accidents or any type of sudden movement to help with training and liability. My dashcam started to go off with every little bump, and I started getting in trouble.

I was reprimanded for my posture while driving or not having both hands on the wheel—all sorts of minor issues. I suppose the handlers hoped I would act out, but I didn't. Eventually, I had the mechanic look at the dashcam, and he confirmed someone had tampered with the settings.

The next series of sabotaged events was mechanical. On two separate occasions, my alternator belt was sliced halfway through the belt. This was clever because this sabotage allows you to drive for a while until the pressure tears through the rest of the belt and power is lost.

The first time, I picked up all my riders, including two wheelchairs, and the belt snapped during morning rush hour on a highway with a narrow shoulder. I needed to pull back onto the right lane of a busy two-lane highway just to get the kids off the bus. What kind of sadistic criminals would go out of their way to jeopardize the safety of mentally challenged kids in wheelchairs?

The second mechanical sabotage was transmission tampering on a very hot day. Because of the heat, I had to take six autistic children off the bus and sit in a parking lot under some shade until a new bus arrived. A few of these children suffered from involuntary mannerisms. Can you begin to understand my stress level in trying to keep my composure while keeping these children safe until the next bus arrived? These attempts to break me only made me stronger.

At one of our quarterly company meetings, we had a guest speaker, our new director of safety. I didn't think anything of it when Dick Fason introduced himself and gave his personal background. He'd been a homicide detective for seventeen years with a police department in New Jersey and had a son who was active military. This caught my attention because I was being bombarded with priming symbols for the Marines, Air Force, Army and retired vets. This was no coincidence—this was psychological warfare. It was also no coincidental that "Fason," was the last name of my old girlfriend, Mandy. Just hearing the new safety director's last name made me start thinking of reasons this was happening. This was gaslighting at its best.

Dick Fason's safety topic for the meeting sent shivers down my spine—what to look for when it came to "mass shooters." He warned the company to be on the lookout for people who complain about being followed or stalked. "These people are mentally ill and dangerous," he said.

I couldn't believe my damn ears. I melted into my seat.

Fason said that people who appear anxious or depressed should be red flags. "Stay away from them," he instructed the team, "and report them to the company to keep everyone safe." Our so-called new safety director also warned the team about personal hygiene and appearance. I started to stroke my beard as I hadn't shaved in weeks. Clearly, he was trying to trigger a response from me.

Shortly after that safety meeting, I was sent to pick up an autistic man at 401 Hamilton Street, which was FBI headquarters— the same place where I had seen the state cop I knew speaking to two guys in black suits. The FBI had a program for mentally disabled people to work part-time.

The guy I took home was a nice man, but he was on his cell phone the entire time, and the tingling sensation in my head grew worse. I just kept it to myself. Dick Fason, Director of Safety, had warned the entire company about people like me.

A few times, I tried taking my lunch break at my parents' house. After a few minutes, though, I experienced unbearable pain and dizziness, so I sat outside. Each time—and I mean every day I sat outside there—I was greeted by a large American flag flapping on the back of a vehicle, usually a Jeep, motorcycle or truck. And not just a little flag—I'm talking about a four-by-eight-foot flag flapping in the wind.

I knew my parents' house had been wired up like a movie set early on. Gena had given that away when I was outside on the front porch one day talking to her. This was when Lala could spend time with me. She was watching TV in the living room, and my parents were on the back porch. Gena suddenly complained over the phone that I shouldn't leave Lala alone in the living room. She was an hour away, so the only way she would know Lala was in the living room would be looking at video transmitted by cameras in the living room.

Lori's house was set up the same way. One day, Lori and I came home unexpectedly and discovered that someone had broken into her apartment. We pulled up, and there was a strange bike leaning against the tree out front. When we walked in, Abby the dog was locked in her room, which we never did. We saw papers scattered around and immediately called the Bethlehem Police.

The odd thing was, someone had broken into the apartment, but nothing was taken. The computer, TVs, jewelry and other things of value were still present. The intruder, however, had taken the time to rummage through paperwork, go through underwear drawers and do other weird shit.

When the police arrived, one of them pulled me into the kitchen and asked, "Why did you do this?"

"That would be a neat trick," I replied, "since I was with Lori the entire day." I wasn't surprised that he had accused me. I was a targeted individual.

I think we had surprised the intruders because a pair of earphones was left on the floor, probably dropped in a frantic rush to depart. The Bethlehem Police did DNA testing of some objects, which led to the arrest of a man named Brice Bocci, who was likely the guy hired to install bugs, cams and other devices.

To give a little more credibility to my intuition, one day I called a company about finding devices in homes and cars. This firm would come out with detection equipment, and if a device was found, the company would trace it back to where it came from. When I tried calling the owner, my phone shut off. When I called back, the call was dropped. Finally, I used Lori's phone, and the call went through. Clearly, someone didn't want me to have that conversation. I learned that this service is very expensive.

One morning, I arrived at work and was barely functional. I had serious sinus disease at this point, with total obstruction of both airways. The congestion alone was maddening but add the constant pain and dizzy spells, and it made it very hard to drive. Somehow, I just kept going like I had an Energizer Bunny stuck up my ass.

I started to take my breaks in a park away from all traffic and people. Again, I kid you not, I saw freaking drones flying over my head. One was in the shape of an airplane with wings, but the rest were circular in shape, and I could hear the buzzing from the propellers. What the hell was going on? I can only assume I was being poisoned because my symptoms just progressed.

One day I was trying to wake up and struggled through the morning routine of checking oil, tire pressure, et cetera. As I stumbled around the bus checking the tires, I noticed an oil stain on the cement by the driver's door. The dimensions and shape were too perfect to be a coincidence—it was the unmistakable shape of a famous cartoon mouse.

My sinus pain got so bad I had to leave work and see a doctor, who diagnosed a sinus infection. I mentioned that I believed I was being poisoned and showed him the text message from Cracie admitting that poison was being put in my car. Predictably, the doctor paid no attention and referred me to a psychiatrist. I never went, of course.

I returned with the doctor's note and assumed I would just go back to work as normal. I was told to report to the main office, where I was told that I needed another physical exam before returning to work. I found it odd that I needed another department of transportation physical.

When I spoke to the second doctor, it became clear that Mr. Dick Fason, Director of Security, had intervened. The doctor said that in my medical record was a psychiatric referral with a question about medication for mental illness. This doctor refused to allow me back to work until I went to the psychiatrist. They got me again, but this time, they had to turn doctors into conspirators.

So here I was again, faced with a very familiar dilemma. I had been terminated from another job and wound up with no income. I knew I would have to play this game a little differently and perhaps make up some of my own rules.

I was no longer fighting to get healthy. I wasn't just fighting to pay support and stay out of jail. I was now fighting for my right to live.

Chapter 27

Good Old Uncle Sammy

I decided to seek a job at a family restaurant near my parents' house. My uncle had done work for them in the past, and they knew my family well. I needed an employer that new our family to help defend against future sabotage. I started working a few days later, and although I was in excruciating pain, I quickly became an asset. I knew, however, that it was only a matter of time before the handlers started to mess with this job as well.

I needed to start thinking long-term and start trying to set up the next opportunity. A coworker, who was also a CNA at a nursing home, told me about the job requirements for becoming a nurse's assistant. To begin, a candidate had to pass a state physical to ensure they were physically and mentally fit to do the job.

An idea struck me like a lightning bolt, and the resulting plan would begin by actively starting the process to see a psychiatrist. The preliminary intake process would take a few weeks and involved working with a counselor and speaking nothing but the truth.

I explained to the counselor how I got sick from mold and how my life had been destroyed by the criminal actions of Don Darkino. I admitted to injecting myself with amphetamines, trying to keep myself employable. I confessed to acting like an idiot at Happy Place. Then I mentioned the stalking, psychological warfare, employment sabotage, poisonings, honey traps, and the 24/7 surveillance and intimidation.

I laughed when my counselor suggested I drive to Florida and apologize to Happy Place in person. I described the no-trespass order and how I felt like I was under a spell, which I learned later was a mind-control methodology called MKUltra. I spoke nothing but the truth and included every detail, even that I believed I'd been implanted.

I was making decent money at the restaurant, but two waitresses were coerced to sabotage me, like so many other people in my life. This was why I had already applied for the CNA position at the nursing home. I went through the background check, got my tetanus booster, had a flu shot, and got an appointment for the on-the-job work physical with my family physician, Dr. Rover.

Finally, I saw the psychiatrist, Dr. Azhal. He had read my file and asked me about some of the salient points.

"I am being stalked and followed everywhere I travel," I explained. After he asked a few more questions, he immediately labeled me a paranoid schizophrenic with delusions. He told me that people don't get implanted without their knowledge or consent. It seems he really didn't know what was going on in this sick world.

I chose to keep the case of *Richard Cain v. DOD* to myself. Cain had been awarded eight million dollars for nonconsensual RFID implants discovered in him and his two kids, a direct rebuttal to Azhal's naïve belief.

As planned, by being totally honest, I received a diagnosis and all kinds of prescriptions for some heavy-duty psychotropic drugs. The most significant side effect of these drugs is suicidal tendencies. Remember, now, a major goal of targeting is suicide. Let that irony marinate for a minute.

Step one of my plan had been completed—I had a psychiatrist diagnose me as a paranoid schizophrenic. Now I needed one more piece for my puzzle to be complete.

I kept my appointment with Dr. Rover for my return-to-work physical exam. My handlers' goal was to prevent me from getting a steady, good-paying job, so I discuss out loud my new job opportunity at the nursing home. The hidden microphones in the doctor's office would transmit that news. Later, I mentioned to my parents in their wired-up house that the pay was great, and the benefits were amazing.

I never really wanted the job in the nursing home, and I knew I would never be cleared by Dr. Rover to return to work. And I was right. The doctor refused to clear me for psychiatric reasons, so my handlers must have celebrated another small disruption in my life. But I had a major victory waiting just ahead.

With a diagnosis from a psychiatrist plus written documentation from another doctor who would not allow me to work, I filed for social security disability benefits again—this time because of paranoid schizophrenia. On the application, I wrote very bluntly, "If I cannot work, I cannot pay support. If I don't pay support, I go to jail. The doctor won't allow me to work. What do you want me to do?"

Within a few weeks, I was approved for SSDI. Honestly, I tried to work—I don't want to live off the state. But at every step, I was sabotaged. I am now getting paid by Uncle Sam to help me fight an invisible war against Uncle Sam.

I sent an email to the FBI telling them to either quit playing games and allow me to work or allow Uncle Sam to pay me for the rest of my life. Once again, I was being totally honest.

To celebrate this victory, Lori and I went to see a band at the casino. I was a bit obnoxious and said hello and gave loving hugs to some of the cocktail waitresses who missed me. As I walked back to the show, I was followed by five security guards. Suddenly, they stopped me and said I needed to leave the casino. They didn't give me a reason. I wasn't intoxicated, but I think the innocent hugs I gave to a few old friends must have rubbed someone the wrong way.

A few days later, I was shocked when I got a court order from the casino stating that I had a no-trespass order and was not allowed anywhere on the property. What the hell! First, I was blacklisted from Happy Place. Then I was told I couldn't come back into Big Foody's even as a patron because people were afraid of me. Now I was blacklisted from the casino.

I figured that preventing me from having fun at familiar places was part of the plan to destroy my life. After landing some secure income, though, these little psychological attacks didn't bother me as much.

For the first time in six years, I no longer had to worry about going to jail. I no longer had to worry about having my employment sabotaged. But it had been over three years since I had hugged my daughter and two years since I'd personally told her over the phone that I loved her.

Lala, I am writing this so you will know that I've been fighting for you ever since I saved you from that mold-infested house. I love you and miss you so badly it hurts. This longing for my daughter gave me the courage to execute the next part of my plan.

I wrote a letter listing all of Don Darkino's criminal charges and made a few copies. I also included all the crimes he had committed that the FBI refused to investigate, the police report from the death of J. Cazonaro, the multi-million-dollar insurance fraud executed on the County Playhouse, and how Don had made his own daughter commit perjury. These letters were mailed to the police, the FBI, and all of Don Darkino's neighbors.

The neighbors showed Don the letter, and he coerced Gena, his daughter, into filing a PFA stating that I had strangled Gena. Every time this scumbag made Gena file a new perjured PFA, the story changed. Nevertheless, I received a contempt order in the mail for violating a previous PFA. Once again, I was at risk of going to jail.

Or maybe not.

In reality, I had not violated any PFA. Just because I, as a good Samaritan, informed the community that Don Darkino was a dangerous Mafia scumbag, doesn't mean I violated an existing PFA. I hadn't contacted the Darkino family. Someone, however, really wanted me in jail. I knew I needed help.

There was no way I was allowing Steven Moore to represent me. Even though my parents thought I was being paranoid, my intuition told me he was contracted to take me down. But I would need cash to retain a new lawyer. Some say, "Everything happens for a reason." I knew there were angels on my shoulder, helping me through this torture.

I decided to ask Louie, one of the Family Restaurant owners, for a loan and explained my situation. I think he helped out because he didn't want to lose me. He agreed to give me $1,500 to be paid back when I could.

I compiled a list of attorneys and made an appointment with Saul Slang. I filled him in and gave him the entire loan. Immediately, Gena's attorney filed a motion to prevent Saul from representing me based on a conflict of interest. It turns out that Gena had contacted Saul a while back about the marital property but never retained his services. Saul got the ridiculous motion dismissed and accepted my retainer.

To make the situation more interesting, Steven Moore started calling me repeatedly like an old prom date. He had never bothered following up with me before, but now he was all over me after learning I had new counsel.

I don't think my handlers ever thought I would be able to legally round up enough cash to retain a new attorney. I don't think my handlers ever expected me to be smart enough to figure out Steven Moore was a setup.

Even though I was approved for SSDI, it took a few months for the checks to start, which was why I really needed the loan. At the contempt hearing, Saul got played a little and didn't realize what was happening. I was hoping for an outright dismissal, but Saul negotiated removal of the contempt complaint in exchange for a new PFA that extended for another year. Saul told me it was worth it. He didn't know how the judge would rule, so this compromise meant I absolutely would see no jail time.

Another year without seeing my daughter! I was so angry and emotionally destroyed my parents had to calm me down. Even as I write this, the pain of missing my daughter is causing me to break down in tears.

Over the next few weeks, the supplemental social security came in, and with that check—combined with some help from my parents—we were able to retain Saul to handle the support obligation, the divorce and the custody. I swear to God, Saul did more for me in one day than Steven Moore did in two years. In a support hearing, Saul not only settled on a reasonable support payment, but he got the entire arrears eliminated.

My divorce was a simple no-fault divorce, yet the Darkinos had dragged it out for nearly seven years. How is this possible? For what purpose? I believe Don was afraid I would file for a disclosure of assets and go after half of the money he'd laundered in Gena's name. Another possibility was games he had been playing with life insurance or viatical settlements. At any rate, Saul was able to finally start finalizing the pending divorce.

I began doing internet searches and not only found many answers about targeting, but also found an entire community of Targeted Individuals going through the same shit I was experiencing—not just in the USA, but also in Canada, Australia and England. I ask you, how can a woman in England be experiencing the exact same stalking, harassment and poisoning that I am dealing with every day in the United States? God willing, if I am still alive to write my second book, I will discuss so much more.

Chapter 28

The Gangstalking Playbook

This chapter provides a well-written manual from one of the targeted individual groups that I have joined. This playbook provides a very good description of this entire COINTELPRO (COunter IN-TELligence PROgram) endeavor.

No matter in which state, country or continent a targeted individual is located, that person is attacked with the same evil tactics using this vile playbook. As you read through this organized stalking manual, please recall certain events that I have written about so far in my story. Reading this manual will remind you of the various intimidation and harassment tactics I have reported in this book and may convince you my reports are not the product of a delusional or paranoid schizophrenic individual.

Organized gangstalking: What you need to know

Organized gangstalking—also known as gang stalking, cause stalking, organized vigilante stalking, stalking by proxy, community-based harassment, and covert war—is essentially harassment and discrediting campaigns waged against a targeted individual. Citizens and neighbors are recruited to participate, often from extremist groups and cults, but also from employees. Coordinated psychological warfare attacks, consisting of stalking, noise campaigns, sensitizing, and the spreading of lies and rumors, are executed in an effort to virtually neutralize and destroy the victim, using people from all backgrounds and vocations to harass and track 24/7, sometimes organizing lethal vehicle accidents, poisonings, electronic harassment, home invasions / property destruction, corrupt or ignorant doctor diagnosis given to stamp the victim as bogus mentally ill with delusions, paranoia, schizophrenia, et cetera.

Everything is done covertly, using a sophisticated, real-time dispatching system to organize the criminals' harassment and attacks, often in the hundreds to thousands of criminals participating as a coordinated mob at any given time while the criminals do their normal routines of work, shopping, commuting to and from work, leisure, etc., using the method of moving foot and vehicular surveillance techniques, and computers, cell phones, verbal and visual cues, and every other conceivable type of communication.

Often, the local network of this mob is connected to a national and international network. When the target travels, the local network will follow the target to the next city or town. When the target arrives there, the networking in that location will stalk, follow, and harass the target in that city or town. Organized gangstalking, also known as organized stalking, community harassment, or community stalking, is a systemic form of control that seeks to destroy every aspect of a targeted individual's life.

Using occupational health and safety laws, warning markers can be added to a target's file. Once a target is flagged, a notification is sent out and the target is followed around 24/7 by the various communities that they are in. A covert investigation may be opened, and electronic means may be used by the civilian spies as part of the covert monitoring and surveillance process. The citizen informants can be parts of these community-oriented programs but are often just average citizens. Everyone in the target's life is contacted, advised as to why the individual has been listed or flagged, advised not to discuss the notification, and asked to be a part of the ongoing, never-ending monitoring (systemic harassment) process.

This process is covertly designed to destroy the target over time, leaving them with no form of support. Since most civil workers are aware of this notification system, it means that targets reporting incidents of being followed around by various strangers should not have been unfamiliar to the police and other agencies that targets reported their harassment to. In most cities, this notification is well-known and used by many workers and employers. Yet targeted individuals have had to have mental health evaluations for making complaints about this structure and the harassment that comes with it.

Organized gangstalking is experienced by the targeted individual as a psychological attack that is capable of immobilizing and destroying them over time. The covert methods used to harass, persecute, and falsely defame the targets often leave no evidence to incriminate the civilian spies. It's like workplace mobbing but takes place outside in the community. It's called organized gangstalking because organized groups or community members stalk and monitor the targets 24/7. (See gang stalking, organized stalking.)

Questions and answers

Does the word *gang*, as in *gangstalking*, refer to street gangs?

No. The word *gang* refers to multiple people who organize/group together for a common purpose.

What is the difference between *stalking* by a single perpetrator and organized gang stalking?

All forms of stalking are physically, emotionally, and psychologically harmful to the victim. With regards to gang stalking, the abuse is particularly invasive, as the victim is not able to distinguish friend from foe. Most of the population is aware of cases such as "jilted lover as stalker" and can readily identify key features of such abuse. The little-known phenomena of organized gang stalking allow the perpetrators anonymity and enables future victimizations, as stalkers are encouraged by the lack of repercussions. Please keep in mind that victims of organized gang stalking must deal with an abuse engineered

to make them appear insane should they complain to authorities. It is no wonder that victims of organized gang stalking
are far more likely to commit suicide than victims of individual
stalkers.

Is organized gangstalking illegal?

Yes! Despite what the leaders or members of stalking and
harassment groups say or believe, all forms of stalking and
harassment are illegal.

Stalking: Definition

Stalking can be defined as a pattern of repeated and unwant-
ed attention, harassment, contact, or any other course of
conduct directed at a specific person that would cause a reasonable person to feel fear. Stalking is against the law in every
state. Stalking across state lines or in federal territories is illegal under federal law. It is a willful course of conduct involving
repeated or continuing harassment of another individual that
would cause a reasonable person to feel terrorized, frightened, intimidated, threatened, harassed, or molested and
that actually causes the victim to feel terrorized, frightened,
intimidated, threatened, harassed, or molested. A person
who intentionally and repeatedly follows or harasses another
person and who makes a credible threat, either expressed or
implied, with the intent to place that person in reasonable
fear of death or serious bodily harm is guilty of the crime of
stalking.

Harassment: Definition

Harassment means conduct directed toward a victim that
includes, but is not limited to, repeated or continuing uncon-
sented contact that would cause a reasonable individual to
suffer emotional distress and that causes the victim to suffer
emotional distress.

FBI Title 18, USC, Section 241: Conspiracy Against Rights

This statute makes it unlawful for two or more persons to

conspire to injure, oppress, threaten, or intimidate any person of any state, territory or district in the free exercise or enjoyment of any right or privilege secured to him/ her by the Constitution or the laws of the United States, (or because of his/her having exercised the same). It further makes it unlawful for two or more persons to go in disguise on the highway or on the premises of another with the intent to prevent or hinder his/her free exercise or enjoyment of any rights so secured. Punishment varies from a fine or imprisonment of up to ten years, or both; and if death results, or if such acts include kidnapping or an attempt to kidnap, aggravated sexual abuse or an attempt to commit aggravated sexual abuse, or an attempt to kill, shall be fined under this title or imprisoned for any term of years, or for life, or may be sentenced to death.

The goal of organized gangstalking

The expressed goal of organized gangstalking is to silence a victim, drive a victim insane, and possibly to the point of suicide, or destroy the victim's reputation and believable responses, as the person will likely be viewed as mentally ill should they complain or report the abuse. To cause the target to appear mentally unstable is one, and this is achieved through a carefully detailed assault using advanced psychological harassment techniques and a variety of other tactics that are the usual protocol for gangstalking, such as street theater, mobbing, and pervasive petty disrespecting. Organized gangstalking is also used to gather information on individuals as well as force individuals to move or leave an area.

Do the stalkers ever question or check to see if a targeted victim is indeed guilty of a crime? No. There is an assumption of guilt among the stalkers. Also, remember that many stalkers are paid for their harassment, so these individuals are not concerned with the innocence or guilt of a victim.

Assuming a victim knows the group that is behind their stalking, should they attempt to openly communicate with them? Absolutely not! For one, the stalkers automatically assume the victim is guilty of an atrocity and thus "deserves" the treatment. Second, many stalkers want the victim to engage them in some fashion. In these instances, the interaction will be recorded and used as evidence against the victim, especially in attempts to suggest the victim is mentally unstable.

[AUTHOR'S NOTE: If a charitable and respectable society practices organized gangstalking on the side, should we assume the victims deserve such treatment? Absolutely not! When people take the law into their own hands, any notion of "law" is destroyed altogether. I should emphasize that most organized gang stalking victims are completely innocent of any crimes. Any group that performs organized gangstalking is not positive in nature, or beneficial to society, despite any charitable works they may perform. Likewise, such societies only remain "respectable" because any and all evidence of wrongdoing is conveniently destroyed or eliminated.]

Motivations for the abuse

Motivations for organized gangstalking vary. Revenge for a real or imagined offense, true or false accusations of a "horrible crime" with which the victim has gotten away, silencing a corporate whistle-blower, defecting from a cult, a perceived enemy of a group or organization, and "knowing too much" are all examples of possible motivations. Due consideration should be used as the motivations of the stalking, and harassment groups are in no way limited to the above.

Who are the stalkers?

The stalkers, for the most part, are everyday citizens. Other stalkers are "street thugs" who have been recruited or hired to harass and intimidate. Some stalkers are actual private investigators who have been hired to gather information concerning the victim. Many stalkers are members of volunteer police groups.

Why people participate in gangstalking

Some stalkers are told lies, either positive or negative in nature, in order to gain their participation. Some stalkers are paid or receive other benefits. Stalkers belonging to an organization may simply be following orders. Some stalkers may use their participation in order to repay a past favor. Racism, prejudice, homophobia, or otherwise. Hatred of a victim, peer pressure/need to fit in. Former stalkers have stated they participated out of fear of becoming the next target should they go against the group. Entertainment value/thrill of participation in an illegal activity. Some stalkers mistakenly believe it is their civil duty.

Who, or what, is ultimately behind gangstalking?

Corporations, government organizations, Military/Air Force, some police, corrupt cops, societies/fraternities/orders, religious cults and destructive new age groups, "concerned" community groups/vigilante groups, criminal organizations, volunteer police organizations, etc.

Examples of organized gangstalking harassment

Slashed tires; threatening phone calls; verbal assaults by strangers; property damage; death threats; being followed on foot or by vehicle; bizarre notes and drawings left; loitering; anonymous false accusations to friends, family, and neighbors; character assassination; smear campaigns; blacklisting; psychological abuse; etc.

Tactics and methods used by these organized gang and stalking and harassment groups

The following techniques are several types that are often used against targeted individuals. There are other techniques used, but these are some of the primary ones.

Anchoring

Anchoring is a technique employed by stalkers to implant a false motivation or reason behind the stalking, preventing the victim from discovering the truth. In more sinister examples, anchoring involves the implantation of evidence to persuade the victim some other group or organization is responsible for the abuse (*anchoring*, https://en.wikipedia.org/wiki/Anchoring). In organized gangstalking, anchoring is used to make the target have fear with things happening in their daily life that's considered to be normal. That can be done with frequent demonstrations. The key is the frequency, just like in other organized gangstalking methods. For example, people show you a pen everywhere you go, and their attitude is rude or crazy against you. You don't know them. You just wonder what's going on. Imagine that happens every day for a week, for a month, for a year, then that makes you have fear with a pen. In this case, a pen is *anchored* with your state of fear. It can be anything. An open car door or trunk, a pencil, a cell phone, a notebook computer, a medical mask, clothes of the same color, anything.

Air Stalking

This is when helicopters or planes are used to track targets that are on foot or in cars. They fly overhead and follow the targets from one location to the next. Some will monitor the targets shortly after they leave their homes.

Baiting/Entrapment

The term *baiting* is a stalking tactic used to lure a victim into environments, or situations, that cause further problems to the victim. Often, *baiting* involves tricking a victim into committing a crime or unknowingly engaging in an illegal activity. To lure into dangerous, difficult, or compromising situations. Members of these organized stalking and harassment groups will try to lure targets into various situations for the sole purpose of setting them up. Setting up targets could involve getting them arrested, institutionalized, set up on fake sexual harassment charges, drug charges, illegal pornographic materials, etc. Once this happens, it puts targets at risk for entrapment into becoming members themselves.

Brighting

Brighting is shining or flashing bright headlights on targets. As targets walk on the street, usually at night, members of these organized gangstalkings will turn on their high beams. This might be flashed once or twice at targets. This might be used to let targets know they are being watched; however, these signals might also be a way for informants in cars at night to communicate with their fellow counterparts. The foot patrols will then communicate back to the informant in the car using a combination of hand signals. You will see members of these groups riding around during the day with their headlights or high beams on. The victim is usually followed and may be "flashed" from either a tailgating vehicle or a passing or oncoming one. Brighting also occurs when bright lights are flashed into a victim's home windows.

Car Accidents

Targeted individuals complain about being cut off, being driven off the road, and having near-fatal or fatal car accidents. Pedestrian targets complain about cars that consistently cut them off, being hit by cars, and other almost-near mishaps.

Crowding/Mobbing

When the target is in public, members of these organized gangstalking groups will usually try to box the target in. Example, they will surround the target in a square-like formation if possible. They will stand too close to the target or swarm them. Quote: "We experienced being mobbed by vehicles from CT, NY, and NJ at the beginning of our trip. Some of the gangstalkers were couples with their children along! Some smirked at us and showed weapons to us through their windows, though none actually fired upon us."

Color Harassment

Color harassment is literally the use of color to harass a victim. Usually, monochromatic color schemes are used, though this choice is pretty much up to the stalkers. An example of color harassment would be a line of stalkers in red shirts, circling a victim. Color harassment is often combined with other stalking tactics.

Convoy

Convoy is a tactic of stalkers referring to the practice of a group of tailgating cars passing repeatedly in front of the home of the victim. Vehicles used may be of the same color, and stalkers may honk the car horn or flash the car headlights as they pass.

Cyberstalking

Cyberstalking, or cyber harassment, is a related group of harassing behavior occurring via internet/online. Cyberstalking includes, but is not limited to, computer hacking, trolling, spamming (often including "porn deluges"), verbal assaults, character assassination, and impersonations of the victim. Online harassment is part of the harassment protocol. If you have a website devoted to organized stalking, you may have people emailing you to flame you or claiming that they are victims and asking for support with the intention of discrediting you. You may receive unsolicited email that parallels a current event in your life. Again, surveillance is used primarily for harassment. Or you may receive covert insults and threats. If you join a support group, you may also receive harassment via threads posted on message boards. Like in other mediums of harassment, the topics of these threads may be about events that are unfolding in your personal life, as well as threats or insults covertly directed at you. This will probably happen repeatedly by the same person or people. They may also employ some gaslighting or jacketing tactics. Jacketing was often used during COINTELPRO to make genuine activists look like informants. Some internet groups that help stalking victims are heavily populated with perpetrators posing as victims. Some of these perpetrators seem to be very vocal and popular members of these support groups.

Directed Conversations

Directed conversation is a term referring to a stalking tactic using strangers' conversation to both intimidate and to convey to the victim that they are under surveillance. During directed conversation, two or more stalkers will approach near to the target and engage in "normal" conversation with each other. The conversation is purposefully made at a level so that the victim can adequately hear what is being said. During directed conversation, personal information concerning the victim is inserted into the speech and emphasized by the stalkers in a fashion that most nonvictims would not be able to discern as harassment. The purpose of directed conversation is to harass a victim as well as make the victim appear mentally unstable should they attempt to complain about such abuse. These are conversations that complete strangers will have out in public relating to the target and their personal situations. Example, they will repeat things a target said in their home or on the phone. They will drop very personal details into the conversation that could only be related to the target. Example: Member 1 says, "It's a shame Uncle Ed won't be able to come." Member 2 responds, "Yeah, since he died golfing on Saturday." The target will just have learned of a death of a favored uncle (possibly named Ed) while out golfing.

Electronic Harassment

Electronic harassment is the use of technological devices to spy on or cause harm to targeted victims. For example, exposure to a high magnetic field has been shown to induce hallucinations in humans, while exposure to intense microwave radiation induces psychotic episodes and causes brain damage. A frequent form of electronic harassment involves beaming a low frequency "hum" or "tone" into a victim's home or general area. Over time, the exposure causes the victim to lose sleep, become agitated, and suffer the effects of prolonged stress. Such tactics are also being used in cases of hostage situations as well as covert government operations. Electromagnetic weapons and frequencies will be used on a target in their homes. The purpose of using the EMF (electromagnetic frequency) on targets and their belongings is multifaceted. Electronic frequencies can destroy electronic equipment. Electronic frequencies can be used for monitoring and tracking inside the home and at work. It can also be used for purposes of sleep disturbance. When those conducting these covert investigations feel that they have psychologically destroyed the target to where they are near breakdown, they will start to use these weapons. They will also use these weapons if targets are not going along with their harassment protocol.

Fake Credibility Reports

Fake credibility reports are being used to subtly discredit and attack legitimate websites regarding organized gangstalking, including the Gang Stalking World website, under the guise of doing good for the community. (From www.gangstalking-world.com.)

Files

It has been indicated that targets will have warning markers placed against their files. The information is then shared with relatives, storekeepers, friends, and the community at large. The files are usually not left behind, but they are used to prejudice and slander individuals against the target. These files can be used to engender the corporation of friends and associates of the targets. The files might have a picture of the target and information about some alleged crime, incidents, that the target has been flagged for or is under investigation for. The information is usually very convincing and helps to further get targets harassed by those around them.

Gaslighting

Gaslighting is a psychological technique used by members of these groups. The purpose of gaslighting is to make a victim question his or her sanity. Doing little things to try to make the target think that they are going crazy. Gaslighting simply is trying to convince someone that they are crazy or "imagining things." Example: If you mention organized gangstalking to someone who knows about it and they tell you you're crazy or paranoid, they *are* gaslighting you. The term *gaslighting* originates from the 1944 film *Gaslight*. In the movie, the character of Gregory Anton, played by actor Charles Boyer, attempts to drive the character Pauline, played by actress Ingrid Bergman, insane. The term *gaslighting* has come to mean similar actions and behavior as used in the film against a victim. (From 1944 film *Gaslight*, starring Ingrid Bergman, http://en.wikipedia.org/wiki/Gaslight_%281944.)

Ghosting

The term *ghosting* refers to the practice of rearranging, or moving, of a victim's home furniture, lawn decorations, desk decorations at work, etc. The purpose of ghosting is to make a victim question his or her sanity. Ghosting is also designed to make others question the sanity of the victim, especially if the victim attempts to complain of the abuse.

Gestures

This includes hand gestures, such as intentionally touching hand to face or bringing fist or hand to face while around a person being targeted. Arm gestures involve members of these organized stalking and harassment groups repeatedly driving by a targeted victim's location or home and holding their arms out of vehicle windows, usually in an unnatural, awkward, low position. As part of the organized stalking crime, victims are being subjected daily to and psychologically harassed by manipulated individuals participating in this intentional bizarre arm gesture harassment. It is a known fact that the individuals involved in the organized stalking and technological harassment crime syndicate are also involved in criminal racketeering/sexual exploitation/human trafficking operations via the criminal utilization of remote neural monitoring satellite technology, where these criminal individuals are illegally profiting (racketeering) off the technological sexual exploitation of victims.

In some cases, these arm gestures are being utilized as a male masturbation sexual harassment reference that is designed to sexually harass and degrade targeted victims. It should also be importantly noted that female victims also report being harassed in a similar manner by individuals involved in the harassment, by placing their fingers in their mouths while around the victim, which is meant to be a female masturbation reference. The fact is the manipulated individuals in-

volved in the organized stalking crime repeatedly and delib-
erately convey things to victims through symbolic references
and numbers, which is also an attempt to cause targeted victims to falsely appear to be exhibiting signs of paranoid schizophrenia, such as delusions of reference, when victims attempt
to explain that they are being harassed by individuals holding
their arms out of vehicle windows or making other gestures
to them. The arm gesture harassment has been continuously
documented by victims and uploaded to the internet.

Illegal Surveillance

This involves setting up audio and some visual surveillance
of the target, like bugging the target's phone, surveillance in
the target's residence, listening to cell phone and hard line
conversations, hacking into their computers and learning all
about what the target is doing, sites they frequent, or planting
things. This also helps to build a profile of the target, and it's
also used for later psychological attacks against the target via
parroting and directed conversations.

Examples of Illegal Surveillance:

- Illegal criminal electronic monitoring

- Illegal criminal phone and computer taps

- Illegal criminal remote neural monitoring

Mimicry

Mimicry, or mirroring, is a specialized form of harassment in
which the stalkers publicly imitate every movement made by
the victim. This is trying to copy things in a target's life. Leaving when they do. Dressing like they dress. Throwing out the
garbage. Going to the bathroom. Doing whatever the target is
doing. This is all designed to be psychological warfare so that
the target again feels like they are always under observation.

Mobbing

Mobbing is a term that describes group bullying. Of itself,
mobbing is not equated with gangstalking. However, mobbing

may be a tactic used by the perpetrators of gangstalking. (Mobbing, http://en.wikipedia.org/wiki/Mobbing.)

Noise Harassment Campaign

A noise harassment campaign is an orchestrated effort to produce stress in a victim through prolonged exposure to significant noise levels. A noise campaign can range from multiple neighbors routinely playing loud music, individual stalkers with air horns or fireworks, or organized "repair work" that involves a high level of noise. This will include anything from loud vehicles, loud mufflers, doors slamming above you and below you, to hammering intentionally, slamming car doors loudly, loud stereos, stomping at specific times, loud coughing, pots slamming, water running, cupboard doors being slammed, fridge motor running all night, power tools, etc.

Number Harassment

Number harassment is literally the use of numbers to harass a target and victim. This can include the brainwashed members of these cults driving by a victim's home at a certain time, exiting or entering the neighborhood at a certain set time, or performing a harassment task or skit at a certain time of the day or night, for the purpose of harassment to the target and victim. The number harassment may be done in synchronicity with other members of these cults. For example, a member of the cult arrives home at 7:07 in the afternoon, and another member of the cult leaves at 7:07 at the same time. The next morning, one of the same members of the cult leaves home at 7:07, followed by another member of the cult. The individuals that belong to these cults are using local police 10 HAM radio codes to harass and to convey harassment-related themes to the individual being targeted for years at a time.

The only logical explanation that can be drawn as to why these brainwashed cult members are using local police 10 codes to harass other citizens is that they have been deluded into thinking that they are somehow police. The idea behind the number harassment is to get the individual being targeted sensitized to certain numbers so that they can be constantly harassed by the use of these numbers. Most importantly, the members of these cults have already been sensitized, conditioned, and brainwashed to these specific numbers and are constantly looking at their watches and clocks to see what the time is, in case they have a harassment skit or order to perform at a specific time of the day or night that has been passed to them by their criminal leader and organizer via a cell phone text. That's correct. These cult members are actually being given a harassment task and street theater scripts to perform at a certain time of the day for the purpose of harassment to another individual, despite the fact that the individual being targeted can easily document this harassment and cult behavior using a video camera with a date and time stamp and sue the individuals for damages of harassment and emotional distress.

Sensitization

Sensitization is a psychological term referring to the forced association between a stimulus and a corresponding reaction. Members of these groups use sensitization to psychologically abuse a victim. For example, if a stalker constantly harasses a victim while wearing a blue baseball cap, then over time, the victim will begin to believe anyone wearing a blue baseball cap is a stalker and is coming to harass them. This is getting targets sensitive to an everyday stimulus, like colors, patterns, or everyday actions, or red, stripes, pens, whistles, loud coughing, clapping, waves, keys jingling, or Joe being mobbed at work and, as part of that daily mobbing, his coworkers will loudly cough at him every time they harass him, by calling him names like loser, worthless, lame, demented. They will slander him and have others, as they are slandering him, show disgust by glaring and coughing at him. Out in public, they will follow him loudly and obnoxiously cough at him. When he goes to stores, they will get others to do the same. After months or years of this, Joe has become sensitive to this stimulus, and it can be used to harass him without the names and the glaring looks. The association has been formed because of all the other harassment. For example, a girl is sexually assaulted, and a sock is shoved in her mouth during the assault. To keep her quiet or stop her from pressing charges, the assailant, his friends, and his family will follow her around and throw socks in her path, mention it everywhere she goes, and show her their socks every chance they get. She will get the message they are sending. Because of the brutal attack, she, and what's happened after, is now sensitized. Sensitization undoubtedly creates an extreme level of fear in a victim, in direct fulfillment of the intentions of the stalkers. (Sensitization, http://en.wikipedia.org/wiki/Sensitization.)

Street Theater

Street theater is a term used to describe the odd actions and behaviors that stalkers, sometimes neighbors, do in public to rile the victim. Such behavior often borders on the extremely bizarre and is aimed at a blurring of the boundaries between reality and fantasy in the minds of the victims. This is running into people that are acting very unusual or people that are putting on a show or production, known as street theater. For example, this could be as minor as public rudeness or people acting out a harassment skit. There will usually be someone nearby to see how you react to it. This is, again, looking for weakness or reactions. If you show an adverse reaction, they will try to embellish on this and use it against you later. Street theater is harassment skits done by strangers and neighbors who have been "recruited" into these stalking and harassment groups. Examples of street theater include baiting, brighting, color harassment, convoys, directed conversation, ghosting, mimicry, noise campaigns, etc.

Synchronized Harassment Activities

This refers to the synchronized activities done by members of these groups to harass a target, which may include, but is not limited to, neighbors arriving home at the same time or leaving home at the same time or strangers or neighbors leaving or arriving home at the same time. For example, one neighbor leaves his or her house at the same time another neighbor arrives home. Another example, a neighbor arrives home, and at the exact same time, a stranger or pedestrian walks by a target's home. This synchronized activity is one of the main techniques used in harassing a target and is repeated. Another example, a target leaves his or her home at the exact same time a neighbor who has been recruited into the harassment leaves their home, followed by an airplane or helicopter flying overhead. This synchronized harassment will turn into a pattern and may include the use of numbers such as two neighbors arriving home at 3:13 and two other neighbors leaving their home at 3:30, then the same neighbors arriving back home at 3:43. Synchronized harassment activities can be done with almost anything: neighbors arriving/exiting at the same time, aircraft flying overhead as neighbors are leaving or arriving home, harassment telephone calls made to the target's home just as neighbors who have been recruited into the harassment are leaving or arriving. The key to this is timing and frequency. The main motivation behind synchronized harassment activities is, again, that if the target complains about this type of harassment, he or she may be perceived as mentally ill.

How these stalking and harassment groups communicate

Signals and Symbols

Communication happens in several ways. When on the street or in cars patrolling, they use baseball or Stasi-like signals. These include things like tapping the side of the nose or corner of the eye, brushing back the hair three times, the infamous double blink, etc. Members of these organized stalking and harassment groups will also communicate with one another on the street by using signals. Below are some examples.

Signals for Observation

1. Watch out, subject is coming: touch nose with hand or handkerchief.

2. Subject is moving on, going farther, or overtaking: stroke hair with hand or raise hat briefly.

3. Subject standing still: lay one hand against back or on stomach.

4. Observing agent wishes to terminate observation because cover is threatened: bend and retie shoelaces.

5. Subject returning: both hands against back or on stomach.

6. Observing agent wishes to speak with team leader or other observing agents: take out briefcase or equivalent and examine contents.

Slander

They will go behind the target's back and tell lies about them. Often, the lies will consist of the target being into something illegal or someone dangerous or just needing to be watched for some vague reason. For example, they will say the target is a prostitute, drug dealer, crazy, terrorist, racist, pedophile, etc.

Sleep Deprivation

Depriving the target of sleep is a really good way of leaving the target stressed out. It's also a way of leaving them disoriented and functioning at less than 100 percent. Then the targets can be baited into reacting in public or getting into a car accident.

Telephone Redirects

When you make a telephone call, get the name and ID of the person that you are speaking to. Covert investigations have redirected phone calls. This means that when you dial a number, they will intercept that phone call and pretend to be the service or repair person you were trying to call. For example, if you call the cable company, gas or phone company, be sure you know that it's actually them that you are speaking to. Also, remember that telephone companies and other businesses are often infiltrated by these organized gangstalking and harassment groups and can be used to harass and cause the targeted individual problems.

Wrong Number Calls

Targets will get wrong number calls daily. These can be automated, or they can be persons pretending to be wrong-number calls. Members of these groups will use this to monitor and psychologically harass targets. They want to know where the target is at all times.

Variations of Gangstalking

Consumer Stalking

Consumer stalking is harassment and abuse directed at a consumer who has either filed a complaint against a company, has filed a lawsuit against a company, or is made aware of illegal activity occurring within a company. Often, companies will fund stalkers simply to prevent the victim from filing a lawsuit, using fear and intimidation tactics. Consumer stalking can also be used to describe certain illegal activities of debt collectors.

Corporate Stalking

The term *corporate stalking* refers to a particularly severe form of gangstalking, where a corporation actually provides funding toward the harassment and abuse of a targeted individual, usually someone who is a whistle-blower, a perceived problem employee, or else an employee who has witnessed illegal activity occurring within the corporation. The most sinister, and downright evil, tactic used during corporate stalking is forcing the victim to see the company psychologist. In most cases, the company psychologist is made aware that the victim is a dissident and a threat that needs to be eliminated. A false diagnosis of general psychosis, schizophrenia, or other mental illness is made, as well as a recommendation of institutionalization.

(Corporate Cyberstalking: http://www.firstmonday.org/issues/issue7_11/b)

(Corrupt Company Psychologist Information: http://www.psychologistethics.net/)

Intimate Infiltration

This is where members of these groups will go out of their way to get into a target's life. They will try to form friendships with targets. They will try to form intimate relationships with targets. They will get close to people that are affiliated with targets. Years before the target ever realizes they are targets, they will try to get into a target's life. For example, if they can't get into your life but you have a best friend, their new significant other might just be a member of the group. The same goes for siblings and the people that enter their lives.

Isolation

For this harassment to be successful, it's important to be able to isolate the target from friends, family members, cowork-ers, and even spouses if they are not already involved in the harassment. To accomplish this isolation, many methods are used, including but not limited to, slander, lies, fake files, sab-otage, anything that will get the target into a situation where they have no support system. This is important for them to succeed.

Profiling

Targets will be observed and profiled long before they ever become aware that they are targeted by this sort of harass-ment. Profiles will be created on targets by certain methods: Following them. Following people close to them. Breaking into their homes and going through their stuff. Listening to their calls. Hacking into their computers. Gathering information from friends and family. Seeing where they like to shop and eat. Knowing what their weaknesses are. Knowing what they can be bribed with. Knowing what they can be blackmailed with. Knowing how they can be bullied. Knowing how they can best be controlled. This will all be used to put together a profile of the target and then to get them into situations for their detriment.

Random Encounters

This will be people on the street whom you randomly and unexpectedly run into. It looks completely natural, and it seems to be a random encounter. They might ask for your phone number after engaging you in conversation. Ask you out or just ask you where you are going. Anything from small talk to lengthier conversations. All with the purpose of finding out something about you or even just getting you to do something.

Ruined Relationships

When targets are in a relationship, the members of the organized gangstalking group will try to ruin that relationship. This could be friendships, family, or significant others. If it's a romantic relationship, they will find out what your significant other likes and try to get them to cheat or leave you. If it's a friendship, they will tell lies to come between you. The same goes for family. This is done so that targets will have no means of support once they do realize that something is going wrong in their lives. When this mobbing continues out in the community, it is called organized stalking. Organized stalking is mobbing that takes place out in public. Deception using lies about the target appears to be the most common method used to get citizens to participate. Specifically, smear campaigns using bogus investigations. Furthermore, it is likely that they take advantage of existing federally sponsored mechanisms, such as community crime watch or community policing organizations, senior citizens organizations, and religious groups, and use them as unsuspecting instruments in their retaliation campaigns. Many people across the country have reported being harassed by these community groups. Some of these people they're using think they're doing a community service. This is a very well-funded and organized service/cult that is apparently condoned or even run by the state. The perpetrators of organized gangstalking are serious criminals who do great damage, and the acts done are very serious crimes by any measure. Organized gangstalking is a highly criminal campaign, one directed at a target individual, and one that aims to destroy an innocent person's life through covert harassments, malicious slander, and carefully crafted and executed psychological assaults. Organized gangstalking deprives the targeted individual of their basic constitutional rights and destroys their freedom, setting a stage for the destruction of a person, socially, mentally, and physically, through a ceaseless assault that pervades all areas of a person's life.

Organized Gangstalking on Foot—Tactics and Methods

Following the target everywhere they go. Gathering information about the target. Where they shop, work, play and who their friends and family are. Getting close to the target, moving into the community or apartment where they live, across the street. Following the target. Mobbing or crowding the target in public restaurants or stores. Having directed conversations about the target. Standing close to the target. Engaging the target in trivial conversations. Intentionally coughing at the target. Repeatedly clearing throat. Using gestures around the target. Intentional staring, glaring, pointing, or whispering at the target. Jangling keys, jangling change. Getting a target sensitized to sounds, colors, patterns, actions. For example, red, white, yellow, stripes. Clicking pens, foot-tapping. Noise harassment and mimicking campaigns. Disrupting the target's life and sleep with loud power tools, construction, stereos, doors slamming, etc. Talking in public about private things in the target's life. Mimicking actions of the target. Basically, letting the target know that they are in the target's life. Daily interferences—nothing that would be too overt to the untrained eye but psychologically degrading and damaging to the target over time. Mass strangers doing things in public to annoy targets. These strangers might get text messages to be at a specific time and place and perform a specific action. It might seem harmless to these strangers, but it could be causing great psychological trauma for the target. For example, blocking target's path, getting ahead of them in line, cutting or boxing them in on the road, saying or doing things to elicit an angry response from targets.

Organized gangstalking on vehicle tactics and methods

Following a target around in vehicles. Tailgating the target's vehicle on the road. Driving or creeping by the target's home. Two vehicles intentionally passing the other vehicle by or in front of the target's home repeatedly. This is a type of street theater and psychological sensitization tactic that is intended to make the target appear crazy or mentally unstable if the target complains of this type of harassment. Driving by the target's home, revving engine loudly. Blowing horns by the target's home. Loud repeated door slamming. Loud stereo systems. Harassment by vehicles with loud or squeaky parts, such as loud mufflers, squeaky fan belts, or intentionally loud, squeaky brakes. Leaving loud vehicles or motorcycles idling around a target's home used as a form of harassment. Pulling in on side streets by a target's home and sitting or backing up. Pulling up in the target's driveway. Reversing vehicles in front of the target's home. Vehicles or groups that travel in cells.

The cells may use vehicle color harassment, using many vehicles of the same color to harass and sensitize the target to a certain color. For example, sending or flooding the target's neighborhood with many white vehicles. This can be done subtly or all at once. For instance, a target may notice eight white vehicles within five minutes driving by his or her home or may see one white vehicle right after the other driving by his or her home. This harassment and sensitization tactic can be done with any color. Vehicles driving by the target's home in convoys. The convoys may be of the same color or similar type of vehicle.

Members of the stalking and harassment group lined up in convoys along a target's route. Positioning long lines of traffic in front of the target. Car accidents that may be staged or set up involving the target. Swarming or surrounding the target's vehicle on the road. Driving at slow speeds in front of the target. Vehicles with vanity plates that may mean something personal to the target that is used to convey messages and harass the target while on the road. Psychological vehicle tactics, such as shining high-beam headlights on the target. Vehicles with one headlight on and the other headlight off. Vehicles with one headlight that is brighter than the other headlight. Vehicles with headlight that can be turned up into a "spotlight" to bright the target.

The crime of organized stalking is perpetrated against targeted victims for two reasons: nonconsensual experimentation or revenge and silencing purposes. Regardless of the motive, organized stalking is a crime! Now that you are informed about it, please help to spread the word about it and awaken others!

Much of my story so far includes many of these examples. The relationship sabotage, the fraudulent PFAs, and the criminal sexual harassment claims came right from their evil manual. The staged accident, tampering with my vehicle, and the break-ins were scripted right out of the book. When I talk to my community of other targeted individuals all over the world, we all seem to experience the same evil acts. No matter where we are in the world, it seems like these sadistic creeps follow the same playbook, and all our lives have been destroyed.

Chapter 29

The Marathon of Execution

I've spoken to many targets already that have been suffering from this cruel and unusual punishment for more years than I have. One poor guy had his wife murdered and his children were taken away. He built a faraday cage to sleep in at night and had medical proof that he had been implanted with body area networking. Despite having proof, he was blocked from getting any medical treatment. He still does not know why he has been put into this program.

I think about my own situation. My mother was just diagnosed with lung cancer and coughs up the same gluey silicone crap that plagues me. I still see trucks spraying poison and truly weird mushrooms growing in the backyard. I see messages everywhere that I am being killed with cancer. I haven't seen Lala in over three years. The program really drives a person to suicide.

Almost all targets experience attacks from directed-energy weapons and radiation. We post pictures of rashes and bruises. We try to protect ourselves, but we all get labeled with the same false mental illness diagnoses, and doctors prevent us from getting real help. Once we walk into a doctor's office and mention we are getting attacked with directed-energy weapons, it's off to a psychiatrist.

Many targets have V2K-induced voices. These people can hear others talking to them and making terrible or threatening remarks. This is an indication to most doctors of mental illness. I know I have implants, and I know that the thousands of perps stalking me every day use a cell phone to trigger the device, which causes me a great deal of pain and agony. I know that devices and technology are installed in places that are meant to be safe. I tried telling my psychiatrist about my implant, and within a second, was labeled paranoid schizophrenic.

I will give you a few examples of how doctors play along with my execution. A CAT scan of my sinuses showed large cysts and complete obstruction of my sinuses. In addition, I had a seriously deviated septum, which was supposed to have been fixed when I had surgery before going to Happy Place. But two different ENT doctors blocked me from getting treatment. A report I came across said I was blocked for non-financial reasons. I didn't owe them any money. Both doctors were affiliated with Pukes Hospital. Was there a connection?

I went to an awesome doctor in the Lehigh Valley Health Network, and as soon as Dr. Karter saw my CAT scan, he scheduled me for surgery. I had been suffering from the sinus issue since I got sick in my marital home. Three days before the surgery, I got a notice from my health insurance that they would not cover the procedure. I was so desperate, I offered to pay out of my own pocket.

A few hours later, the hospital notified me that they would not allow the surgery until I got a medical clearance from both a primary care physician and a psychiatrist. Why the hell did a psychiatrist have to approve my sinus surgery? Even Dr. Karter was confused.

I changed primary care doctors and got Dr. Sattus to sign the release. He also thought it was strange that I needed to have a psychiatrist approve sinus surgery. Starting over meant I had to go through a new intake procedure, taking two months to see a psychiatrist. When I finally saw the psychiatrist, she refused to sign off the sinus surgery. She said if I agreed to be injected with psychotropic drugs and wait six months, she'd review the surgery again. How was this ethical?

I later discovered that my medical report contained a note saying that a call had been made to the hospital by someone claiming to be my father. This person said I was in a barn trying to hang myself. Fortunately, when reviewing this record, my dad was right there to witness the false report.

After a few more months of counseling, I was finally able to meet with another psychiatrist. When I told the doctor I just needed a signature to get sinus surgery, she told me they didn't do medical releases. This was a complete lie! My counselor had just told me they did medical releases all the time.

Dr. Carter appealed my case to the head of the hospital and was denied. I decided to try my luck with a psychologist, which took fourteen months to schedule. At last, I finally had the surgery. Perhaps psychology was out of the handlers' extrajudicial network of collaborators. Although I can breathe through my nose again, I am still getting this painful, gluey substance that is suffocating me. Obviously, I am still being attacked.

When I tried to get disability income in my own name, the handlers apparently were angry at my work-around and managed to mess with me by requiring a payee on the account. To this day, my father must approve all my payments.

When I say the entire community has been involved, I am talking about neighbors, businesses and groups. The police have been called on me multiple times. When a woman who had a state university sticker on her car followed me out of the Home Depot doing the usual community-based stalking, I decided to turn the tables. I followed her car for several miles. When I finally got home, three Bethlehem Police cars pulled up with lights flashing. The woman had reported me for stalking her. Yeah, I'm the stalker.

One time, I was rollerblading, trying to exercise and stay alive. It was a little chilly out, so I put on my mouse Santa hat with the big ears. I guess "they" didn't think I was funny because someone called the Bethlehem Police again and told them that I looked like I was cracked out. At this point, I think the police started to feel bad for me, but since I had been smeared with some evil crap, no one wanted to offer me help.

My parents' neighbors, and Lori's too, were coerced into participating in noise campaigns. Every time I walked onto the deck, a neighbor would come out and crush cans. I'm amazed how many cans these neighbors go through in a day. All day long, I get psychological attacks from fathers with little daughters. Sometimes, the perps play out street theater and use the name "Lala."

One day, I went to Walmart to cash my check. The mentally challenged customer support woman counted the money four times but added an extra hundred dollars to the cash she handed me. The goal clearly was to have me walk out with the extra money and then charge me with taking advantage of a mentally handicapped employee. The handlers have even gotten local funeral homes involved and stalk me frequently with hearses. A few times, they have staged fake funerals with numerous cars driving around me.

While I was driving the bus, I flash perps a handwritten sign: "Why?" Then a black pickup started pulling alongside me with the handwritten message, "Why? Because Fuck You, That's Why." When Lori and I would go to different towns, military personnel would already be checked into the rooms next to us. Large black trucks with huge antennas would be in the parking lot, and as soon as I tried to relax in my room, I began to experience awful pain and have dizzy spells.

When I went to see my sister in Oregon three thousand miles away, I was shocked they let me on the plane. I figured they would have wrongly labeled me a terrorist. The first night there, two cop cars and two federal agents drove by my sister's house. My brother-in-law said, "That was odd. We never see police cars drive by here."

It took the Lutterschmidt targeting program six days to get up and running in Oregon. At that point, I started having excruciating sinus and chest pain. I learned later that satellites were triggering a response to my implants, and the entire community was just beginning to gangstalk me. My execution will be carried out no matter where I go or what I do.

I know that I am not alone out there because I actively communicate with an entire community of targeted individuals.

Since I have no charges, no warrants, and no way to discover why I am being executed, I am left to utilize whatever brain I have left that has not been damaged by the attacks.

Chapter 30

Happy Place

After my unhappy episode at Happy Place and the no-trespass order they issued against me, I started to do deeper research on Happy Place. Immediately, I was terrified. I make no direct accusations here, but I will reveal what I have learned.

The CIA works with Happy Place and helped them get their parcel of land in Florida. Even more astonishingly, Happy Place was granted permission to govern themselves. They not only work with the Department of Defense, but Happy Place has been given numerous military contracts for various types of experiments. The military even has its own resort on the grounds.

What had I fallen into? Suddenly it was less surprising why I was getting bombarded with mouse ear symbols and stalked by members of the Air Force, Marines and Army.

I read the section about surveillance of individuals with drug abuse issues in the DOD manual. I believe that my history of methamphetamine use was a major qualification for my targeting. Many of the other victims of targeting have had similar histories.

I have no way of proving it, but I'm convinced I've been implanted with electronic devices and nanotechnology, and that these devices allow my handlers to hear through my ears and see through my eyes. I'm not sure how "they" benefit from my torture and death.

I believe that while at Happy Place, and after, I was influenced by mind control, perhaps using these implanted devices. In addition to feeling mentally manipulated on the grounds, I also felt strongly influenced against my better judgment to leave the White Bear rehab facility early. At times, in my own house, I could feel the strong effects of mind control technology.

I could never understand why Happy Place would be willing to spend a lot of money to intimidate and harass a guy who was going through a very traumatic time in his life. Just because I got intoxicated on their grounds and stole some food and a fifteen-dollar stuffed animal?

At Happy Place—and most other places too—if someone gets drunk and obnoxious, someone will prevent that jackass from causing more of a disturbance. Not only did Happy Place continue to serve me alcohol when I was obviously drunk, but no one said anything to me until the no-trespassing order. Were they observing the effects of a mind control experiment?

Many books have been written regarding dark secrets at Happy Place. I learned that Happy Place has been around the porn industry for a long time. I knew they did some sick illustrations in their movies, one being a penis for a castle, but I didn't think they were peddling pornography.

There was a huge scandal about employment of pedophiles and outrage when a little boy was attacked and killed by an alligator at the park (why did that family never file a lawsuit?) I found a lot of troubling information, but nothing about a guest being executed for acting like an idiot while in the park.

I discovered an article from a guy who once worked as a security guard in the park. When I read his first paragraph, describing how he had been stalked by mouse silhouettes, everything became real for me. I have not edited or changed one word of this online post.

> Good morning! I am writing this on my phone, so please
> have patience with any grammatical or formatting errors.
> This post got removed originally, and I messaged the
> mods. They said they have no idea how it happened, but

I've been finding small silhouettes of a mouse outside of my house. Here's the repost, and an update is in the works.

To start off with, I now reside in a completely different state after leaving my job with the Happy Place Resort in Asto Luego, Florida. I used to be what one other Redditor described as a "suit"; I am one of the guys that walks around the park in plain sight yet hidden to the public. I am part of the elite group of black-polo-sporting undercover security officers that specialize in worse things than shoplifters and unruly park guests. You see, as stated prior to this post on /r/nosleep, if you are at Happy Place and you see more than a few guys in one place wearing black polos, then you are most likely in danger and you should leave the area immediately. The sad part is, we are so good at blending in with the woodwork that you wouldn't even notice us. Anyway, let me cut to the chase here. I have seen some pretty weird things at Happy Place during my time. These "anomalies" that everyone speaks of, well, they are true, but the least of our concerns. See, the thing is, when you take hundreds of thousands of people and cram them into a relatively small space, weird shit is going to happen. We have had kids, even adults, get lost in the park and cryptozoological sightings, alien sightings, ghost sightings, and just generally unexplainable things happen all the time.

I was a senior special security officer during the height of my time there and got called for some pretty dark shit. Many of you think we, as in the security detail I was in, were covering up for Happy Corp., but in our true nature, we were damage control and were kept out of the loop on things and were trained not to question but to diffuse. There was one thing, though, that, to this day, still bothers me. A cast member called us on the Nextel to report that a group of four children had gone missing on the Land. Of course, I thought, another one of those anomalies. For those of you who don't know the eerily calming nature ride called Living with the Land, it is in the Land and the Sea pavilion over by Soarin'. The odd thing about this report is that we have never received one of these complaints before, and of course, we are issued cover-up stories to tell cast members or guests to calm them down. My colleague calmly came up with a story and explained that the kids were part of an educational program and they exited the boat with a guide and were escorted into the botany lab that exists on the ride. I told her not to ask any questions or talk about the incident as to not spread "false rumors" and had my colleague escort her to a near-by security office to have her sign some forms. My human nature took over, and I got curious and entered the ride on the next boat alone.

Living with the Land is boring and not particularly popular, so I can understand how the kids would be on the boat alone and how I could get on the boat by myself. I noticed absolutely nothing until I came to the part of the ride that has the prairie farmhouse. It looks like a faux house, but something about it just never sat right with me. As I have done hundreds of times before on rides, I jumped off the boat and onto the scene where the house is. I noticed something funny, though. There were no pressure mats, and the boat went away, allotting about a good thirty seconds before the next boat got to the scene. I have never seen a ride with no pressure mats to detect if anyone disembarks the ride.

So quick recap: Kids disappeared on ride, I showed up and fed the cast member who reported it some story about how they disembarked midride and were on a tour of the lab and for her not to question it. A colleague of mine took her away to debrief. I contacted the new cast member operating the ride and told him to put some space between the next boat as I was looking for a lost wedding ring. Bull, I know, but so what?

I slowly started to walk up to the faux house. Climbing the steps up to the porch, I noticed a small emblem on the left window. It was a small square and compass symbol. Interesting that a Masonic symbol was hidden here. I figured whoever built the ride was a Freemason and brushed it off. I looked in the windows of the house, and it was nothing but curtains with black plywood behind them. I thought that there was nothing to see here, but still, something inside me decided that wasn't good enough. The front door glided open to a bright room with a black-and-white checkerboard floor. There was a marble altar-like table on the opposite end of the room, with a weird, throne-like chair built into the front of it and a gold cup on the tabletop. The only other thing that was noticeable was a heavy wooden door on the other end of the room that was locked; there were no windows or anything else. I thought it was weird because I was always under the impression that this house was fake. Human nature took over again, and against my better judgment, I tried the door in the room, but I was relieved that it was locked. I tried my keys, but none of them worked. Here's the thing: At Happy Place, we use a lock system called Best. This had interchangeable cores that have assigned numbers and/or letters. This is so we can issue keys only to certain areas. I have the general master key, which essentially is the real key to the kingdom. Interesting thing about this lock was that my master didn't open it. I looked closer, and it was a Best Lock, but the inscription said "CC." on it, which I've never seen before. Since the door wasn't open, I decided to just leave. On my way, out I noticed in the floor there was a fast pass printed out for Soarin'. I picked it up and pocketed it; it's amazing how trash works its way into odd places. I'm going to figure out where these kids went.

I rode the boat back out to the platform and went back to the E——T security office to play back some footage from the DVR. It took me a while, but I zeroed in on the period where the kids entered the Land and Sea Pavilion and followed them. There were four kids total, three girls and one boy. The girl's actions were almost robotic, and it sent a chill up my spine. They walked in a straight line through the pavilion, but what scared me was, there was a man with them escorting them through the place. I paused and looked closer when I realized the man was wearing black polo and khakis, the same thing I was wearing. Holy shit! I even recognized him—it was one of my colleagues.

Allen is the guy that was at the scene before I got there, the same guy who fed the cast member at the control podium the bullshit about the kids going on a tour. I thought maybe he sent them on the tour of the botanical lab and lost track of them, until I hit Play on the film. The boy was not walking in line, and I could tell he was giving Allen problems; he kept venturing away and getting distracted by various things in the Pavilion. The benefit of the doubt I gave Allen subsided when I saw the kid go press the button for the fast pass on Soarin' and take the paper fast pass almost like a prize. Allen then tugged him away and stood back and observed as the kids walked to Living with the Land. I saw them get on the boat. I saw them through the storm scene, through the rain forest scene, then through the desert scene. After the desert, I lost the boat on camera. The ride stopped momentarily; you could see it on the other scenes. And once it resumed, I saw the boat again in the scene with the pictures of farmers. The boat was empty. I also saw freakin' Allen looking down off the observation deck, which explains how he responded so quickly. I switched the cameras back to live view and left that area. I haven't been exactly honest with you thus far. I know a lot of the things that Happy Place does and things that we respond to that a regular security officer wouldn't deal with. I have seen them experiment on so many things, such as eugenics, pharmaceutical engineering, even experimenting with gas. Have you ever noticed that on both Spaceship Earth and the Monorail, you get a strange, calm feeling on those rides? Well, they are pumping low doses of laughing gas in those areas. Ever heard of Room 0? They were wearing gas masks for a reason. Ever hear of Gascots? Well, that's not important right now. I would encourage you to research it. I never thought that what we did was okay by containing these dark secrets, but it paid well. I have seen them quickly inject some experimental drug on guests and throw them back out there. Our job was to monitor and contain them if things went haywire. I know that I am the bad guy, but this wasn't normal. This wasn't procedural.

First thing I did was go over to the room where we keep the keys. I looked through the logbooks for the core labeled "CC." I found it, but it had no zone or specific location issued to the core, and the number of copies was marked as 1. This key was in our system, but my master key didn't open it. I grabbed the "core key" and a few zone 1 cores. The core key is a specific key that, when inserted into the lock, will remove the core so it can be replaced with another. I put this in my pocket and made a beeline for the Land and Sea Pavilion. I may be paranoid, but I swear I saw Allen following me in the shadows.

I got to the ride and got to the house and back in the front door to the Masonic room and locked the front door as I entered. I inserted the core key into the lock on the wooden door, removed the core, and inserted the zone 1 core into the lock. Now, my master key will open the door, and boy did it. The door glided open. It was heavy and steel on the other side of the wood face. There was a red-velvet-carpeted staircase leading down to some kind of utilidor, but we are in E——T. What the hell. There is one small utilidor in E——T, but it doesn't go this deep. I descended the stairs and walked down the red-carpeted hallway to these two double doors. Behind these doors was my answer and the truth as to what happened to these kids. Through these doors was the darkest side of

Happy Place, a side of Happy Place that even I couldn't believe. Would Walt be in favor of this? Or was this one of Eisner's little idea of making more money off his guests?

Behind these doors was an empty, dimly lit room with a small circular platform in the center. The carpet was the same lush red velvet carpet from the hallway. There were six leather armchairs around the circular platform, all with telephones and card readers on the table next to the chair. Inside I knew what was going on. I knew what was happening here. This is one thing I will not cover up for the Happy Corp. I stood there in disbelief and horror and noticed a small door toward the back of the room. I went over and popped out the "CC" core, put it in my pocket, and put in a zone 1 core. I heard someone clear their throat from the front of the room. It was Allen. He had an annoyed look on his face and held a gun trained at me. I slowly propped the door open on the latch and turned to face him.

"You never should have come here," he said to me when he was stepping toward me.

"So, this is what you and your scumbag friends have resorted to? We did some pretty fucked-up shit, Allen, but this is a new low for you and your disgusting friends." I had my hand at my side and blocked the view of me slipping the zone 1 core out of the handle and into my pocket.

"It's not going to matter, because no one is going to find out."

He raised the gun, and like something out of an action movie, I ripped the door open as he pulled the trigger and a bullet hit the door. I jumped backward through the doorway and shut it behind me. That asshole was stuck because I had both cores in my pocket, so there was no way he could open the door. He started shooting the door, and I moved forward. I walked down a hallway with these small cell-like rooms lining the hall, and inside were those playschool chairs and a few toys. I checked every one of them, and they were all empty. I got to the end of the hall, and there was this huge vault-like metal door. I popped the last zone 1 core into the door to replace the "CC" core and pulled the steel door open to be hit in the face with sunlight. I was outside on some side utility road off premises of E——T. The road led away. I was too late; they were already gone for good.

I called the police, but they never came. I called the FBI, but they never took me seriously. Hell, I even called the CIA, but they said they didn't deal with domestic issues like that and referred me back to the FBI. I showed up at the Orange County Police Department HQ, and they took a report, but I heard something fall in the trash when I was leaving. Happy Place is good at what they do: they are good at keeping secrets, and they are good at controlling any outside force that attempts to bring their secrets to light. I am lucky I saw the sunlight again and am lucky to have had time to leave the state before they got to me. If you go there, please keep your kids close. Watch out for the guys in the black polos. They may be monitoring you; they may be responding to something that will put you in danger. As far as I know, they aren't the ones that pick out the merchandise. I don't even know who does that.

The second story of the house is seemingly normal, but I don't know how they access it. You'll also notice that there is an observation deck; this area was undergoing "maintenance" at that time. It was closed off to guests, but CCTV footage revealed nothing was happening in that area. The camera points back onto the observation area and not at the house. There are no cameras in that portion of the ride.

Chapter 31

Epilogue

I believe that I've survived despite the torture and pain for two reasons. First, the love for my daughter provides me strength and the courage to endure my suffering. Second, I feel that I have been guided through these last several years with angels on my shoulder. I believe God is protecting me in many ways, shapes and forms.

I have a friend who knows every part of my story, and that the events I've described are true. He outlined for me his best guess at why I am being executed, and how all these characters and staged events fit together. I can't disagree with his conclusions, but they are only one possibility. Perhaps you have other ideas—you certainly have an abundance of facts. I leave you to reach your own conclusions.

If you are frustrated by not having a clear-cut wrap-up to this murder mystery, then you understand the intense frustration that I and thousands of other targeted individuals live with every day. We all have theories about the motives but no obvious and proven answers. So, we all live with uncertainty and without closure. We fear execution while clinging by a thread to a painful and frightening life. We resist suicide, if we can, because we refuse to give the handlers what they most want.

Gangstalking is a fact, and targeting is real. We are in the early days of a new kind of intimidation and torture perpetrated by the wretched behavior of legions of co-conspirators. Today's divisive political climate shows how open hostility can cause millions of people to justify—even enjoy—cruel acts of punishment, manipulation and suppression.

God help us all.

In the absence of a tidy conclusion, I have assembled some examples of communications that illustrate the mindset and methods of the handlers. I fear we are only seeing the beginning of an epidemic.

If you believe that you are a victim of targeting, have been involved with gangstalking or other targeting activities, or have knowledge about the targeting process, please contact me at TI@ calumeteditions.com.

Appendix

Here is a short collection of internet ads that reference targeting activities and devices. If you see others, please copy and send to me at TI@calumeteditions.com.

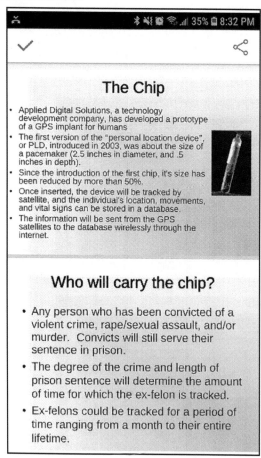